Charmian Clift was born in Kiama, New South Wales, on 31 August 1923. She became a journalist on the Melbourne *Argus* newspaper after the war, and in 1947 married novelist and journalist George Johnston.

Early in their marriage they collaborated on three novels: *High Valley* (which won the *Sydney Morning Herald* prize in 1948), *The Big Chariot* and *The Sponge Divers*. Then, in 1954, having lived in London for the previous few years, they took their family to live in the Greek islands. During this period Charmian wrote two accounts of their life there, *Mermaid Singing* and *Peel Me A Lotus*, and two novels, *Honour's Mimic* and *Walk to the Paradise Gardens*.

In 1964 the family returned to Australia and Charmian began writing a weekly newspaper column which quickly gained a wide and devoted readership.

She died in 1969.

Also by Charmian Clift in Flamingo

Mermaid Singing/Peel Me A Lotus
(one volume edition)

CHARMIAN CLIFT

SELECTED ESSAYS

edited by Nadia Wheatley

flamingo
An imprint of HarperCollins*Publishers*

Flamingo
An imprint of HarperCollins*Publishers*, Australia

First published in Australia in 2001
by HarperCollins*Publishers* Pty Limited
ABN 36 009 913 517
A member of the HarperCollins*Publishers* (Australia) Pty Limited Group
http://www.harpercollins.com.au

HarperCollins*Publishers*
25 Ryde Road, Pymble, Sydney, NSW 2073, Australia
31 View Road, Glenfield, Auckland 10, New Zealand
77–85 Fulham Palace Road, London, W6 8JB, United Kingdom
Hazelton Lanes, 55 Avenue Road, Suite 2900, Toronto, Ontario M5R 3L2
and 1995 Markham Road, Scarborough, Ontario M1B 5M8, Canada
10 East 53rd Street, New York NY 10022, USA

National Library of Australia Cataloguing-in-Publication data:

Clift, Charmian, 1923–1969.
   Charmian Clift selected essays.
   ISBN 0 7322 6887 7.
   1. Australian newspapers – New South Wales – Sydney –
Sections, columns, etc. – Women. I. Wheatley, Nadia, 1949– .
   II. Title. III. Title : Sydney morning herald.
A824.3

Cover design by Katie Mitchell, HarperCollins Design Studio
Cover photograph by Jill Crossley
Printed and bound in Australia by Griffin Press on 70gsm Ensobelle

5 4 3 2 1
04 03 02 01

Contents

Introduction

Through the watershed years of the latter half of the 1960s, Charmian Clift was a household name to many Australians. Every week from November 1964 until July 1969, the author produced a newspaper column of approximately 1200 words that challenged Australians to think in a new way. Her regular 'pieces' were like a breath of fresh ocean air after the long dry spell of the 1950s and early 1960s. Clift herself had fled that political and cultural aridity in 1951, to spend over a decade of exile in Europe. On her return in 1964, she was able to look at her homeland with a loving but critical eye.

Her concerns covered an extraordinary range of topics including suburban architecture, military conscription, censorship, the need to develop a local film industry, Australia's participation in Asia, the changing role of women, the division between the Haves and the Have Nots, the iniquities of the Greek Junta, the right to protest, Australia's relationship with America, and the need to extend full citizenship rights to Aborigines. However, while sometimes the columnist felt provoked into politics, on other occasions the column might take the form of a classical essay about dreams, or moonshine, or the sounds of summer.

While many of Clift's opinions were so radical that they could not be found at this time in other Australian newspaper columns, just as astonishing was the fact that these passionate arguments were expressed in beautifully cadenced prose. Indeed, Charmian Clift must be regarded as one of the consummate prose writers of Australian literature of the twentieth century.

Both her political attitudes and her passion for literature were the result of her rather unusual upbringing in a straggly little settlement on the outskirts of the coastal township of Kiama. It was in the last house in a row of quarry workers' cottages that Charmian Clift was born on 30 August, 1923. Charmian was bequeathed a double legacy by her home town. On the one hand, there was a sense of freedom and wild beauty, encapsulated by the beach, which was so close to the cottage that there was sometimes seaweed on the front fence after a big storm. On the other hand, there was the sense of living on the outside, on the edge—at 'the end, rather than the beginning of somewhere'. Through most of her life, Charmian would retain a feeling of being an outsider, looking in.

While the Clift family did not fit into the middle class respectability of the town of Kiama, they were also an anomaly in the North Kiama settlement, for Charmian's father, Sydney Clift, held the position of engineer at the gravel quarry on the nearby headland, while all the neighbourhood men were labourers. A self-educated English migrant, Syd was an eccentric figure who had 'Strong Opinions' about every topic under the sun, and whose political ideas were always radical, if sometimes inconsistent. It was from him that Charmian learned how to argue. Syd also developed his daughter's mind with the eclectic range of reading (which included authors such as Sterne, Balzac, Rabelais and Cervantes) that he 'force fed' his three young offspring. At the same time, Charmian's mother Amy Clift (née Currie) was introducing her children to a love of poetry, both by her habit of quoting long passages from Tennyson, Byron, Shakespeare and other favourites, and also by her practice of scribbling away late at night at her own verse, which she would subsequently poke into the kitchen fire.

Charmian herself began writing poetry and stories at an early age. At school, she excelled at sport but did not make friends easily and was mostly unhappy. She left with her Intermediate Certificate in 1938, at the age of fourteen, determined 'to get out into the big bad world and do [...] something [...] better than anyone else could do'.

It was beauty, rather than brains, that won this ambitious young woman her chance to escape from the small town. In May 1941, a photograph of Charmian in a swimsuit won a Beach Girl competition run by *Pix* magazine. With the money, Charmian was able to move to Sydney 'on the search for glamour'. This first foray into the world led to disaster. At the end of 1942, Charmian—aged nineteen—gave birth to an illegitimate daughter; under pressure from family and social values, the young mother offered her child for adoption.

In April 1943, Charmian made a fresh start by enlisting in the Australian Women's Army Service. Within eighteen months she was made a Lieutenant and transferred to Melbourne, where she was given the job of editing a news sheet for the Ordnance Corps. The beautiful young lieutenant attracted the attention of Brigadier Errol Knox, Director General of Army Public Relations, who in civilian life was managing director of Melbourne's *Argus* newspaper. He invited her to join his staff, which she did as soon as she was demobilised in May 1946.

On one of her first days at her new job she met up with George Johnston, a thirty-three year old journalist who had established his reputation as the newspaper's leading war correspondent. They immediately began an affair which was seen by colleagues as 'the *scandale* of the office'. Within weeks, Clift was summarily dismissed. Johnston resigned in protest. This was the beginning of a partnership that would continue through twenty-three years, thirty books and three children.

By early 1947, the couple had moved to Sydney; Charmian was pregnant. In the hope of making some cash, they began a collaborative novel, *High Valley*, using the exotic setting of a valley in Tibet which George had visited during the war. Work on this novel was completed in time for the birth of the couple's first child, Martin, in November. Their daughter, Shane, was born in February 1949.

In early 1951, George Johnston was posted overseas to run the London office of Associated Newspaper Services. Although initially exhilarated at being in London, Charmian Clift quickly began to feel that she was losing her identity. A holiday trip to Greece in the spring of 1954 held out the promise of a new world and a new way of life. At the end of that year the Johnstons rented a house on the island of Kalymnos—a barren and isolated place where sponge diving was the only industry. Over the first few months in Greece, Charmian began to write a sort of journal in which she incorporated notes about the people and place of Kalymnos and the seasonal rhythms and religious festivals alongside descriptions of how she and her immigrant family were settling in. As this developed into the book *Mermaid Singing*, the author used for the first time the personal and lyrical voice which she would later employ in the essays, and which would become the identifying feature of her unique prose style.

Towards the end of that year the Johnstons moved to the island of Hydra, which was only three hours away from Athens and already featuring on the tourist trail. Although their finances were precarious, the couple decided to blow their small reserve of cash on a house on the island. Their third child, Jason, was born in April 1956 in the house that would be the family's home for the next eight years.

On Hydra, Charmian Clift at last felt that she was an insider, because, in the island's small town scene of resident foreigners, her status and role were acknowledged. She also felt that she was able to manage a successful division of her time between her domestic life, her professional life and her social life. Under these circumstances, Clift's writing developed. Over the next eight years she completed a second personal travel book, *Peel Me a Lotus* and two novels, *Walk to the Paradise Gardens* and *Honour's Mimic*.

Through these years in Greece, George Johnston's health had been deteriorating, owing to the tuberculosis which he had contracted during the war. In the autumn of 1962, believing that he might have time for only one more book, he made a start on a first person narrative about growing up in Melbourne. Clift put aside work on her own autobiographical novel so that she could assist her husband. Every day, until the book was completed the following March, she sat on the step next to his desk and acted as his sounding board. Her input into the work was so great that George Johnston would describe *My Brother Jack* as 'virtually a collaboration'.

This novel provided a pathway home for Johnston, who returned to Australia for the book's launch in March 1964. Although Charmian Clift still passionately loved Greece, she would follow in August, together with the three children, and the family would settle in Sydney.

During George's initial scouting foray to Melbourne, after his homecoming, he had met up with an old journalist friend, 'now an important newspaper editor' who had got in touch with Charmian to ask if she would write 'some regular pieces'. George later noted:

> He was not at all sure what these pieces were to be
> ... sort of essays, he thought ... anything she liked.
> The point was, he explained, that he was not looking
> for a woman journalist, but a writer. The daily press
> needed some writing, real writing, from a woman's
> point of view.

It was the Melbourne *Herald* which initially employed
Charmian Clift as a columnist; on 6 November 1964 her first
piece—appropriately entitled 'Coming Home'—was published
in that newspaper. At that time the Melbourne *Herald* and the
Sydney Morning Herald had an agreement whereby they could
use each other's material. Thirteen days later, on 19 November,
this same essay appeared in the *Sydney Morning Herald*. Over
the coming months, Clift's column would become a regular
weekly feature of both these newspapers. As the pieces were
commissioned at the Melbourne end, they were also subedited
there, and at this stage it was the Melbourne paper that paid
the author.

The most important thing was the brief: it was a job
description that was perfectly tailored for Charmian Clift.
Although writing at short length was something that she had
never done before, the mode of the essay—with its
idiosyncratic point of view and its apparent discursiveness—
was akin to the mode that Clift had practised in the travel
books; and of course 'real writing' was right up her alley.
From her first column, Charmian Clift immediately found her
voice: assured, intimate and intensely personal.

In this initial essay, the writer assessed some of her
impressions gained over the first two months in her homeland.
It was an unusual viewpoint, for someone to be both native-
born and newcomer. In the short time since her return, the

writer had noticed how 'over and over again' a certain statement was reiterated with complacency. 'The old place has changed quite a bit since *you* saw it last.' The author would turn this statement into a series of questions. Had Australia changed since the early 1950s? If so, how? Were these changes superficial or profound? For better or worse?

When Charmian Clift had left her homeland in 1951, the reason was partly to find 'the Big Thing, [...] the wonder or the sign that it was her inalienable right to claim as her own'. At the same time, she saw her departure as a form of exile, because she felt herself to be stifled by the social and political climate of post-war Australian society. The election in December 1949 of the first coalition government, led by Robert Menzies, had been the final straw.

When she returned, in August 1964, Sir Robert Menzies was still the Prime Minister. In other ways, too, the country felt like the same place that she had fled. Women were excluded from public bars and many jobs, and working wives were still the subject of criticism and controversy. It was hard for unmarried women to get the Pill, and there was no social security for single mothers. Pubs and cinemas were closed on Sundays, the film industry was non-existent, certain stage plays (or parts of them) were banned, and *The Trial of Lady Chatterley* was a prohibited import.

Perhaps the most significant indicator of the lack of progress was the fact that the White Australia Policy was still in place. Insofar as the composition of Clift's fellow countryfolk had changed, the new arrivals had been either English immigrants or 'Continentals'. The latter were expected to assimilate into the dominant Anglo-Australian monoculture. Indigenous Australians were also expected to assimilate; at this time they were not even counted in the census. Under Menzies, the country still looked towards the northern hemisphere and particularly to Britain, and there was little sense of being part of the Asia-Pacific region. Although the war in Vietnam sometimes made the headlines, Australia had no military presence there yet, and the people of Australia had little awareness of what was going on in that conflict.

Thus when Charmian Clift returned in 1964, the overall feel was of an affluent, settled, self-satisfied society. And yet there was a feeling of 'imminence' (she perceived)—as if something was *about* to happen. In fact, a social commentator could not have arrived at a more interesting or more significant time. Over the next few years, as Australia began to go through a profound political and social metamorphosis, Charmian Clift would turn her rare skill of social observation and analysis upon her own country and compatriots, just as she had examined the people and place of Greece in her two travel books. Indeed, these *Selected Essays*, if read sequentially, form a kind of third travel book.

The first harbinger of change occurred as early as 10 November 1964, when the Prime Minister announced sweeping changes to the country's defence program, including the introduction of conscription—and moreover, conscription for overseas service. In April of the next year, the federal government announced that Australian troops would be sent to Vietnam. Whatever side people took over the issue of Australia's military role in Vietnam, this involvement would have the effect of bringing Asia into every Australian living room on a nightly basis. The Vietnam War would be the catalyst for a change in Australian society more profound than the changes wrought by World Wars I or II, for the very composition of the population would be affected, as well as the political consciousness.

While this shift was beginning, Charmian Clift was in the front seat—not just as observer, but as an agent of the transformation of attitude. The columnist publicly opposed conscription and Australia's role in the Vietnam War long before such attitudes were respectable, and she was also one of the first voices to urge that Australians extend friendship and welcome to Asian people, and to see Asia as 'the place where one lives'.

In July 1965, the first National Servicemen went to camp, amid protest by women from the Save Our Sons Movement. Around the same time, Clift received a significant affirmation of the popularity of her column. The senior journalist John Douglas Pringle had recently moved from the position of editor of the *Canberra Times* to the editorship of the *Sydney Morning Herald*. Fairly soon after Pringle's arrival at the new job, the managing director, Angus McLachlan, came up with the idea of employing Charmian Clift on a permanent basis, rather than just taking her copy from the Melbourne *Herald*. Pringle relayed this decision to the paper's redoubtable Women's Editor, Maggie Vaile, who declared herself to be 'delighted'. Under this new arrangement, both the pay cheque and the subediting were the responsibility of the *Sydney Morning Herald*. After this, Clift's copy went to Maggie on a Saturday, was published in the *Sydney Morning Herald's* weekly Women's Section on the following Thursday and appeared in the Melbourne *Herald* on the subsequent Saturday.

The important aspect of this story is the fact that the decision to employ Clift on a regular basis came from the top: not many freelance columnists are engaged on the specific orders of the newspaper's managing director. This is particularly significant because by this stage Clift's column had shown itself to be considerably to the left of the editorial policy of the Fairfax-owned *Sydney Morning Herald,* which was committed to supporting the Government position on Vietnam.

For the Fairfax management, the bottom line was that Charmian Clift attracted readers, and this in turn helped sell newspapers and advertising. In September 1965 the Clift column was moved to the prime position of page 2 in the Women's Section, opposite the social notes. At the same time the large retailer Grace Bros, which had formerly advertised only intermittently in the *Sydney Morning Herald*, bought the major advertising space on this page 2/3 spread on a regular basis, specifying that its advertisements were to be placed near the Clift column. This support from a major advertising subscriber, coupled with the regular volume of Clift's fan mail, all helped to strengthen Charmian Clift's editorial freedom. She herself was in no doubt about how subversive her column was. A couple of months after her engagement by the *Sydney Morning Herald,* the author summed up the year since her arrival in a letter to her London literary agent:

> This has all been so new and so invigorating in a mad sort of way. I think I like it. At least it is a country where you can still make things happen instead of waiting for them to happen. I have been making my own sneaky little revolutions [...] by writing essays for the weekly presses to be read by people who don't know an essay from a form-guide, but absolutely love it.

The columnist's first piece for 1966, 'On a Lowering Sky in the East', revealed a new strength of political concern. This change in emphasis was in keeping with the times, for if the political turbulence of the sixties had already started, the retirement of Menzies that same January marked the end of the old era. For Charmian Clift, this had a deep symbolic significance. However, with Harold Holt at the helm the country would tend more and more to woo the friendship of the United States, offering increasing commitment to the Vietnam War as proof of our fidelity. In late April 1966, 4500 more troops, including the first overseas conscripts, were sent to Vietnam amid (a *Sydney Morning Herald* headline noted) 'Mounting Controversy'. A couple of weeks later, in 'Banners, Causes and Convictions', Charmian Clift applauded a change in attitude from the apathy and mental flabbiness of 1964.

While protest was starting to become vociferous (especially during the visit of American President Lyndon Baines Johnson), the majority of Australians still supported the Holt government. Indeed, in November 1966 the coalition was returned with ten more seats after a campaign fought mainly on the issues of conscription and the Vietnam War. No wonder it sometimes seemed to the columnist that the change of social and political climate that she had felt to be coming had somehow turned direction, or had maybe been a matter of wishful thinking.

Of course, hindsight shows that Charmian Clift was not wrong.

While her attitude and beliefs were at odds with majority opinion, if we read the Clift column for the period 1964–69 we get a different picture of the society from that given by the voting figures. Instead of noting the number supporting the government and the war, we see the size of the minority that was in conflict with the old 1950s political and social values. We see, too, that this minority was composed, not just of long-haired student demonstrators, but of a wide range of people who shopped for 'gear au gogo' at Grace Bros, or who were seen as the target market for Rhu pills and wrinkle cream; teething aids and wigs; splayds and serviced ranchettes. Less than a year after Charmian Clift died, these were the people who would provide the groundswell of the Moratorium movement. Two years after that, the majority of Australians acknowledged at the ballot box that it was time for a change.

In every generation of writers there are certain figures who function as national weathervanes, recording change to the social and political climate. Charmian Clift was one of these. Yet as well as recording political change in the volatile years of the 1960s, she was also instrumental in helping Australian society discard many of the outdated and xenophobic values which it had held through the Cold War period.

It is frustrating for a writer to live in advance of her or his time, because it often means that the writing is misunderstood, and under valued. Yet one of the benefits of writing from a vanguard position is that the work tends to remain relevant. Three decades after her death, Charmian Clift continues to win a new readership, both for her travel books and for her essays.

Nadia Wheatley, 2001

Editor's Note

In selecting these essays, I have drawn from the four existing anthologies of Charmian Clift's essays—*Images in Aspic* (1965), *The World of Charmian Clift* (1970), *Trouble in Lotus Land* (1990) and *Being Alone with Oneself* (1991). Between them, these contain virtually all the 'pieces' which the essayist wrote in the brief but highly productive period from late 1964 until mid 1969. In choosing eighty out of the author's 225 essays, I have tried to give a representative sample of her concerns and interests. I have arranged the pieces pretty much chronologically.

The text of these essays has been based, in most cases, on the author's typescripts (rather than the printed newspaper column). While occasional inconsistencies in the author's punctuation have been corrected, I have retained Clift's idiosyncratic punctuation style overall, and I have not 'modernised' her usage in regard to capitalisation et cetera. In places where the author did not provide her own title on her typescript, I have occasionally changed the title provided by the newspaper's sub-editor, particularly when there would otherwise have been two essays with the same title

As the column pieces were often written in response to current events, I have provided notes for some of the contemporary political references at the end of the book. However, I have not explained the literary allusions or unusual expressions which Clift expected her audience to understand. Readers seeking more background to the essays could consult the introductions and notes which I wrote for the anthologies *Trouble in Lotus Land* and *Being Alone with Oneself*.

Coming Home

For years now, in the whitewashed house at the cobbled square by the public well—'The Australian House', the islanders called it, and enthusiastically directed any and every casual Australian tourist up the lane from the waterfront as though to a national monument ('Blue door and red bougainvillea. You can't miss it. But ask anyone for the children if you are not sure,')—my countrymen and women, Europe bound but not quite there yet, still, one felt, tugged by uneasy thoughts of irons left on and bath taps running, would say, daringly accepting a glass of Greek ouzo or retsina—or more prudently refraining—'How many years did you say? That's a long time. Why, you'd never even *know* the place now.'

And since I have returned to my native land, here but not here, still tugged by my own uneasy thoughts of shutters left unbattened against the *meltémi* and rainwater pipes flooding the underground cistern and whether in fact I paid Stamatis the muleteer for the last two tins of drinking water from the Sweet Wells, the statement (and it is a statement, never a question) has been reiterated over and over again. With assurance. Even complacency. 'The old place has changed quite a bit since *you* saw it last.'

My husband came back to Australia six months before I returned with the children. He did the trip jet-propelled in about twenty-three hours flat and arrived a rather shattered man. It was not so much a question of distance as of different worlds: it takes a little more time than twenty-three hours to adjust from donkey-amble to the screaming blast of city pace.

But I—because of immense quantities of household baggage, including three children who could not remember anything other than a way of life that moved at donkey-amble—returned to my homeland by sea, in what was meant to be a leisurely way of transition from one world to the other. A corridor, if you like, between a room and a room—the one room, familiar by constant and recent usage, closed and locked behind, the other, at the end of the corridor, remembered as a childhood room is remembered, with many distortions in proportion, bright emphases like splashes of sunlight, and some shadowy corners.

I suppose that once it would have been a journey like that. But the ship on which we travelled was a migrant ship, and filled with other families also travelling hopefully or apprehensively from one world to another. It was a queer feeling to be part of a nomadic horde—more than a thousand souls (at sea one is inclined to think in terms of 'souls' rather than plain 'people': whether this is a sort of spiritual insurance policy or just plain gruesome thinking I haven't decided).

Anyway, there we all were, our worldly possessions reduced to what was portable, but still tied emotionally to what we had abandoned. By the time a migrant—and I am including myself and my Australian-born children in the term—actually boards the ship that is to carry him to his brave new world the audacious bite of decision has long since been blunted, if not altogether gummed up, on the toffee-apple of bureaucracy. The freshness of adventure has worn off and uncertainty, alas, is practically all that remains.

There were times when it was necessary to support each other in sadly faltering convictions.

In a special sense it seemed actually miraculous to arrive. 'I can't believe we're here,' was a literal statement. Australia did in fact exist, and we were one family under one roof again. Our windows, as ever, looked out on the water. Only the water was not the blue of the Aegean but the blue of the Pacific, equally beautiful (comparisons, as they say, are odious, and in any case I have no intention of sticking my neck out so soon) but more daunting. It is, after all, so terribly *big*. More than all the weeks of travelling, this view of the Pacific makes me realise how far away Australia is from the world we have left.

But all the old friends were there to greet us, friends I have not seen for fifteen years, and it was comforting to find that one did not, in fact, need white carnations or name tags for identification. They were all still recognisably themselves, that much older certainly, and that much more prosperous, or at least established ... 'assured of certain certainties,' I thought with a sneaking envy. They were all so very much at home in this land where I am still half alien and certain of nothing, and where it seems to me that only we are precarious. I do agree with Laurence Sterne that 'the balance of sentimental commerce is always against the expatriated adventurer' because Nature 'has effected her purpose in the quietest and easiest manner by laying him under almost insuperable obligations to work out his ease, and to sustain his sufferings At Home'.

Well then, since I did not stay at home, and did become an expatriated adventurer—how misleadingly romantic that sounds—since my continuities (by my own choice, to be sure) are snippets and lengths of many various experiences, I must get on to this question of change. Or statement, rather. 'The old place has changed quite a bit since you saw it last.'

Has it? There is a sort of dreamlike quality in returning to a place where one was young. Memory is as tricky as a flawed window glass that distorts the view beyond according to the way one turns one's head. Change there is, certainly, but in these first few weeks it seems impossible to judge whether the change lies in the place or only in myself. Shamefully, I find that a tourist map is necessary if I am to make my way successfully from point A to point B, and yet there have been days when I have turned a corner with a sharp bright shock of recognition and fifteen years have disappeared; it has even seemed possible that I could meet my own young self walking towards me. This sort of thing can be spooky.

Certain aspects of urban life have been urged upon me as indicia of change. City skylines, for instance. But surely it would be a matter of marvel and wonder only if skylines had remained exactly as they were fifteen years ago. How curious if our Australian cities had slept on, brambled under tangled thickets of oblivion, through all the technological advances that have thrown skyward the new palaces of Brasilia, let alone Omsk, Tomsk, and dear old Pimlico. Even on a small Greek island one was aware that architectural fingers were signposting progress all over the world.

And, yes, there is an obvious European influence—in shop signs, in the variety of wares on display in innumerable delicatessens, in flavoursome scraps of conversation overheard on buses and street corners, in restaurants where the food has improved out of mind and one may drink wine with a meal without being suspected a plonko. But may I suggest that a Continental 'way of life' which so many Australians consider we have achieved (rather, it seems to me, like earning a boy scout's merit badge) cannot be printed on a menu card. It is a matter of the spirit. It requires that a lot of things be taken for granted, including cultural heritages, traditions so ancient and unquestioned as to have become instinct, the crowding proximity of other cultures, other races, other traditions, other languages. And hazard.

Australia seems to be such a safe sort of place, or perhaps this only strikes me so forcibly because for so many years I have been an alien living on police residence permits that could be revoked at a day's notice. Perhaps it is also the fact that I have grown unaccustomed to plenty that makes this land seem such an incredible cornucopia: I feel ever so slightly sinful in supermarkets loading up with more goodies than I have ever seen all together in my whole life.

In a few weeks I have collected a whole cupboard full of empty screw-top jars, not because I shall foreseeably need them, but because it seems downright immoral to throw them out. Admittedly this is ludicrous (like never having had a washing machine or a telly before, or cappuccino served in a plastic takeaway cup) but it indicates habits of frugality that were a matter of course in my mother's generation, and common enough in my own, at least in those years just after the war, which was the last time I lived here. From Australia I went to a still-rationed and very austerity-minded England, and from England to poverty-stricken Greece. So the habit of frugality just stayed with me. Saving screw-top jars, or tins, or bits of string, only becomes ludicrous in a society where children can no longer be bothered to take back empty bottles for refund money, and where, a taxi driver told me, the only reason every family doesn't own an elephant is that nobody yet has thought of advertising them for ten pounds down and a quid a week.

Safety, plenty, prosperity, jobs for all, a television in every lounge room, a car in every garage, steak for breakfast, youth-worship with its attendant permissiveness, and what appears to be the emergence of a new sort of aristocracy based on non-migrant birth. What a fabulous, Utopian land it is.

Now, during all the years of my expatriation I have kept a cliché image of my countrymen and women—frank, fearless, independent, astringent, tough, highly original—an image sustained and even nourished by the picture Australia presents of herself abroad in film, theatre, novel, and migrant-snaring picture book: the lean drover, the overlander, the sundowner, the digger, the surf lifesaver, the lonely man on his horse in the big big land.

Admitting my own presumption (and, yes, I know I can go back to where I came from if I don't like it), and admitting too that national pride in prosperity and material achievement is justified, I am nevertheless led to wonder if these qualities of fearlessness, independence, originality, etc., are thriving noticeably in an affluent and predominantly urban society.

Australian faces have changed perceptibly, softened in some way (city faces, that is, because as yet I have seen only city faces), or perhaps this only seems to be so because at the time I left, most faces—in cities or out of them—were still looking bitter and exhausted from war and its immediate disillusioning aftermaths. But certainly the qualities one has always associated with Australians do not appear to be reflected to any marked degree in cultural achievements as opposed to material ones. Not only techniques but also ideas seem to spring timidly from borrowed or transplanted roots.

Do these qualities in fact exist or have we all been fooling ourselves with a 'Mirror Mirror on the wall, who is the bravest of them all?' attitude?

I suppose that what I have been really looking for is evidence of a spiritual change—a burgeoning and a bursting of the image qualities into a real cultural and social flowering, spiky and wild and refreshing and strange and unquestionably rooted in native soil. Not just Australian singers, but Australian singers singing Australian songs, not just Australian dancers, but Australian dancers dancing Australian dances, not just Australian actors, but Australian actors acting Australian plays written by Australian writers expressing the Australian ideas and challenges in Australian idiom. Not a 'Continental way of life' but an Australian way of life developed naturally from its landscape, climate, and its own heritage.

Yet I do sense deeply a hope and an expectation of such a natural wonder. There *is* a feeling of imminence here. One seems to recognise—perhaps through over-eagerness?—all manner of signs and portents that indicate a mustering of forces for what I have heard referred to over and over again as 'the breakthrough'.

If this is true—and it will not be easy to bring to birth or to sustain without dedication and vigilance—*then* it will be time to say (with assurance, even complacency):

'Yes, the old place has changed quite a bit since I saw it last.'

Social Drinking

For reasons that seem insane in retrospect, but were doubtless sound enough at the time, we spent a wet green winter a few years back in a Cotswold village, so old, so mellow, so authentically Jacobean as to be breathtaking.

In this village it was our invariable habit, every Saturday at midday, to plod up the miry sheep-track to the grey stone pub that crouched picturesquely under bare and dripping elms (English country pubs, I swear, are all prefabricated in film studios and staffed by extras filling in the time until the next version of *David Copperfield* or *Tom Jones*). There, steaming out in front of the log fire, we would have a couple of pints and listen to the slow blurry buzz of talk about fields and crops and farms and fox-hunting and fences and guns and dogs and lambing seasons past and to come. Village talk, like village pubs, is just too authentic to be quite real. There was always a certain fascination in waiting for some rustic in leggings and flat cap to slip up and reveal himself as bogus. Nobody ever did.

Anyway, we had never managed to swallow even the first pint when there was a sense of diversion, grins and nudges and winks and a delighted slapping of gaiters, and there, on the far side of the misted window, noses pressed to the glass like three forlorn waifs most wickedly abandoned, were our three cunning children, hatless and coatless, sopping wet (they confessed long afterwards that they often rolled in the long grass in the apple orchard on the way) and with noses and cheeks and fingers cherry-red with cold.

It was, of course, flagrant moral blackmail, and instead of ransoming our warm and pleasant social hour by paying up in pineapple juice—which they drank outside in the rain, with many exaggerated shivers and pathetically yearning glances at the bright and cosy parlour denied them—we probably should have fetched them a crisp backhander apiece. That they escaped was only due to their continuing and quite genuine bewilderment at being forbidden access to a perfectly ordinary public tavern where people were only drinking. If we could take the dog inside and welcome, what was the matter with them?

Summoning our rather frazzled patience we would explain again that the discrimination against our children was not of our doing. It was the Law. And in England the Law supposed that young persons of less than eighteen years were liable to corruption if given free access to licensed premises. The children, like Dickens' Mr Bumble, gave us clearly to understand that if the Law supposed that, then 'the Law was a ass'. Had they been corrupted in Greece, where the dogs were shut out and the children made welcome? Sighing—perhaps a little wistfully by this time, for we, too, were missing things—we explained that Greece was different.

Partly, of course, this is a matter of climate. There are no deceptions possible in the sun. Everything is open. Everything revealed. Almost all drinking in the Mediterranean is completely public and unregulated by any law except that of good taste and regional custom. Thus, on Kalymnos, the first Greek island where we lived for any time, I was the first woman ever to drink in a taverna, only because the women, by ancient tradition and preference, restricted their social activities to the purely domestic world (where, heaven knows, they conducted some of the gayest parties I have ever attended). In the tavernas the men were invariably warm to me, gentle, considerate, and totally unresentful.

On the next island, less formal in tradition and because of tourism undergoing a minor social revolution, both men and women were quick to see the advantages of mixed public drinking, and—shyly at first, but with increasing confidence—the men brought their wives with them in the evenings to taverns and restaurants and waterfront cafes. As far as an outsider can judge, nothing but good came of it.

In the Mediterranean there are virtually no secret drinkers, either women or men, and while every village or community will have a regular drunk or two—usually set great store upon as a 'character'—regular drunks are the exception even if regular drinking is the rule, and this seems to be less a matter of weak heads than natural good sense and moderation. Where there are no authoritarian pressures or wagging fingers of warning there is no need for defiance or proof: people, left alone, are usually so much more sensible about their own needs and pleasures than they are ever given credit for.

In any case, moral authority in Greece belongs to the church, and wine is part of the church ritual, the sacrament to the great mysteries of birth and mating and death. When the wine boats of Hydra set off for Attica at the end of summer to bring back the new season's vintage (each empty barrel scoured with sea water and every bung stoppered with bay leaves) the priests in a mist of incense flock to the waterfront in brocades and embroidered silks, carrying bowls of holy water and bunches of rosemary with which to bless boats and barrels and to ensure good wine and the safe homecoming of the vintage. There is both reverence and joy explicit in this ceremony, and looking at the high-prowed boats whose decks were so anciently and beautifully murmurous with leaves, I always thought of the ship of Dionysus, bringing the new religion of wine.

Now, in a community where normal drinking is regarded as both a joy and a blessing, as the indispensable accompaniment to food and conversation and song and dance, and to ceremonial too, the public places in which one drinks—being untainted by even the whiff of shame or secrecy or the imposed regulation of officialdom—are inclined to be unselfconscious and charming, whether a whitewashed courtyard blazing away with geraniums growing in kerosene tins, a couple of painted iron tables under a vine or an awning (sun-faded and caught in a moving mesh of water reflections) or, in winter, the back room of some grocery shop festooned with plaited garlic and cotton waste and bags of nails and old galvanised bathtubs and that wonderful smell of hot honey coming from the corner where the proprietor's wife is pouring melted beeswax over revolving threads of string to make church candles. Yes, and children coming or going on errands, cadging money for sweets or ice-cream or chestnuts, listening in on adult conversation until noticed and cuffed out of the way: nuisances, certainly, but uncorrupted—at least uncorrupted by the fact that their elders happened to be sitting around drinking.

So we were wistful that wet winter in the Cotswolds for such an easy, unrestricted, pleasant way of having a social drink together with mutual friends. But in these first weeks of my return to Australia I am wistful even for the restricted public drinking of an English village, let alone a host of other places where we have talked whole nights away over magic bottles without stay or hindrance. There was the wine town of Alf on the Moselle (little fires burning under the vines to protect them from the spring frosts, and although a cuckoo in the woods said 'cuckoo' in the most impeccable English, nobody ever said 'Time, please', and the landlord stayed with us till nearly dawn wondering how the cuttings he had sent to the Barossa Valley in South Australia were flourishing). Or Telfs, in the Tyrol (wooden inns with great hot porcelain stoves and the beer in ornate tankards and bunches of forget-me-nots in copper pots and at three in the morning the vintner insisting on cooking sausages as a bedtime snack). Orvieto (getting a bit tight on Montefiascone too early in the day and driving up the hill to the town in perfect and sublime agreement with Dante—'Orvieto is high and strange!'). Oh, and Christopher Wood inns in Brittany and all those 'Never on Sunday' cafes in the back streets of Piraeus and the strange illuminating encounters in strange taverns on strange waterfronts, Naples and Marseilles and Dieppe and Venice and Lerici and Paros and Patmos and Canea.

I know that this is romantic stuff and I am very lucky to have had it, and I don't really expect landlords in my own home town to stay up all night waiting for us to finish our drinks and our interminable talk. But I *do* think that we are all missing something somewhere along the line, and that there should be any number of pleasant accessible places, and unpretentious too, where men and women can eat and drink and talk together without necessarily making a great occasion of it. I am not thinking in terms of city restaurants, and I agree that they are good if you can afford them (although in Melbourne recently I was *agape* to see the wine whipped off tables at ten o'clock, and later, attempting to alleviate the embarrassment of my hosts over this incident by inviting them to have a drink at my hotel, to be asked for my room number and to have to wait, like a suspect call girl, for its confirmation by the desk clerk before a waiter would take the order: that's really nasty stuff to my way of thinking, and it occurred in quite one of the smartest and most sophisticated hotels in Melbourne).

Anyway, a nice cosy little local pub would do, if there was one, but we are living in one of those desirable residential areas that don't hold with local pubs, in spite of the stupendous beaches and bays and yacht harbours and boat sheds and wharves right on the doorstep that knock most of the Mediterranean for a loop.

No, if we want a drink and a chat outside 'the Home'—and I am playing Barry Humphries' records again with a new and enthralled fascination—we have to walk several blocks, take a bus (if we can get one) for several miles to a shopping centre where there is a fancy red brick hotel embedded in much plate glass and chromium. *I* am not allowed into the white-tiled, aseptic, toilet-like bars, and my husband is not allowed to escort me up to the Rainbow Room or whatever it is (and sleazy and horrid it is, too—a phoney roof garden with plastic jungle, fancy parquet floors, a tired three-piece orchestra playing to groups of tired women talking about ailments—but the only place where we may drink together publicly) unless *he* wears a tie.

Last week, tracking down a furniture restorer we had heard of, we found ourselves at lunchtime in a suburb that was closer to town and not so 'desirable' as the one we live in. It could be, we thought, it *must be* the place where some enterprising foreigner had started a beer-and-sandwich garden, or a vino-and-spaghetti cellar, or even an English-type local with toad-in-the-hole and warm beer (which we would drink if necessary). Exhausted with searching we ended up in the Lounge of yet another red brick chromium and plate glass monstrosity. A furtive, illicit-seeming room it was, sickly pea-green in colour, decorated with dismal ceramic ducks wallbound in a travesty of flight, lit by an innuendo of light from central pink plastic fittings (and the day outside the most tender piercing blue with a fresh little breeze and a scud of vehement cloud) and patronised by dimly seen couples of uncertain ages talking in whispers over short drinks on glass and chromium tables.

I dared not look into any of the art-nouveau mirrors: I knew that we would appear to be as furtive and illicit as everybody else ... and we would look as unnatural and as joyless, too.

We had a beer and what was called a 'sizzler'—a great big toasted sandwich that was really terribly good—and we said to each other: all right then, it's the winds ... give up the idea of tables on pavements. Still ... if you could rip up the wall-to-wall just in that one room, release the poor embedded ducks, pour gallons of white paint over stripped bricks, consign the glass and chromium furniture to the Salvation Army and set up a few plain benches, plank tables, stools, windsor chairs, replace the pink plastic arrangement with cheap white paper Japanese lanterns, trade the plastic jungle in for one real geranium in a real kerosene tin ...

'Awfully sorry, dear,' the blonde waitress whispered conspiratorially to my husband. 'Gents only in this lounge after half-past one. If you'd like to buy your good lady another drink you'll have to go to the Tudor Lounge upstairs. On the third. Quite nice it is really—panelled and all that— and there's a nice orchestra comes on in the afternoon and plays ...'

Second Class Citizens

I am one too. And, being one, I feel entitled, like Laurence Sterne's Uncle Toby, to climb on my Hobby Horse and gallop away at exhilarating pace over any and every obstacle in my path.

This has been sparked by a letter published in a newspaper recently under the heading 'Australian Women 2nd Class Citizens', which is signed by three women university students who complain bitterly—and I believe with justice—of continuing sexual apartheid in employment, wages, social standing, and moral judgements. More fascinating even was one of the replies, from a man, headed 'Woman's Place', and a more pompous, peevish bit of nonsense I have never read.

So the battle is still on. Here and there, anyway.

I have read much and heard much about the Australian social habit of the boys sticking with the keg of beer at one end of the room and the girls in a gaggle of gossip at the other. Honestly, I have not yet encountered this social phenomenon—the only men and women I know intimately share a community of interests that would make such a social segregation unlikely, to say the least—but there can't be smoke without a flicker of fire somewhere, and so many reputable writers and thinkers have commented upon this aspect of Australian life that there must be a truth in it somewhere.

I have lived in very primitive places where the segregation of the sexes was absolute (except for bed and board), defined and dignified by ritual, custom, tradition, and law, where each sex had its separate duties and obligations as well as its own privileges, and also (and this I think important) its inviolable mysteries.

In a primitive community it is likely that a woman will bear many children and that a man will have to engage in hard physical labour to support them. But the divisions in duties are practical and clear, and the dignities are maintained on both sides. There are no first and second class citizens. The sexes are different and that's that.

But no such conditions exist here. Women are not doomed to bear hordes of children, nor are men doomed to support them by wrenching a living from unfriendly soil. We have moved very far from such a basic simplicity, and there isn't an Australian I have met yet who hasn't pointed out to me—with enthusiasm, pride, and sometimes a profound pessimism—how big and complex and modern our civilisation has become.

Granting that, one wonders a little impatiently how much longer it is going to be before society faces up to the inescapable fact that women are fully-fledged members of the human fraternity, and as such entitled to participate in its economic, social, and cultural life on terms of absolute equality. That such an acknowledgement is inevitable eventually is clear enough; theoretically it was made when women won for themselves the right to vote in a future that concerned them as closely as men, and as directly.

The old arguments about women's comparative physical frailty and biological limitations are not only hypocritical but just plain silly in a civilisation where brute strength is scarcely the gauge of a person's usefulness to the community, and where women are being liberated constantly from domestic tyrannies by more and more efficient labour-saving devices and the right to choose the number of children they will bear at the times most convenient to bear them. Women can, if they want, organise their lives in such a way as to make their specialised feminine superiorities available to a society that needs them as much as specialised masculine superiorities if it is not to become lopsided.

This is all so obvious—indeed, so elementary—that one is forced to turn the penny over, as it were, and to wonder also whether the fact that the acknowledgement of equality so far is only theoretical, partial, and without conviction isn't due to a certain half-heartedness, a lack of stomach for the fight, in the ranks of the women themselves.

The assumption of rights automatically entails the relinquishing of some privileges. One of the comforts of an inferior position is the lack of responsibility that goes with it. Any ranker in the army knows this; it's the poor harassed bloke with the pips on his shoulders who has to make the decisions, and take the blame for them too if the decisions happen to be wrong. Inferiority implies weakness and weakness implies protection. Now protection might at times be suffocating, irksome, or even humiliating to a free and enquiring spirit, but it is terribly cosy for all that, and chivalry and solicitude are such charming words.

It has been suggested by one writer whom I respect that Australia's relatively small female labour force is partly due to suburban housing—that rosy encrustation of blushing bricks that spreads out over leisurely miles around every city, each separate plot a hallowed domestic kingdom so comfortable and secure that the reigning housewife has little compulsion to stir out of it into the harsh, demanding world of competition and decision-making. She does not need any justification for declining to enter the income-earning lists as long as the old man is earning well and the household gods—car and telly and washing machine and motorised lawnmower—are getting their monthly tithes. If she does feel a sneaking need for justification, she has it in her domestic duties.

There are some of us who find housework, although necessary, to be tedious, dull, repetitive, and negative in that it aspires to no end but the perpetuation of the present. It is a maddeningly dreary cycle of making things clean to get dirty again, a sort of running-on-the-spot that uses up a tremendous amount of energy in not getting anywhere at all. In fact, far from achieving anything, one is actually slipping back all the time, since everything deteriorates and wears out eventually, entirely in the process of being kept clean and in use.

Fortunately—and my cynical children have christened the new washing machine Zoe in memory of the doleful Greek girl who was its predecessor—labour-saving devices have liberated us from drudgery ... and, yes, I know it is all very well for me to talk about drudgery in the same breath as a Greek maid, but I only mean that the washing machine is actually cheaper and more efficient, and golly how we used to have to suffer for her aching back, and how sadistically she tyrannised over us! Every washday was Euripidean—Greek tragedy on the full scale: the cistern, the bucket, the pump, the tin tub, the green soap, even the clothes pegs became animate and fraught with malevolence ...

Well then, we may now, if we please, regard our household duties as negative and more or less inconsequential, to be got over as quickly as possible so that we can use our time to some more exciting and rewarding end. It has often occurred to me that men are much gayer about household chores than women are, because in fact they regard them as simply that—

chores—and not an end in themselves: for them the really important things tend to happen outside.

Having leisure, we also have the incomparable luxury of choice as to how we use it. In the suburb where I am living at the moment I am fascinated by the number of collective female activities that seem to be going on every day. There are bridge clubs and bowls clubs and tennis clubs and luncheon clubs. Cars filled with ladies in sparkling white uniforms and bosomed badges whizz along the Groves and the Avenues and the Crescents between the desirable brick residences and the lawns and the groomed azaleas. Healthy young women, tennis racquets in hand, healthy babies on sturdy hips—all of them looking like breakfast cereal advertisements—meet on corners and pile into smart station wagons. In front of a rather opulent Spanish style bungalow a long line of very shiny cars disgorges an older and more sophisticated group of women, elegant in luncheon dresses and pearl chokers.

In the Rainbow Room of the pub where my husband and I occasionally seek a kind of subdued social sanctuary for the want of somewhere better, we listen in unashamedly to 'the girls' (this is their own term, not mine), six of them, all much of an age, with children grown up, or earning anyway. This isn't idle eavesdropping—we really do want a clue or a sign, a word of illumination.

And, yes, it's true, the conversation *is* of their own and their children's illnesses and ailments, of specific cures and household appliances, of clothes, daughters' pregnancies, personal gossip with a high moral tinge, and through it all an ironic, faintly derisive putting down of men. There seems to be a real complicity in this, a collective affirmation of the female universe they hold in common where they can convince themselves and each other that purely domestic values outweigh the values of their men, who are tiresome, inept and clubby little boys, really, but have to be humoured.

'The girls' are of a generation, and one must admit, in fairness, that they have kept their homes and raised their families and battled through their separate domestic difficulties, and are now entitled to meet and chat about the things that are most important to them. Certainly it does not seem very likely that Australia will develop a matriarchy of the American type—those powerful, neurotic, terrifyingly efficient blue-rinsed women who dominate that business world by capability and energy and sheer implacable will, women to be placated and feared and admired too because of their enormous influence and their control over so much of the country's purchasing power, to say nothing of its mores.

What then of the legions of young women—better fed, better educated, better dressed, better paid than ever before in Australia's history? One sees them swinging along the city pavements, crowding mornings and lunchtimes and evenings with a sheen of clean loveliness, flocking to the universities, clear skins and shining hair and beautiful healthy bodies dressed in clothes that have as much flair and style and good taste as anything in Europe's capitals. They are tremendously impressive in their young sexual arrogance—yes, and let's face it, their lack of mystery.

How many of them, one wonders, have the desire and the tenacity and the confidence to carry on the fight for the dignities and responsibilities of a real equality? How many are going to be discouraged along the way and settle for something less, but easier? How many talents are going to come to full fruition, and how many atrophy and be lost to a society that needs all the talents, especially the young talents, it can muster?

And how many, when all's said and done, still see as the prime goal the safe protective custody of some suitable man of sufficient income to provide the red brick haven, the shoulder to lean on, the reassuring moral authority on which she can prop herself, secure in the approbation of society, a self-elected second class citizen?

Youth Revisited

My late father, a dogmatic man and something of an armchair philosopher, used to be given to saying—among other trenchant pronouncements—that the air of our home town would be worth a quid a whiff if some quack could bottle it and get out a patent.

At that time, being young and eager to breathe more exotic air than that of a small country town, I put it down to his parochialism, for he was indeed a very biased man about all things local—possibly because he was English anyway, and therefore the town was his by choice rather than any accident of birth.

Now, having just returned from a sentimental pilgrimage to my birthplace, I am inclined to think that a quid a whiff is a bargain basement rate.

Sentiment is heady seasoning, I know, and hometown air is unique whether it is flavoured with factory soot or eucalyptus leaves. But it was incredibly good to breathe it again—something between tangy and sweet, such clean country air, spiced with smells of kelp and clover and cow-dung, mixtures of sea brine and rich loam turned in the sun.

My home town is small as towns go, three thousand people perhaps, and for some reason industry has passed it by—or never quite reached it—for to the north there are tall forests of chimneys belching progress and around them the fibro scabs of the housing developments are creeping out over the paddocks.

Because of its lack of any big industry it has failed to attract migrant settlers, and the sturdy local names—English,

Irish and Scottish—are untainted by unpronounceable foreign terminations, as its way of life is untainted by unmentionable foreign habits.

So the town has this curious air of timelessness, preserved under the sky as under one of those old-fashioned glass domes which in my childhood still protected such mementoes as decorations from wedding cakes, golden keys from twenty-firsts, babies' shoes, bridal wreaths, funeral ribbons, and small bullet-dented bibles that had been worn over soldiers' hearts. (I remembered, standing in the cemetery by the graves of my parents and grandparents, with the sound of the surf beating back from the hills, how absurd once had been the notion of death in connection with any one of us.)

From the blue bulk of the mountains to the blue expanse of the Pacific the hills tumble down, round hills plotted with fields, veined with old stone walls of convict origin, fuzzed with lantana and crowned with crests of cabbage palm and umbrellas of Moreton Bay fig. ('Do you remember,' they said, 'how we went rabbit-shooting on Saturday afternoons?')

The town is on the sea, where the hills end their tumble in purple bluffs that separate casual mile-long sweeps of salmon pink sand frilled with surf and starred with aloe clumps. ('Do you remember,' they said, 'racing over the sand dunes after school? Digging out the lagoon? Worming at low tide?')

It grew around its little hand-hewn port, where the whalers called once and timber-boats loaded up with cedar and later—in my youth—the coastal steamers berthed under the hoppers to fill up with blue metal from the quarries that are worked out now—vast lonely faces of rock shafts cut into the hills and the headlands like excavated temples of ancient and savage origin. (Remembering the vindictive scream of the knock-off whistles, the blast of the detonators, and trotting out to the headland in school holidays with my father's crib-tin.)

When I was growing up the crushed metal was conveyed from quarry to port in a mad little Emmett train that rattled enchantingly up the main street between the old wooden shop fronts and the austere Norfolk pines that march along beside the sea. ('Remember,' she said, 'how we sat on that balcony and set each other's hair and practised the latest songs from the *Boomerang Songster*?')

The train is gone, and the sulkies and buggies are replaced by cars, but the wooden shop fronts are still there, most of them with the same proprietorial names ('Remember the ice-cream sodas, and choosing a length of material from the drapery?') and the pines—taller, straighter, more majestic than remembered—still lace the town together with precise verticals, black against the sky. The cedar is gone too, but that was all gone long, long ago, except for what remains in old barns, and the doorframes and verandah posts of the colonial houses and cottages still preserved in all their grace among the later bungalows of weatherboard and brick and stone (remembering how funny and old-fashioned one had thought those houses to be).

It must always have been a prosperous place, because there has never been any need of new public buildings. The original ones still stand, solid dignified examples of late nineteenth century architecture—nothing temporary there—courthouse, post office, bluestone schoolhouse, banks, council chambers, School of Arts.

The old Oddfellows Hall, where we danced on Saturday nights (first long dress, first romance, first desperately awkward attempt at sophistication) has made way for a spanking new Leagues Club, the Drill Hall has been painted and rechristened the Municipal Annexe, there is a tennis clubhouse, and on the hills above the town a new modern high school ('Our kids get it easy,' they said. 'Do you remember how we had to catch the train at half-past seven every morning?').

But these are superficial things. The spirit is the same. Prosperous without being smug, placid without being somnolent, a summer resort now but without a touch of scabbiness. It is beautiful enough to be a national monument, except that it is too intensely—although quietly—alive. Dairying country now as it always has been, cocky-farming country, with the fat-uddered cows wading through drifts of clover, and in every hollow among willows and peppercorns the remembered rose-and-silver shimmer of homesteads that were built, some of them, a hundred years ago.

We sat in the same old family hotel, catering now, as then, for families on holiday, commercial travellers, club meetings, twenty-firsts, and wedding receptions (there was one in progress, very floral, and a tenor singing 'Where e'er you walk').

We were, all of us, a little soggy with nostalgia.

'Do you remember,' they said, 'how you always swore you'd get out of this town and go and see the world?'

'Yes,' I said. 'I remember. Do the kids these days want to get away too?'

'Some of them,' said one of the gathering, and looked at me with a sort of quizzical aloofness, as at one who had passed long ago out of their community and understanding. 'Funny, isn't it? I mean, there's everything here.'

On Debits and Credits

Since I have come back to Australia I have been asked many times about the advantages and disadvantages of bringing up my children on a Greek island.

Because yes, of course, there *are* disadvantages as well as advantages. But observing those same children now—after two months in a land that is their homeland and yet virtually a foreign country—tearing off in a last-minute spurt to catch school buses, telephoning new friends, bickering about who is going to see what television program, making plans for weekends, practising Twist and Shake until the house rocks, I realise that the debits and credits have balanced out as nearly evenly as if they had spent the last ten years in a more conventional way.

Fortunately for parents, children are such incredibly adaptable creatures.

I remember with what doubts and misgivings I watched the two eldest (seven and five then, and the third one not even thoughts of) during our first few months of island living. Dislodged so suddenly from the familiar, comfortable and utterly secure London pattern of home and school and nursery tea, ordered outings in ordered parks, toys and treats and special family rituals, and thrown into what must have seemed to them to be a barbaric chaos of harsh landscape, strange and unappetising food, uncomfortable housing, savage and barefooted children who patently regarded them as interesting freaks, and without any means of communication whatever, they sickened, grew thin and nervous, and rather pathetically unconfident out of our presence for even a moment.

We hardened our hearts and sent them to school. And an outlandish school it was too—called, for a reason I have never been able to discover, The Black School—catering for the minimal educational needs of the swarms of island children who testified to the virility of their tough, sponge-diver fathers. It was built on the ruins of an ancient Temple of Artemis, and had turned out rather Byzantine in character if not in fact, with an elaborate tinselly chapel, and rows of plain plank benches under hand-drawn charts of primitive husbandry—reaping and threshing and winnowing. The woman teacher wore a long skirt and an apron and a headscarf, very medieval. The male teacher carried a birch rod. The little girls wore patched and faded blue smocks and long hair tied in bows, the little boys also wore patched and faded smocks, but their heads were shaved, and their arms and legs (and their shaved heads too) were scored and scratched and bruised and cut with new and old wounds. They were indeed formidable.

What was interesting was that within a month our pampered little darlings were spurning shoes, neglecting their toys (those they hadn't given away or used as bribes or paid out in blackmail), wolfing bread and oil and olives and goat cheese with every appearance of enjoyment, and jabbering away in Greek with a whole horde of shaven-headed snot-nosed little savages, with whom they raced away every afternoon to shin up ships' masts and rigging, to explore rocky mountain trails, to help with the goat-herding or to trample bales of sponges in the shallows, to fly kites from the high golden rocks that soared over the town. They were playing fivestones, they were fishing from the harbour mole, they were beating an octopus on the rocks, they were triumphantly swimming at last without touching the sand with their feet, they were in and out of houses, sponge-clipping rooms, warehouses, they were following wedding processions and funerals, they were awed spectators in the gruesome slaughterhouse, they were here, there and everywhere—everywhere, that is, except home.

By the time we moved on to the island of Hydra, where we were to live for the next ten years, they had forgotten that any other way of life existed other than one of rather spartan frugality in the way of comforts, and absolute physical freedom. They could sleep on the hardest planks, in shepherds' huts, on the decks of caiques, they could ride donkeys like cowboys, they could swim like fish and fight like tigers. They were beginning to be slightly ashamed of us for our distressing Greek and our *foreignness*, which they felt to be rather humiliating to them personally. We had to get down to serious maintenance work on their English.

But the new pattern was established, and was to be maintained for the next ten years.

The only break in it came after we had been living in Greece for six years or so, and decided to take a trip back to England for six months. Now we had another child, born on the island, and it was uncanny to see the whole thing in reverse. He spoke only Greek, and he had never been off the island of Hydra in his whole four years. He had never seen a train or a car or a neon sign or a hot-water service or a real bathtub or a modern shop or any traffic (other than a mule train or a string of fishing boats) or a vacuum cleaner or a garden hose or a lawnmower or a kitchen gadget.

And yes, of course, he panicked, grew thin and nervous, unconfident, clinging, whiny; rallied, and came back to Greece at the end of six months speaking English with a quaint Gloucestershire accent and no Greek whatever, to the horror and dismay of his Greek nurse and all his little Greek friends, who could neither believe nor understand it. So we had to go through another couple of months of readjustment.

After that we stayed put.

Now, on the debit side, I think it has been trying for the children to have foreign parents. Children are really conformists, and I think they found it quite hard work to live down the fact that their mother wore pants and smoked and frequented the waterfront taverns, and that both their parents spoke Greek lamentably enough to make them targets for childish ridicule. They were particularly vulnerable during the Cyprus troubles, when all their little friends were being valorous about EOKA, and they, for the life of them, didn't know which camp they were in. They solved it characteristically, the elder with reason and some moral courage, which was appreciated and worked not only in his favour but in ours too, and the second by throwing in her loyalty absolutely with the other children and leading bands of them round the back streets shouting 'Death to the English', which worked in her favour and ours just as much as her brother's moral stand for justice.

There were religious difficulties also, since there is only one religion in Greece, and nobody even has a name or an identity until he is baptised. Also, religion is a compulsory school subject. We left it up to them. One decided to stay outside the Greek Orthodox Church but to take religion as a school subject, one decided to be baptised and take a new Greek name, and in the case of the baby we decided to have him baptised without his consent, since it seemed desirable he should have a name rather than not, the neighbours and townspeople were thrilled, and it tactfully sidestepped another possible charge of parental peculiarity against the older children. It was a very happy baptism, at which all the islanders were present, and none of us has ever regretted it.

On the debit side also, from my own point of view, was the total lack of medical facilities, and the ever-present nagging worry about accidents, emergencies, teeth and tonsils and appendix, mule kicks, mad dogs, and the fact that there was only one steamer a day, which took three and a half hours to make the journey to Piraeus. We kept our fingers crossed and I learnt first aid and kept a well-stocked medicine cabinet, and luckily nothing ever happened that I couldn't cope with.

The credits are good. Once the children got through primary school and entered *gymnasium*, they received as fine a classical education as one could wish anywhere in the world. Old-fashioned certainly, terribly disciplined, without hobby or play periods or consideration of their psyches, but very sound. Also they have grown up with basic and real values, and probably for as long as they live they will never quite take for granted water and food and warmth and shelter, because they have lived for so long in a place where people have been hungry sometimes, where water depends upon rainfall and is often rationed, where the household roof is almost a sacred thing, where a shady tree is precious, where life is lived to an ancient pattern of ritual that grows out of man's constant and continuing battle with the earth and the sea. They each have two languages, and a deeply ingrained knowledge of another culture. They have standards of comparison which will be of value to them as long as they live.

I am glad to have brought them home again, and they are glad to be here, in a world of modern marvels that is their own to evaluate and to make of what they can and will. Now it is up to them.

On Painting Bricks White

Idling around the neighbourhood blocks just a little time ago we noticed a piece of construction—or alteration, rather—in progress on a private garage that fronts one of the avenues. A couple of men were busily bricking in the entire opening. This in itself was not very interesting and I don't know why we even remarked on it, except that it is a little curious these days to see someone sealing off car space rather than building extra, and one wondered (vaguely) why. Had the owners come to what is called The End of the Tether with all automobiles? Or were they nobly sacrificing car space to a growing family's need for living space? Making a rumpus room? An extra bedroom? A garden shed? Another few square feet of brick doesn't matter much one way or another around these parts.

Only, the next time we passed that way we really did stop and stare. Because the couple of men had a brush apiece, and a big pail, and they were sloshing whitewash all over the completed area of raw brick. Real whitewash. We both stifled a mad impulse to cheer. Instead we walked around the corner to look at the house (which the garage obscured) for the first time. An ordinary house, brick, of course, of the post World War I 'bungalow' period, uninteresting architecturally, but soundly built, probably very comfortable inside (one imagined plaster ceilings with mouldings, and vaguely William Morris fanlights), and transformed from ordinariness into grace by the fact of being painted white.

This was like being given a bonus, or an unexpected Christmas present, and led us to some further explorations, and some further thoughts on the pleasingness of painting bricks white.

Australian suburban architecture is without doubt or question the ugliest in the world. There is nothing to come near it on the civilised globe—or uncivilised either, for that matter: grass huts are beautifully cohesive and harmonious.

Approach any capital city from the air and just look at the rectilinear grids of terracotta ruled out in a stupendous monotony of elementary geometry, a statistical nightmare of raw repetition. Actually, if one makes the urban approach by road instead of air, it is all too horribly apparent that the sameness is deceptive. How in all the world do Australian brick manufacturers manage so many variations on such a painful chromatic theme?

Over and above the dominant Humours—Choleric, Sanguine, Phlegmatic, Melancholic—there are Splenetic bricks, Liverish bricks, Apoplectic bricks, Bibulous bricks (those purplish ones like old drunks' noses), and bricks which appear to have been steeped before baking in the Pancreatic Juices for a special variegated effect.

This is all the more fascinating since bricks aren't (or shouldn't be) in themselves hideous. Bricks are a good honest form of building material and have a long and distinguished history.

Men have been building with bricks for at least five thousand years and probably a good deal longer. Bricks were the very first prefabricated building material. The Egyptians used them, and the Mesopotamians, the Assyrians and the Persians. The Etruscans brought their ancient craft knowledge to Italy, the Romans passed it on to the Byzantines, who, in turn, influenced the Seljuk and Ottoman Turk. Byzantine brick buildings furnished prototypes for the great Lombard development of brick buildings in the eleventh century, and bricks came to dominate the architecture of northern Germany, Denmark, the Low Countries, and England.

Bricks were good enough for Ur of the Chaldees, the Tower of Babel, the Pyramids of Dashur, the Palace of Sargon, the Sassanian dynasty palace near Baghdad, the Colosseum, the Church of Agia Sophia in Constantinople, Brunelleschi's dome in the Duomo in Florence, Michelangelo's in St Peter's, Wren's in St Paul's, the palace of Hampton Court (as well as a thousand other brick castles, manor houses and chateaux all over Europe), whole cities such as Amsterdam and Copenhagen, and the supreme grace and elegance of the Georgian period of architecture in England.

It can't be just age (and soot?) alone that produces that effect of quiet, mellow vibrancy. Perhaps it is a peculiar quality of light? For, certainly, whether one approaches an Australian city by land, sea, or air, all that brick gives a sort of *inflamed* effect.

Very distinguished architects and authorities have talked a lot and written a lot about the Great Australian Ugliness, and fulminated (with justice, I think) against the architectural errors of the past, and the architectural delinquencies of the present. I have just been reading Robin Boyd (whom I would recommend as required reading to anyone really interested in what makes us tick as a people and as a country) and agree with him absolutely that it is the uses to which perfectly honest bricks have been put that is the core of the ugliness.

But—alas—what's done is done, and we can hardly, even in the cause of aesthetics, bulldoze down whole square miles of errors and delinquencies and start again. No, the double-fronts and the bow-fronts and the feature windows and the sundecks will have to stand now, and the 'contemporaries' and the 'semi-contemporaries' and all those 'home units' that look like tall, ransacked chests of drawers. Perhaps, one golden day soon, people will begin planting trees to replace those that have been hacked down by the subdividers—those great Australian axemen—to make way for the bare building plots, and then branches and leaves will mercifully soften and disguise the nude brick boxes.

In the meantime, what we *could* do—and I know this is a revolutionary thought—is to get out the whitewash brushes.

In the course of our explorations (begun on the fact and the hope of one whitewashed garage) we happened upon some lovely individual discoveries of white houses—old, new, beautiful, ugly-made-beautiful—and finally a whole street of white houses. I would think they were built in the 1920s, not one of them pretentious, not one of them beautiful, with the usual old half-verandah and projecting gabled front room, all standing back at a decent number of feet from their front gates and lawns.

But because they were all white the whole street was cohesive. It had a harmony and unity and dignity far beyond the architectural worth of any of its individual components. No house was competing with its neighbours for attention, and all that clean white under the blue sky made a tranquil background for pretty gardens and green grass and a few spectacular blood-red bracts of bougainvillea.

I was reminded, naturally enough, I expect, of Mediterranean towns, towns of Calabria, towns of any Aegean island, towns that are really only huts made of mud and daub riveted to bare treeless hillsides and breathtakingly beautiful because they are painted white. Property owners (and tenants too) are compelled by law to whitewash their houses once a year. On Mykonos, an island busting out at every cobbled seam with civic pride and tourist-awareness, it is *twice* a year.

The point is that the tourists—Australian tourists, many of them, straight from the inflamed brick areas—make the proper gasping responses and start in frenetically with their cameras.

Perhaps it *is* all a question of the peculiarities of light. Naked brick becomes mellow and vibrant under soft European light, but just wouldn't do in the Mediterranean, where whitewash works better, for harmony and beauty (and camouflage too).

I know it's a daring suggestion, but I'll make it anyway. Might not a poultice of whitewash reduce the inflammation of our brick areas also?

On Lucky Dips

The occasion of my elder son's seventeenth birthday the other day was also the occasion of the first party the children have given since their return to their homeland, and the first opportunity I have had to observe a big group of Australian teenagers socially.

They swarmed—gaggles of dewy girls hopefully beruffled like Tom Jones wenches, alarmingly elegant young men with stylish bangs and winkle-picker shoes who had all, apparently, been melted and poured into their pants before setting out. However, contrary to what the newspapers had led me to expect, they all had manners ranging from good to impeccable, really preferred soft drinks to hard, and were uninhibitedly young, and joyful rather than blasé or just rowdy in their singing and dancing. No couples, packs, or mixed teams disappeared at any stage into the bushland that surrounds our house, and there were no gate-crashers.

Far from being decadent, I found them rather poignant, particularly the young men—most of them in their senior school year or first year at university and tentatively positioned on the launching pad for the big take-off into adulthood.

Because this was a birthday and these were young men, one thought inevitably of the coming lotteries and wondered which of them—any of them? all of them?—in two years' time or three or one would receive among the cards and gifts and congratulations and sentimental commerce appropriate to the day that other official acknowledgement of manhood that will demand two years out of their lives.

They themselves were discussing the subject with a fairly good attempt at cynicism, but none of them really seemed to believe in it as a probability, at least not as a personal probability. It was, after all, years away and ten to one against. Still, there was a certain uneasiness, and one or two of them were almost sheepish, as potential victims of an unseemly practical joke.

Their elders, however, some of whom were hiding out with us in a relatively soundproof room, were vocal about reactions that ranged from bafflement to outrage.

Nobody objected in principle to national service if it was proved to be really necessary. A couple of parents thought that most kids these days (including their own) were overindulged and that a period of camp life and discipline would foster self-reliance and initiative. (Here there was discussion of street gangs, rape packs and gate-crashers.) Everybody was in agreement that two years was excessive and that it should be possible to arrange training periods that did not interfere too drastically with the important business of a young man establishing himself in a tough and highly competitive society. (University long vacation was suggested, and the Lebanese system of making military training a compulsory subject in the last two years of high school.)

Having established their reasonableness as parents and citizens they then gave vent to their feelings, and it was illuminating to see in these prosperous, middle-aged, middle-class, and in the main conservative people a copybook illustration of the Australian mystique—the authentic, fiercely independent spirit of the cabbage tree hat and the Currency Lads, rebellious against officiousness and authority, refusing to be pushed around.

Firstly, they were angry in varying degrees that they, the people, had not been consulted on the matter. I had no feeling that there was any particular political basis in this, but a reaction against authoritarianism generally.

Secondly, although the word 'honour' was not used, they appeared to feel—some obscurely, some deeply—that Australian honour had been slighted, if not insulted. If the cause was just there had never been any lack of volunteers to go and fight for it. National pride was involved here, shades of Anzac were invoked, the Depression and the Sixth Divvy, examples of selflessness and outstanding courage cited, and the draft systems of other armies derided or condemned. They appeared to be in agreement that an integral part of the national charter of liberty was their right to decide themselves the justice of a cause and their degree of participation in it.

But most perturbing of all was the fact that the choice will be random, and I wonder if this might not prove to be a toad just too nasty to swallow. Someone (perceptively, I thought) mentioned Kafka. And indeed there *is* something extremely sinister about putting lives in a lottery barrel, suggesting as it does that THEY consider human life to be inconsequential. The point was made that such a system was open to manipulation by the unscrupulous, and it seems a fair point—I know that in other countries where I have lived it is common practice for the rich to buy their sons' exemption from military service, and the influential always find a way out.

It seems to me too that it is bad, psychologically, to wantonly divide a whole generation of young men into Fortunates and Unfortunates. For even if a couple of years of military service might prove to be actually beneficial to a young man, he will be considered unlucky to be compelled into it by blind chance, with the stigma of humiliation that attaches to bad luck. Compulsion is degrading, and it seems a pity to degrade youth at the very moment when it is struggling to achieve the dignity of adulthood. This quite apart from the fact that the Unfortunates will be forcibly restrained from competing with the Fortunates for two whole years, which is a fairly sizeable handicap in a fast, modern society.

'All of them or none of them,' said the Cabbage Tree Hat mob in the back room, and out on the verandah the very young dandies laughed uneasily at the concluding verse of a Tom Lehrer song ...

> It makes a feller proud to be
> What as a kid I vowed to be
> What luck to be *allowed* to be
> a sol-ol-ol-dier!

Christmas

The harbour view from my study window, so cool and magical until now, offers nothing at the moment but intimidation. The sea is dull and battered flat by the burning wind, and in the foreground my favourite eucalypts are streaming sorry parched banners. My daughter, wilting, reports that the sea is unpleasant to swim in, like bathing in sticky soup (if one can wiggle through the half-naked crowds milling there in the hope of relief and get to the water at all), and the sand is too hot to walk on barefoot.

The city is ringed by bushfire smoke—one gets the sharp, dangerous, acrid smell every now and again, and the sirens of the fire engines have been wailing hysterically all the morning. In this house we flounder about gasping, like landed fish.

It is really rather strange to be having a hot Christmas again.

Not that it *is* actually Christmas at the time I write this, but the parties started weeks and weeks ago, and the advertisements are now so urgent as to make one fearful of forgetting or missing, or being late with the suitable emotions as well as the expensive gifts. Shop assistants are looking really harried, young mothers exhausted, children fretful, fathers worried (for their bank accounts undoubtedly). It is difficult to imagine cheer and goodwill eventuating from it all, although one knows from experience that it often does, like those wobbly stage productions where everything comes right on the night. I suppose Christmas is about miracles anyway.

I will never forget our first Christmas in Greece. We had arrived only a few weeks before, filled with our own audacity but bewildered nevertheless. Rainstorms were raging and fuming on every day, our temporary accommodation—unfurnished—leaked, our children were punch-drunk with unfamiliarity and discomfort to the point of near imbecility. No more dismal or disillusioned little band ever stumbled into its Promised Land.

The approaching feast and the indisputable fact of Christmas was to the children the one familiar safe beacon beckoning in a world that must have seemed then to be on the point of disintegration.

But the imminence of Christmas was for us parents a nightmare. For as the days passed and the rainstorms gave way to that deceptive December sun of Greece and we scouted around the little island desperately for a single sign of festive preparation, it was gradually made apparent that the Christmas celebration, as we mindlessly knew it, did not exist.

Easter is the great feast of the Greek year, New Year is the time for gift-giving. Christmas is a religious day, honouring the birth of Christ, but definitely not a spree. Nobody, alas for the children, had ever heard of one S. Claus.

There were no gewgaws, bells or decorations for sale in the few island shops, no children's toys, no greeting cards, no bonbons, coloured lights, tinsel, holly wreaths, or imitation snow. And—Mother of God!—what could we possibly want with a *tree*?

Nevertheless we found one, or, rather, our new and completely mystified Greek friends found one for us. Not exactly a tree, but the branch of a tree—a salt tree branch still encrusted with hen droppings and with a couple of tentacles of dried octopus hanging from it. And on this precious bit of greenery we hung poison-coloured sweets, hundreds of sweets, kilos and kilos of sweets on poison-coloured ribbons. Both sweets and ribbons seemed to be in plentiful supply.

And we found (miracle of miracles) five tiny and rather dented celluloid dolls forgotten in a dusty box marked 1921 below the counter in a coffee house (bought for what child, when, and why never given, we wondered), and we dressed them, Mary, Joseph, the Kings and the Baby, in scraps of material cut from underneath the hems of my dresses and more poison-coloured ribbons, and we carefully undid the links of all my brummy bracelets and earrings and necklaces for jewels to deck them with.

We made haloes from chocolate wrappings, silver and gold, and a flock of sheep from scraps of sponges and matchsticks for legs, and a manger from bamboo and straw, and frost from a packet of coarse salt, and we painted—from the children's watercolours still surviving—a backdrop of kneeling shepherds, Hark Herald Angels (with trumpets) and a marvellous wobbly five-pointed star.

The children didn't have any Christmas presents that year, but they gave a wonderful party for the swarms of island young who had tagged them since their arrival. All the tree decorations were eaten as well as the peculiar assortment of food I had been able to assemble, and the party stood in front of the crib with its bank of church candles and sang the one Greek Christmas carol over and over and over again.

I don't think Christmas was ever quite as basic for us after that, but the crib survived year after year, refurbished, redecked, and the backdrop repainted by artists famous now, but not then. And it became the custom for the carol singers to sing their one carol in front of it, at four o'clock in the morning usually, which could be distressing—snotty-nosed tots, bands of high-school girls sweetly conducted by one of their mistresses, village drunks, wharf labourers carrying a gramophone with an ancient horn to do their carol-singing for them. It was part of Christmas ceremonial.

So was the tree. On Christmas Eve Barba Yanni the muleteer brought two donkeys and left them at the gate of our house and our neighbour lady graciously gave the children permission to climb to the top of the mountain and cut two small fir trees from her grove. One for us and one for her. We used to make an all-day picnic of it, experienced children, bewitched guests, loaded with food and straw-covered wine flasks, climbing for miles in the crisp and sun-dazzled weather to the thicket high above the highest monastery. Not many Christmases passed before it was common to meet other tree parties out on private or communal forays. A tree had become a status symbol.

Fortunately the gradual seeping through of the true commercial spirit of our western Christmas saved the little fir thickets of the island from total destruction.

Last time Barba Yanni brought his donkeys the neighbour lady said wonderingly: 'Of course you may have a tree, but why put yourselves to so much trouble? Look, I have such a pretty plastic one. See? It goes up and down like this. Put it away after. Use it next year just the same. You can buy one from Mitso.'

Indeed one could buy a plastic tree from Mitso. A miniature plastic tree or a little plastic tree or a middling plastic tree or a plastic tree so tall it wouldn't fit inside the shop. And from Yanni also. And from Sotero. And from every tobacconist, grocer, fruit shop on the island. And one could buy gewgaws and bells and coloured lights both plain and flower-shaped, and bonbons and tin toys and imitation snow and holly wreaths and Christmas stockings and celluloid figures of that recent saint added to the Greek calendar—S. Claus. Caique-loads of turkeys were being unloaded onto the waterfront, where they paraded before prospective buyers with ludicrous elegance, gobbling. And one could, if one wished, buy greeting cards depicting a map of Cyprus with S. Claus himself shaking hands across tinselled barbed wire with a gallant *evzone* in a frilly skirt on guard.

And one could buy plastic cribs anywhere.

Before we left Greece we gave our crib to the little girls next door who had loved it for so long. Every year they had helped with the redressing and decking of the dolls, and suggested further additions and fancifications to the manger, and saved silver paper for haloes and stars and angels and cherubs. Every year they had been the first of the pre-dawn carol singers.

And the last we saw of it—as we dropped in next door to say goodbye to their parents—was a ruin of cardboard and bamboo and bits of sponge, and Mary, Joseph, the Kings and the Baby, haloes skewwhiff, robes definitely awry, sitting down to a nice meal of bread and oil served on bougainvillea petals and drinking retsina out of yellow bell-flowers.

The Joys of a City

'The man who is tired of London is tired of life,' said Dr Johnson. E. B. White had much the same feeling about New York. And who hasn't said, written, painted, or set to music everything sayable about Paris? And Vienna. And Rome. And there exist, undoubtedly, jealous lovers of Prague and Budapest and Madrid and Istanbul and Beirut and Tehran and Rio and Hong Kong and Athens and Chicago. Rat race, petrol fumes, poisoned air, population explosion and all, cities are mostly filled with people who really like cities.

I was touched, on my arrival back in Australia, by the number of troubled friends who had tried to help with our housing problem, and more touched by the fact that all their efforts were directed towards finding us a habitation as far out from the city as was compatible with children's schooling and our own work.

In fact, one doesn't voluntarily renounce the donkey pace and lazy charm of island life to seek a pseudo haven on the outskirts of a big city. One renounces it—or at least we did—for the Big City itself, not for its hems and fringes. Rather like people on islands transposing themselves in wistful imagination into the big ships passing, and the people in the big ships gazing speculatively out at islands. The other way is always enticing. Island life and city life are to each other unique, and I love them both wholeheartedly.

Now I have had time to unfreeze from my first paralysis of terror at unremembered size and noise and pace, I find that urban life is as diverse and exciting and rewarding as I had hoped it was going to be.

To begin with, it is so very nice to be comfortable again when one hasn't been really comfortable in years. For me it is still the sheerest luxury to run hot-water taps, to see a bath filling without uneasily wondering about the level of the underground cistern, the contents of the gas bottle, whether my son really *did* pump the deposit tank full on the appointed day, and what horrors might be in store if Tassos the plumber had underestimated the capacity of the cesspit dug illegally under the cobbled lane outside.

There is a permanent sense of the temporary about all island sanitary and electrical arrangements—and about much else, too—and while one was fatalistic there, it is pretty marvellous to be surrounded by desirable amenities that actually do work. Hot water that runs, electric light switches that respond to a touch and don't have to be supplemented by oil lamps or candles, flushes that flush, gas on tap instead of from a bottle that always ran out halfway through baking, refrigeration instead of the howling scrum at the ice plant at five o'clock in the morning, household gadgetry instead of a fallible and dependent girl, telephone calls instead of droppers-in and hand-delivered messages, delivery vans instead of the burdened baskets.

Apart from the novelty of comfort, these things free me—or will, I tell myself, when I can free myself from the pleasures and interests and necessities of work—for the enjoyment of all the other urban pleasures I've missed for so long, like hailing taxis, and window-shopping, and lunching out, and idle browsing afternoons in bookshops, or going to the hairdresser, or gawping at men digging a hole in the road, or sifting through junkshops on the chance of a discovery, or riding on top of a bus, or just looking at a skyline and wondering.

There is so very much to enjoy in a city, bizzare, original, strange, appealing. Yesterday it was an Australian accent emanating improbably from a Chinese face across a stall of bananas, and coming home the taxi took me through a mid Victorian street of terraces hung with banners—Save Us From the Bulldozers. Preserve Your Own History. 'The bugs were so fierce in those houses,' the taxi-driver said, 'that if they couldn't finish you orf in the bed they lugged you behind the skirting boards for later. Gawd!' he said. 'Preserve our history! Just wait till they excavate the *bones*!'

And today the typewriter repair shop I was searching for turned out to be a cubbyhole under a gigantic insurance building, crammed with machines and parts of machines and skeletons of machines that looked as though Caxton might have experimented in their construction. The typewriter mechanic was one of those spare stringy old men with sun-cured leather for skin and vapoury blue eyes who must have gone adventuring once to get to look that way. And yes, he had. To the Americas in his youth and the Mediterranean in the First World War and the desert with the Light Horse. And the trouble with the world, *he* said, was that there were no standards any more. Go into a shop and ask for a tin of red paint, he said. Do you think you can get it? No. They'll give you Fuchsia or Pillarbox or Magnetic Flame or Danger or Pirate or Cyclamen Glow. But plain *red*? Never heard of it. Nor blue either. Nor yellow for that matter. The standard of blue was the sea, he said. He'd worked that one out long ago in the Med. And the standard of yellow was gold. And the standard of red was *blood*. He knew a lot about typewriters, too, and one day I shall go back and ask him about the standards of white and black and what it was like in the Americas when he was young.

And tomorrow it might be anything. Rows of chimneypots, cranes on the skyline, wharves and ships with wonderful names, trees growing out of the asphalt, neon lights fuming on at dusk, garish wall signs, a market, a secondhand shop, a group of buildings with something about them, some shabby backwater the home units have bypassed, a European family on a stone doorstep, a front room seen into from the top of a bus, an unexpected invitation, a face in the street.

Whatever it is I'm prepared to enjoy it. Spike heels after bare feet, hair lacquer after salt-dried tangle, formal dresses after old pants and patched shirts, civilised drinks after the rough and resinated island wines, the company of people actively engaged in their own society after the company of people who had repudiated theirs.

I love first nights, last nights, shady bars, sooty spires, glittering parties, stalls of flowers, overheard conversations, beggars who play music, balloon sellers, the backstage of every theatre, delicatessens, subways, the new beauty of TV towers, students' demonstrations, mouldy museums, lights smeared on wet pavements, brass nameplates, glass offices, air terminals, famous people glimpsed in hotel foyers, sailors' pubs, art openings, pretentious intellectuals, tarts in tight dresses, lovers in parks, and in parks, too, the Sunday soapboxes, empty early morning streets, eccentrics, brass bands, ambulances, police cars, fire engines.

Only in cities can one live in daily expectation of the unprecedented. That, I think, is why I love them so much ...

The Sounds of Summer

Whatever has happened to the sounds of summer? The lazy sounds, the drowsy sounds, the indolent sounds?

To those who have time to mark variety in a world where the pace is accelerating at such a rate that variety tends to blur and lose any real definition, the four seasons, rotating still in their own capricious, disorderly, and untamed fashion, act as slyly on the senses as perfume or poetry or that haunting tune one cannot quite remember.

I was thinking, the other day, how much of the essence of a season is embodied in sound. The rustling of breakfast cereal in a plate can evoke for me autumn in Kensington Gardens and idle scuffing about in dead leaves, hail on a tin roof is spring and any force of water roaring brings back wild winter days and the excitement of the rains pouring into an underground cistern. Cicadas are summer.

Last summer, and for many summers before that, in Greece, we used to lunch in the garden, and after luncheon, in siesta time, we often sat on under the thick green hang of the grapevines, immobilised in time, like the figures on Etruscan sarcophagi. Not talking. Listening.

The cicadas would shrill their chorus, and stop, and start again. From the bronze-plated mountain there was the occasional thin drift of bells ... a pad of mule steps or the patterings of donkeys in the lane outside and the soft jingle of harness ... the clank and gurgle of a bucket at the well. Sounds just distinct enough to emphasise the silence; it washed over us like healing poured from some immeasurably vast receptacle. The scent of roses was almost audible, and every yellow nasturtium shouted glory.

I remember, one summer, watching the face of an English guest we were entertaining at the time. He had come to us a week before, from London, neurotic, pasty, anxious, drinking too much. Now in the garden his face wore an expression of rapt contemplation, like a child listening to a seashell. His hand no longer shook. The smoke from the cigarette held in brown relaxed fingers ruled straight up. His glass of wine was still untouched. He had mislaid his pill box two days before. He did not seem to feel the necessity to project any longer. He was as silent as we were, or the summer day around us. One saw how infallible was the panacea of that hot silence to the tense and troubled ones.

This summer in Australia, my first here for many years, is nearly over now and they tell me it has been a very unseasonable one. Certainly it has been different, but then with two summers strung together across the width of the world it was bound to be very different. But the most different thing about it has been my inability to find the old evocative summer sounds.

It should have been so easy, too. We live high, on a rock outcrop that is ancient and was once a tribal meeting place for Aborigines. It is an old house, many streets removed from busy traffic, and insulated against noise by an overgrown, dank, and rather mysterious garden. But sound rises, and there are swimming places below, so that it is holiday sounds, the sounds of an Australian summer, that come up to us.

Now, if I close my eyes this is what I hear. Four—no, five—separate motor-mowers, each with a distinct engine note, one like a buzz saw, which my children call The Screech, and of the others one might even be a motor scooter. Engines of cars swelling and fading. Somewhere a pneumatic drill. Television in one room and record-player in another. When these are shut off for the purpose of the exercise, I hear a Cessna droning overhead, the snarl of a jet, motor launches chugging, the whine and roar of speedboats. As I open my eyes to check on the speedboats (there were two of them, each towing water-skiers) four young people pass with a transistor turned up full volume. The telephone rings, a gust of wind bangs the door, and the ice-cream van turns into our street playing a chime of 'Greensleeves' on a public-address system.

Somewhere under all this, several layers down, there are other summer sounds. Birds burbling and laughing and chiming (they are so numerous and so wonderfully exotic here that sometimes it is a little like living in a fantastic aviary), dogs barking, children calling to each other, and beneath them again, but unheard, there must be, I suppose, other unmechanised sounds like the thump of a ball or the slow wet slap of sails, neighbours chatting, ice chinking in long glasses, waves brushing on sand, perhaps even lovers whispering (if lovers do still whisper). And under all this there is silence, which must have been the essence of this ancient place from the beginning.

Silence, I know, can be disquieting as well as therapeutic. There is no deception in silence. No distortion. If you ask it a question you might only hear the pounding of your own heart. It will allow you nothing but the rare and difficult consolation of being alone with yourself, and your joys and your agonies and longings whether painful or perverse or immortal.

But I think that people probably came to this place once because of the silence, which would have been all the more profound for the bird calls rising and falling in it and the heat tripping the switch of the cicadas.

Now they bring their transistors.

It is strange to think of the immense power for invasion that lies in that tiny little battery thing, everywhere infiltrating the silent places with the noise that summer holiday-makers are trying to get away from. Does silence make them uneasy now, disquieted, one wonders? Or is it that the sense of hearing has suffered permanent disablement under a surfeit of mechanical sound?

A careful watching and hearing of television commercials might offer some clue. There are some soft-voiced wheedlers, of course, but there is no continuity of employment for *sotto voce* on any of the networks, and the lure of the tempter is usually offered at a pitch well above that of ordinary human speech. The point is that from these vocal enticers one is led to believe (if one can put any faith in the fact of *some* sort of psychology motivating the advertisers) that summer fun, summer success, summer status—boy getting girl, girl getting boy, hostess getting praise for picnic food, Dad getting a day Away From It All or even just being admired for smoking the right cigarette, kids getting a square meal—lies in a mass of people pursuing their holiday hobbies or each other at a demented pace with stretched smiles and deranged gesticulations, singing extraordinary snatches of song to the accompaniment of the loudest possible noise, usually in a racket of highly modern machinery.

But doesn't anybody want to sit quietly any more in a quiet place, or lie in the sand or on a carpet of leaves, sun-sodden, drugged with heat-torpor, and listen to the soothing lap of water, a keel scraping on shingle, or a bird or a single voice calling or a leaf dropping or a footstep passing or a chorus of cicadas starting and stopping and starting again? Indolent sounds. Lazy sounds. Therapeutic sounds. Sounds that used to mean summer ...

The Law of the Stranger

When I came home they said expansively, with an honest self-congratulation I admired: 'Ah, it's the European influence that's made all the difference. Look at the way our eating and drinking habits have changed. Look at the restaurants we've got now. Wine with your meal as a matter of course. Look at the delicatessen in any suburb. You've got to admit we've changed to a Continental way of life.'

And I thought then, well, that's a really pleasant and praiseworthy modulation of the old screeching note. When we left this country Europeans were still 'bloody reffos', untrustworthy, unsanitary, un-understandable, undesirable. Un-Australian, in fact. How very nice, I thought, that in these passing years the old attitude has mellowed into tolerance, and that even, generously, Australians are actually giving Europeans credit for effecting improvements in the everyday business of living.

I am beginning to wonder whether, in fact, the tolerance is as genuine as it first appeared to be.

There seems to be a weird sort of ambivalence about it, as about so many other Australian attitudes. As far as I can make it out we are, on the one hand, to commend Europeans for their civilising influence on our way of life, and on the other we are to feel superior because they are, after all, Europeans, and will never quite fit in to our way of life. The indigenous, dinkum Australian Way of Life we are so proud of, that is. Or is it the Continental Way of Life we are so proud of?

'Yes, well look at the way they stick together,' someone said by way of explanation. 'Like burrs to a blanket. Whole streets of 'em. You'd never hear a word of English spoken. They don't even *try* to fit in, if you follow me. Not that I've got anything against them, mind you, and I'd be the first to grant you that they've made a wonderful difference to our way of life—look at the restaurants we've got now'... and so on, all over again.

There isn't even a whisper of the old active hostility in all that, but is it good enough?

The other day I chanced upon a letter in a newspaper from a migrant who had been living with his family in this country for eight years and had not yet set foot inside an Australian home. He wondered about that. So do I. Is it superiority on our part? Is it inferiority? Is it indifference? Or is it really shyness? Because I think that many Australians, contrary to their own image of themselves as an extroverted people, *are* shy, and timid of making a gesture that might be misunderstood, or 'taken the wrong way'. It is so much easier to believe that the Europeans are completely happy 'sticking together' and wouldn't want to know us anyway.

I believe that they do want to know us. And they want us to know them. The fact that they have come such a long way indicates a positive desire for at least a nodding acquaintanceship. And they, unlike us, are accustomed to living in propinquity with other races, other cultures, other languages. It must be very puzzling to them to be excluded because they speak a different tongue and have different domestic customs. There are so many tongues in Europe, and if a man is worth knowing it doesn't matter which one he speaks.

How many hundreds of times in Greece have I heard an Australian visitor exclaim in delighted astonishment: 'But I have never encountered such fabulous hospitality in my life! I hadn't been in (wherever) a day before I was invited into three (or four or five) different homes. They couldn't do enough to make me feel welcome. And the questions they asked! I really felt as if they genuinely wanted to know me.'

Quite right. They did.

In Greece the law of hospitality goes back to Zeus, who decreed it. It is a moral law, not a written one, but none the less binding because of that. And it goes far beyond amiability and ordinary courtesy. The law enjoins that a stranger is to be honoured positively, in whatever way lies within one's power, and not for one's own self-esteem, but for the good name of every citizen of one's village or town or city, for the good name of the state and the honour of the country. A man who failed in his obligation towards the stranger would feel himself to be disgraced. It is a beautiful law, of superb and classic simplicity, and even in these days of moral dinginess, when the tourist-shark has international teeth, he still pays at least lip-service to the ancient law and calls his most comfortable new hotels 'Stranger' and pretends that his services are bestowed from his overflowing heart.

I remember that when we were leaving the island of Kalymnos, where we had lived for a year, to move on to the island of Hydra, the Kalymnians were horrified. 'If you must leave us,' they said, 'don't go there. We beg you. Go anywhere else in Greece. But on that island—you have never heard of such a thing—they *close their doors*!' (It wasn't true, actually. The Hydriots proved to be a little more restrained than the Kalymnians, that's all, and strangers weren't quite such rare birds there.)

'That's all very well,' said somebody else. 'But most of them only come out here to make money anyway. They live on the smell of an oily rag and aren't interested in anything but filling up the sock under the floorboards. They work their kids like slaves, you know.'

Alas, I do know. For the underprivileged of Europe the endless unremitting struggle for economic survival can only be maintained by the efforts of every member of the family. I have gone through every stage of outrage, indignation, anger and pity at the fact of a ten-year-old waiter working from six in the morning until two or three the next morning, or an eight-year-old girl from the shepherd country being handed over as a servant to a matron of the town, or the two bright sons of a local mason, aged nine and eleven, being kept away from school to labour as hod-carriers for their father. And I have been properly sentimental about ragged donkey-boys and fisher-boys, and thought it tough that most of my children's school friends had to do a job either before school or after. It took me a long while to realise that because children work it doesn't follow that they are unloved. Of course it is not desirable that children work, but there it is a stark and necessitous fact of living. And I expect that it takes quite a number of full socks under the floorboards before security is familiar enough to even be recognised, let alone taken for granted.

Certainly a lot of Europeans make money here. They are accustomed to working harder and for longer hours than we are. They are accustomed to living more frugally. And they are more inclined than we are to work towards the future, for the good of the next generation, and the generations still unborn. Perhaps they find the set of Aussie rules relating to labour and leisure difficult to understand, if not incomprehensible.

But I do know that we wanted them to come here, we needed them to come here, we asked them to come here.

Tolerance isn't enough, or even praise for their influence on our way of life. Somehow we have to make them *part* of our way of life, and a good step in that direction, I think, would be to open the doors of our domestic havens and put out the Welcome mat. It might be illuminating for everybody.

The Rare Art of Inspiring Others

Most of my adult life has been spent in the company of so-called (and sometimes self-called) creative people. That is to say, writers, painters, actors, poets, sculptors, potters, musicians—established, hopeful, would-be, deluded, people swimming hard in deep waters and people splashing pretentiously in the shallows.

On the whole they are a fairly zany lot. Often neurotic. Mostly egocentric. Outsiders. Special people, in a way. Quite often sad people too, since there is no defeat more bitter than that of aspiration by inability. But of all the ones whose paths have crossed mine at one time or another there are a few that I would rate as great people, and I was trying to analyse this. I mean apart from public recognition and that bubble reputation and the transient fashions, the validity of which will only be decided with the passage of time.

The quality these few have in common, and which I think of as great for want of a more precise definition, is an ability to communicate an original vision in terms as positive and startling as a hypodermic ... that's not a bad analogy, actually, because ideas can rage around in the bloodstream as potently as any fever.

These thoughts arise from a recent encounter with one of these rare people, and if this piece turns out to be the portrait of an artist I wouldn't be at all surprised.

Our encounters with this man have looped like an arabesque through fifteen years, several countries, and a whole set of different circumstances.

In London first, when he was quite poor and young and nobody much had heard of him, and we were just a bunch of Australians in our first year abroad, bursting with discoveries. He and his wife had just discovered Spain, and he talked about hot rocks and burning light in the autumn gardens at Kew, with the mists draped in the cedars and our assorted children playing tag around the red lacquer pillars of the Chinese pagoda.

There were other later encounters in London, and hours of talk that ranged wide and sometimes wild. Always he communicated to us his own excitements. But it is that day at Kew that stays most vivid to me, perhaps because I had never seen rocks and light like that before.

Later, when we had found our own hot rocks and light in Greece, he came one winter to share them with us. It was a strange winter for us, primitive, uncomfortable, and hazardous, both financially and emotionally. There were six of us foreigners wintering there, but he was the only one who seemed to inhabit himself with any certainty. I don't think he was really very well known even then, although he was on his way, and one knew, unquestioningly, that the way was going to be far. I used to have a queer, shamed compulsion to touch him for luck.

We all worked hard in the day but at night we would meet in the window table of Spiros Papathanasiou's taverna. It couldn't have been as totally a dramatic winter as I focus it now, but I remember that window as being storm-embattled nightly; the sea sloshing across the pavement outside, and the boats heaving and the wind shrilling in the rigging and the bone-white bust of a marble admiral weathering it all with his back turned to the taverna and us in the lighted window huddled around a deal table and the picked-over platters of octopus and goat cheese and olives.

We had been reading Robert Graves' *Greek Myths* then, and W. Grey Walter's *The Living Brain*, and had passed these on to the artist for his interest ... and what was curious, and in a special way intoxicating, was to have this vast field of mythology, and even vaster field of experiment within the human mind, given back to us, transformed, made applicable quite personally to each of us. To say that he gave us courage to go on is trite, and probably untrue, but what he did do so often was to fan the flickering convictions of a group of very uncertain protestants into a healthy crackling blaze. He helped us to believe in our different talents by showing them to us in a quite new and unexpected way. He acted as a catalyst for our own tentative ideas and theories.

I seem to be giving the impression that we used him mercilessly to bolster ourselves up, and perhaps this is true in a sense. Although he took from us, too, because he had (and has) a genuine and absorbed interest in other people, particularly people struggling towards any sort of self-expression. Some nights we used to talk around that taverna table until the town's electricity plant had cut out and the cook, Gregori, still smiling his sweetly uncomprehending smile, would bring us a single kerosene lamp and another carafe of retsina to sustain the torrent of words and ideas and laughter on which we rode so buoyantly.

I do know that we all thought better for his presence among us, talked better, actually worked better. 'On with the dream,' he would say, and things like that never sounded pretentious coming from him, because he would grin mockingly and say, 'They'll get your kidney fat anyway.' To one pessimistic Irish writer he said, 'You want to fly? Then jump up and bloody well fly!' Once I said, 'Why wish for the moon?' And very firmly he replied, 'Why not? For heaven's sake why *not*?'

He went on with this, and it led him away from Greece and through a series of wanderings (although 'wanderings' is wrong, because he pursued his dream at a pace and over distances that would be exhausting to anybody else) and when we next saw him it was in London again, and he was very famous indeed, although not so young any more, and he had given up drinking and anything else that impeded the work in hand. We had been told he had become inaccessible, and certainly there was some strange little air of loneliness about him, as there always is about people who have climbed a bit higher than the rest of us ... I expect because they can see farther than we do, and also find the blows a bit more bruising. The old excitements had developed into new excitements, and he shared them with us as generously as ever, even, I thought, with a touch of urgency. One had the impression that he was no longer static; he was poised where he was only momentarily, to get a good view of the new distances unfolding before he was off in pursuit again at that breakneck speed that nobody else could quite keep up with. And although that encounter with him was necessarily brief, it was long enough to give us the courage to make a decision that had seemed, until then, too dangerous and difficult to contemplate.

Last week, all together again back in Australia after all these years, we dined rather luxuriously in a penthouse room with a breathtaking view from its wall of windows. (It was his little moment of pause; he was anxious to get off to New Guinea, to Cooper's Creek, to the Snowy, to Indonesia, the Himalayas, China.) We talked a bit about that other window at Spiros Papathanasiou's taverna and the lamplight flickering and the wind howling outside, and the dreams we had had then. He never once said 'I told you so,' but he talked about having been down to the Antarctic, right to the South Pole, and the space-fiction qualities of the life of the men there, which excited him tremendously.

And then he gave us his little conspiratorial smile as we sat there guzzling lobster mornay. 'Of course,' he said quite matter-of-factly, 'what they're really doing down there is having a trial run at living on the moon.'

An Exile's Return

When the Greek liner *Ellenis* left for Europe the other day one of its passengers was Yanni Tsakrios, aged about forty-five (give a year, take a year, because he isn't quite sure when he was born), a Greek carpenter, house-painter, plasterer and handyman, formerly of the island of Kalymnos in the Dodecanese, and for the last ten years a resident of Melbourne, Australia. A resident but not a citizen, because he had never been naturalised.

Until he called—so very unexpectedly—to say goodbye to us, we had not seen him since the last goodbye more than ten years ago, and we examined him with some awe. The eyes were the same; soft, and tempered with inquiry, as though looking out from his own world and wondering what the devil was really going on in ours, but the external man had changed. It wasn't just that he looked prosperous. He looked distinguished. He had put on weight (but just enough for sleekness), his thick black hair was frosted lightly with silver (but only at the temples), his shirt was of the white executive type, his tie was dark blue, narrow, and of Thai silk, his suit was dark too, very conservative, very expensive, narrow lapels and narrow trousers (but nothing extreme—what the Victorians would have called an 'unexceptional' suit). On his well-manicured fingers he wore, beside his wedding ring, another gold ring made in the form of two snakes intertwined, with rubies for eyes: it was the only flaw I could find in him.

'Crikey!' I said, remembering the lean brown young man with the calloused hands and the bare calloused feet, patched pants hitched up with a piece of rope, tattered green shirt billowing as he led a dance at some wedding or christening, thin throat always throbbing with the sad sad island songs. Remembering the little one-roomed house with the bedshelf where all the family slept in a row on piles of handwoven rugs—Yanni nearest the door, his wife Polymnea, and the four shy children, Petros, Sanpicos, Anna, and the baby Drossos. Remembering when Yanni had perhaps two days' work in any week, or three if he was very lucky, and usually there was only bread and oil for the children to eat.

The migrant ships were taking the young men away from the island then in batches of hundreds, for the sponge-diving industry was dying and there was no agriculture or work of any kind as alternative employment. In fact there was, about that time, a most marvellously imaginative and audacious scheme to transport the entire population of Kalymnos— aunts, grandmothers, cousins, great-uncles, babies, and the crippled and halt and lame as well—holus-bolus to Australia, and convert the able-bodied men from sponge-divers to divers for pearl and shell. The scheme fell through, for reasons too silly to talk about, but the fact that there *was* such a scheme illustrates the lamentable plight of an island whose seafaring continuities go back (recorded, even, by Homer) to the siege of Troy.

Yanni was one of those ineligible for government-assisted passage to the Promised Land—and Australia was the Promised Land then, dreamt of and wished for with such fervour, prayed for with forests of candles blazing before indistinct ikons in dim old churches—so we made him our personal migrant, and arranged his sponsorship and paid his passage, and ten years ago poured a libation of retsina on a tavern floor and wished him good journey and good luck.

And he, like all the other young men, threw a stone into the sea as he left, meaning that he would never come back.

So, 'Well!' we said, and, 'You look marvellous!', edging up to the inevitable and difficult question. Because he *was* going back. And why?

Well, he said, with that old evasive trick I remember of lowering his lashes right over his eyes, Anna was going on sixteen now. Time to be thinking of marriage. Dowries. He would like to look over the candidates personally, because it was, we understood, an important business.

'But why?' I asked, getting shrill in spite of myself, 'didn't you bring Polymnea and the children out here? After all, you brought your brother Mike and his wife and all their children.' (This was part of our original thought—that in sending one migrant, we would eventually send dozens, as one got established and could sponsor another, and so on.)

Oh yes, he said, seizing on the diversion. Mike and his family are very well. Very happy. Owning their house. Kids at high school. Calliope to be married. Oh yes, very well. But Polymnea ... he carefully turned his wedding ring round and round, round and round, as though it were a rivet on his finger ... Polymnea, we knew, was old-fashioned. Didn't want to leave home. He had, he said quickly and proudly, sent plenty of money back. Plenty. The house was all concrete now, and two new rooms built on. Terrace. Everything. New furniture. Gas stove. Everything modern.

'Then you've done well here, Yanni?'

'Oh yes. Very well. Lots of jobs. Lots of money. Good government here. You make a mistake they look after you. Show you how not to make that mistake again. Oh yes, good place. Good for children ...'

'Then *what*?'

Then ... 'Look!' he said, 'where is the life here? The *life!
Then ekhei zoe etho.* There is no life here. Me, I understand
the life. You, you understand the life. These people are dead.
Where is the little taverna, drink some wine, eat some fish,
sing some songs, sometimes break a glass or two? Everybody
asleep nine o'clock. No singing, no dancing, no nothing.
Where are the Australian peoples I knew in the war? They
knew the life all right. But gone now. People here no good.'
(Yanni escaped from Leros when it was held by the Italians,
got to Gaza, served in the Western Desert with the AIF, and
went on fighting until he was wounded at the Battle of
Rimini.) 'Now they all worry worry worry. Not laughing.
Not singing. Not caring about one Greek wanting to be
friendly. I feel like nothing here. I am sorry,' he said. 'This is
not for you. But there are thousands like me. Thousands.
Want to go back.'

'But, Yanni,' we said, remembering, 'go back to *what*?'

And he explained to us the changes that had taken place in
Kalymnos since we knew it. By some strange technological
twist the sponging industry is in boom. Japan is buying the
lot, the synthetic is no longer competition, the industry is
prosperous, and divers are making big money. Tourism has
arrived. There is building everywhere. New hotels, new
houses, new shops, new roads. Tons of work for everybody.
And the money is good.

'There is a good living there for a carpenter,' he said. 'And
life. Most of all, life.' And he smiled a gentle apologetic smile.
'So I go.'

So there we are. Rejected. And not just by Yanni. By
thousands of Yannis. I remember talking with an Australian
migration officer in Athens about the increasing difficulty of
getting enough migrants of the right sort. I remember the

swift moves to take advantage of the situation in Kenya, another in Algeria. Bid 'em in! Bribe 'em in!

The milk and honey of the Promised Land seems to have curdled. The Land of the Wide Open Door still has the door opened, but just suppose nobody wants to come in? Where is that eager stream of hod-carriers, cement-mixers, road-workers, oven-stokers, heavy labourers, dirt-carters, who should be so humbly and gratefully getting on with the really dirty work of the country in return for living room?

'Excuse me,' said Yanni diffidently, 'it isn't really living, you see. Not living at all.'

A Death in the Family

I was writing about something different entirely when the telephone rang and I learned that my only brother was dead.

He was forty-two years old and he died of a coronary, brought on, probably, by overworking at work which he neither liked nor disliked particularly, but which he accepted philosophically enough as the inevitable tribute he had to pay to the society he happened to live in. He said: 'When that is done I'll stop,' and he said, 'When this is done I'll stop.' And now he has stopped anyway, whether this or that is done or not.

He was not, therefore—except in dreams, perhaps—an insurgent or a revolutionary. He accepted society and came to terms with it. Society's terms, not his. He never whined about this. He was, so everybody tells me, the most loving and devoted of husbands and fathers, the best of citizens, the finest of friends. These are the things that people are going to say about him anyway. I want to say something else.

He was my first and best friend. Being, as we were, a year apart in age, an inch apart in height, and a class apart in school, we were almost like twins.

We were frowzled, freckled children, skinny and hard, with our front teeth coming down like half-lowered blinds. We had the same long bony arms and legs bruised and scarred and scored and scratched from the violence of our games. We could swim like fish and fight like tigers, we could walk a post-and-rail fence on our bare horny feet like acrobats, we could skin a rabbit as well as shoot one, we could gut a fish or tar a canoe, we could send signals by Morse or flags and knew every knot in the scouts' book. We preferred each other's company to any other in the world. We were an alliance, wordless but unquestioned, against the world of adults and authority. We had, as far as we knew, no limitations whatever.

We had cubby-houses in those days where we retired with loot we had filched or acquired, rice-papers and ready-rubbed with which we practised rolling our own, tomatoes or peaches or strawberries we had nicked from the painful cultivation of our mother's back garden, speck fruit or broken biscuits we had wheedled out of tradesmen, tins of condensed milk we had knocked off the factory lorry.

One cubby-house was on the beach, just above the dunes and under the shadow of the cliff. It was made of four huge old aloe plants whose fleshy spears, broad-based and thick as paddles, were brushed with bloom and edged with rose-pink thorns. They made a palisade that arched up to meet over a mat of decaying fibres feet thick, where ants and spiders and sometimes lizards crawled; it was as springy as a carpet. The light was always greenish silver inside the cubby. It was a still place, an away place, a place made for secrets. We would always talk in whispers there, and my brother's yellow eyes seemed phosphorescent through a haze of Wild Woodbine smoke.

There were other cubbies: a lantana cave just by Jacob's Ladder; a stamped-down place, dry, scratchy, and filled with insects in the bullrushes beside the creek; a carefully constructed cubby of stones in the Bullring on the top of the hill above the farm; another of boughs right up the creek under the lilli-pilli tree. But the aloe cubby was our favourite, according to some mysterious law of preference which we understood perfectly at the time.

'What are you going to be?' he said, and when I had expounded my grandiose schemes, 'What are you?' I asked, and he answered, predictably, according to the laws of excellence that our parents were busily instilling into us. 'Oh, I'll be a test cricketer,' he said casually, 'or someone like Zane Grey, or Kingsford Smith.' And very carefully he carved our names and the date into an aloe spear, whistling nonchalantly as he did so. And then he turned a face tight with urgency: 'Would you care,' he said, 'if I never did anything wonderful at all?' And I laughed, because the possibility of anything other than grandeur was too ridiculous to contemplate.

What did he know then about himself? More than I did, certainly, bound unquestioning as I was in the family compulsion to excel. To be less than first was to be nothing.

He was wiser than I. Under the defensive savagery of our childhood games he was a peculiarly gentle boy, more-than-average good at everything if he had a chance to work on it laboriously and in secret, but excelling in nothing except his instinct for what was kind and generous and brave and true. He was sick with apprehension before any competition, and when he came first it was by virtue of will and endurance and to please us, who valued such things. For himself, I don't think now that he ever cared about the trophies and prizes and the gold stars in exercise books.

He had too what is rare in a child—acceptance. Whether it was a cut with a tomahawk that sliced off the end of his finger, or the messy and ugly death by motor-lorry of his beautiful and devoted dog, or a belting with the razor-strop for some particularly dangerous piece of devilment I had led him into and left him to take the blame for, he accepted it without fuss. When he cried or raged it was always alone.

So he was at his happiest and most relaxed with animals and smaller children, who always recognised him instinctively and didn't care about first prizes any more than he did. Or fishing on the beach at night, with the dark sand still warm from the day's sun and the beating surf luminous with light that seemed to pour upwards into that vast sky hung with such a blazing majesty of stars as I have never seen since. And I can still see him like that, a boy of ten, skinny-frail and big-headed, advancing and retreating against the luminous frills of foam, arched rod tip dancing delicately, whistling softly his own little counterpoint to the great grave cadences of the surf.

He cultivated that whistle, and that easy slouch of the shoulders, against the world of the Depression into which he emerged at sixteen with a Leaving pass for which he had worked most of every night for most of a year. An Honours pass, which entitled him to nothing, as was soon evident, except a clerk's job in an industrial plant, for which he had to get up at four o'clock in the morning to catch the workers' train. You could say he was just unlucky to have been born into that time, although I never heard him complain of it.

'How can you stand it!' I used to rage, and he would smile at me diffidently while I ranted on about all the things he should be doing if only there was money to send him to university where he belonged. 'But there *isn't* the money,' he would say without rancour, 'and there *is* this job,' and then he would slip me half his pay to buy something that I just couldn't do without for another second.

I lost him somewhere there, obsessed as I was by my own feverish impatience to get on to the first prizes he didn't seem to care about. Until last year I hadn't even seen him for fifteen years, and in this last year I have seen him twice.

They've been telephoning me all day, friends of his, weeping about some wonderful man who I don't even know. All I have is an aloe cubby, and a skinny big-headed boy with yellow eyes looking phosphorescent in Wild Woodbine smoke, and two names and a date carved with a rabbit-skinning knife into an aloe spear that has probably long since decayed into the mat of decaying fibre feet thick, where ants and spiders and sometimes lizards crawl. And I hope that children still crawl in there and talk of grandeur to come, or even doubt the possibility of it, but carve their names on a new spear. My brother would have liked that.

Things That Go Boomp in the Night

Lately, having galloped up all unwitting and unprepared to one of those crossroads that are forever complicating the straight and simple way of things with the necessity for pause and choice and decision, I have been awake often at night.

I don't know whether I have something positively nefarious in my nature—and am reminded suddenly that one of my ancestors was reputedly hanged at Tyburn Tree for his midnight exploits as a gentleman of the roads (I say reputedly because all my family were terrible liars and inventors and embroiderers, and could well have made it up)—but I have always loved nocturnal prowling in a house where everybody else is sleeping.

Perhaps, in a busy and eventful life, these night watches are the only times when one can ever be truly alone, and there is a sort of elation in this, a sense of quickened heartbeats, of heightened perceptions, of self-surprise. Of complicity even.

Lodged in my head is a line from a poem read somewhere once in some anthology and never tracked down since. I read it then and remember it now with a sharp sting of recognition.

'How strange we grow when we're alone and how unlike our other selves who talk and laugh and put the candles out and say good-night ...'

And it is not only that we ourselves grow strange. Our familiar surroundings grow strange too. A house at night, at the full ebb of the tide of human activity that has crashed and surged through it all day, is eloquent with its own life. It breathes and sighs and creaks with relaxation. You can hear it easing itself out at the seams, as it were, and settling a fraction more comfortably on its foundations. The loose window you had so firmly and definitely closed has opened itself enticingly to the night insects, the cupboard door to the ants; there are scuttlings and scurryings and rustlings it would be better, perhaps, not to investigate. If you flick a light switch suddenly the revealed room has a look both bland and furtive, as though it had composed itself just in time not to be caught out.

I don't find these manifestations of a house's individuality at all frightening. Much more inimical are the mechanical noises, especially in an old house where machines have been imposed on it long after the personality of the place has declared itself and developed its own eccentricities.

Padding quietly down the darkened hall towards the stealthy indulgence of coffee and cigarettes one is paralysed into immobility as the low purr of the refrigerator changes to a sort of shuddering snort and all the milk bottles chatter dementedly. Downstairs the hot-water system makes an intermittent gulping sound, wrathful somehow, biding its time, and—after fifteen minutes of pretending not to hear it—that soft sinister intrusive whirring from the living room is identified as the record player that somebody, carelessly, forgot to switch off.

Streets away there is the wild high agonised squeal of tyres and brakes. With dry mouth and prickling scalp one waits for the hideous crash of metal and glass ... and waits ... and waits ... and the room heater thrums on, indifferent and unwearied, and the clock fills up the silence neatly and with precision: so loud: one had never noticed before.

Yet under the mechanical sounds are the reassuring human ones, close and familiar, breathings and turnings and sleep-mutterings, and the coffee is scalding and bitter and good—

better than it ever tastes at any other time, like the cigarette—
and one can let one's thoughts go nosing down strange new
corridors of possibility, never suspected in all the busy day, or
drift back in exploration of old stores of experience without
urgency or haste or distraction.

I was thinking, on one of my prowls the other night, of
other cups of coffee, other cigarettes, other wakeful hours in
other places.

Ships' decks and shepherds' huts and pebbled beaches and
herb-hung kitchens and terraces dazzling with moonlight.
Then the coffee was thick and black, brewed Turkish style on
a few coals still glowing in the charcoal brazier, and the
cigarettes were that sharp acrid Macedonian tobacco to
which one so quickly becomes addicted, and the night-light
was the moon or the stars or a kerosene lamp turned low.

The night sounds were of bells mostly, thin drifts of them
from high sheepfolds, or the clamour of cockerels gone a bit
mental and hurling imprecations, dogs howling, the demoniacal
screaming of love-maddened cats swarming on roof tiles and
garden walls, and sometimes, in the spring, the pure sweet notes
of a little night owl, Athena's symbol of wisdom, dropped
separately into the darkness from a mountain top.

I am glad of all those wakeful nights. I might never have
got to know the Pleiades so well otherwise, or plotted the
nightly course of the *gri-gri* boats. Over against the mainland
their acetylene lamps made as lovely a constellation on the
black silky water as the Pleiades overhead, and I used to wish
that I might go with the boats sometime (only I was too
constrained by being a woman and a foreigner ever to ask)
and spear octopus in the moving cones of water lit before
every prow like brilliant green glass, and eat olives and cheese
and drink retsina and listen to tall fisher tales. Or tales of

love and revenge and supernatural happenings, which are the proper things to discuss in such a setting at such an hour.

I used to think about the *gri-gri* boats years later, at a very troubled time when we were staying in a Tudor farmhouse in the Cotswolds. It was spring then, too, and aching cold in the prowling hours with the fires sighing and whispering, and there were more noises in the walls and the wainscotting than I could ever identify, and Mau-Mau the Siamese cat with the crumpled ears used to prowl with me, arching and purring: she knew what I was about.

And instead of the *gri-gri* boats there would be the crackle and scrunch of boots on the frost-spiked grass outside, and the low buzz and burr of voices, and that would be Jack and Harry back from the lambing. And sometimes they would come in and let me look after the damp new lamb in front of the fire, and I would give them mugs of tea and cider, and we would sit and talk, as I knew we would, of lambing seasons past, and country lore, and tales of love and revenge and supernatural happenings.

So much of life goes on in the night. Here, in a city, I think of boats hooting and the melancholy sound of train whistles at sidings, of people hurtling through the night at impossible speeds, of destinations and departures, people running away from things, hurrying towards things. I think of border police and customs barriers, conspirators, lovers, city markets, hospitals, air terminals. I think of people watching, people waiting, people hiding and people searching, people dying and people being born.

And people, like me, who have talked and laughed and put the candles out and said good night, and are prowling around in dark houses all over the place, being as strange as they please.

A Birthday in the Kelly Country

My mother, whose natural love of the dramatic inclined her towards ceremonial and ritual whenever possible (even the exchanging of a child's tooth for a fairy sixpence had its strict form of ceremony), used to say that the two most important dates in anybody's calendar were the one on which he entered this world and the one on which he left it. She always thought it most extraordinary that any of us should be here at all—'Look at the odds,' she would say, 'against such a thing'—let alone being our very own selves and not somebody else entirely.

So that, in our family, birthdays were always regarded as being singularly potent days, to be observed with some state. One celebrated one's exceeding good fortune in having made the evolutionary scene, as it were, and at the same time gravely took a sort of spiritual audit of the year past and read the omens for the year to come, for she never let any of us forget that the celebration of the one date brought each of us closer to the inevitable trysting time with the other, terminal and unknown.

She has long since kept her own tryst, as ardently as she ever revelled in the surprising fact of being alive at all, but she left behind in me this deeply ingrained sense of the significance of birthdays.

Last year my birthday (and I always count it from twelve o'clock midnight as she did, and make a point of being awake to greet it) found me struggling off a migrant ship on to home ground for the first time in fifteen years, filled with astonishment that I had actually got here, and a bit apprehensive about rehabilitation into what seemed then to be a completely foreign country.

So this year my birthday took on double significance because it was also the anniversary of homecoming. I'm sure my mother would have had a field day with the omens, because twelve o'clock midnight this year found me quite alone on a railway platform in the heart of the Kelly country, of which my previous acquaintance had been limited to those interminable pages of erudite backgrounding to Sidney Nolan's paintings that are forever appearing in the London glossies.

Beginning my birthday on a railway platform was quite contrary to my intentions, which were that I should spend it at home, wallowing in rich gifts and self-indulgence and being waited on hand and foot. But the transport strike had intervened between me and my intentions, and my intentions had to be postponed like those of everybody else who had been caught. The fact that I was philosophical about it was proof of a year's conditioning to the mores of my native land. I had had a bonus day in the country, which was perfectly lovely, and even if my reserved seat for the non-existent express of the night before was not valid for this night, the stationmaster thought he could get me on the second division.

The snag was this. My hosts, who had driven me forty-odd miles to the station well in time to catch the express my ticket wasn't valid for, could not, because of baby-sitters, wait with me until the second division. This left me with three and a half hours to occupy with my own devices, and anybody else who has ever been stranded in an Australian country town at night will recognise the bleakness of the predicament.

The station refreshment room, naturally enough, was barred and padlocked. I've been home long enough now to accept that as normal. So in all innocence I suggested to my hosts that they drive me back to the main street and leave me at a café or a restaurant where I could read for a couple of hours over a meal and cups of coffee. They seemed very dubious about the possibility of anything being open at nine o'clock at night, but I reminded them of the succession of gigantic transports passing through the town every couple of minutes. There would be, I was sure, a truckers' café, or some all-night pie and tea bar attached to one of the service stations. Anywhere in the world, I said, where the trucks pass through regularly, provision is made for their drivers.

Anywhere but Australia, obviously. The wide streets of the town, flatly and precisely geometric, were bright enough with lighted shop windows, but there was not a single human being to be seen anywhere, and every door was locked. At nine o'clock it was like a town under a spell, or rumoured threat that the Kellys would be riding again. Every shop closed. Every café closed. Every milk bar closed. We tried further up the highway, where the flossy garages lined each side of the road with all their brilliant bowsers and garish advertising. The garages were closed too.

Bereft of any possibility of warmth and refreshment, and beginning to be acutely embarrassed at so embarrassing my poor hosts, who had to get home, I watched the huge trucks and trailers roaring through the indifferent town and thought of stage coaches and the Kellys riding and that then there would have been, at the very least, a bustling inn to welcome traveller and bushranger alike. Even, perhaps, a stranded wayfarer like me.

And marvellously enough in that apparently spellbound place, there was an inn. You couldn't have called it bustling, but there were lights in the downstairs windows and the door was open, and after ten minutes of knocking and prowling and calling and trying doors we roused the landlady, who was very sorry for me and said I could sit by the fire until ten o'clock, when she would have to close. And after a while of talking she said I could sit as long as I liked, if I let myself out the side door because she would have to lock the front one. And after my hosts, reassured, had started home, the landlord came and talked too, and after a while I was transferred to the comfort of their private parlour, with a good fire and a good drink to go with it, and kinder or more hospitable people I have never met in my life. Their talk was that enthralling country talk of personalities and local gossip and dramatic bushfire stories and even Kelly lore, and they told me that the little parlour in which we were sitting was the room in which the body of Aaron Sherritt had been laid out. And all this was so entrancing that I might have missed the train altogether if they hadn't reminded me that that was what I was waiting for.

So I reached the station platform and twelve o'clock and my birthday in a mood so pleasurable and grateful that it didn't surprise me as much as it should when the station assistant told me he had lit a fire in the Ladies Waiting Room and I would be very comfortable there, he was sure, until the second division came in, the second division being, he said, a little late.

I thanked him and installed myself in front of the fire, and now being alone seemed very desirable because I had so many pleasant and intriguing things to think about, and I thought that this was the time only a year ago when I had been struggling off a migrant ship, and I thought that Australia was still filled with nice surprises as well as nasty ones, and I wished myself many happy returns of such a singular day since there was nobody else there to wish it to me, and I stirred up the fire with the toe of my shoe and read omens in the coals and waited for my train to come in.

On Letting Asia In

We were having a wallow the other night in the nostalgia of a stack of old photograph albums, some of them of wartime vintage. One of these photographs shows a group of war correspondents in uniform, posed rather self-consciously near a Chinese temple in Yunnan province. The temple is shadowed gracefully by an Australian eucalypt, and this does not look at all incongruous. The tree is as right in its setting as the temple.

The correspondents, naturally, look impermanent. They are all middle-aged now—some of them old, even—and some of them are famous and some of them are not, but every one of them would have photographs pretty much like these and every one of them would have, in daily use or in daily view, some personal little oriental object or objects—a jade paperweight, a personal seal in a black lacquer box, a small Ming porcelain that has become talismanic, a silk scroll, a carved screen, a bronze incense-burner, a set of painted plaster theatre masks or wafer-thin wine cups. Their wives (or ex-wives) would still wear the pink jade and silver and the ivory hair ornaments. The souvenirs.

What is interesting is that the giant old eucalypt which so gracefully shadows the graceful temple in the photograph began as a souvenir too. There are eucalypts growing all over the plateau country of China, brought back as saplings in pots by coolies returning from the Australian gold-fields, or sent back with the coffins of the dead returning to the *feng-shui* of ancestral burial grounds.

At the time of the great gold rushes, thousands of Chinese coolies, mostly from Canton, were brought out here as cheap indentured labour. They were, in effect, slave labour, and as such one might think that their case should have had strong appeal to that embittered colonial mentality that was so basically concerned with the plight of the underdog.

What happened, in fact, was that the unfortunate Chinese were assaulted, stoned, mobbed, robbed, beaten up, murdered, and even scalped for the novelty of their pigtails. Three of the worst outbreaks of mob violence on the gold-fields were organised against the Chinese diggers.

Although this savage reaction could have been caused partly by ignorance (the reviled coolies were suspected of bringing leprosy and smallpox into the colony, of following heathen practices, of luring white women into opium dens and there indulging in unmentionable, and even unimaginable, vices), the real basis of the Australian attitude was undoubtedly economic rather than racial. The earliest union work codes excluded Chinese, Kanakas, Japanese and Afghans, but accepted American negroes, New Zealand Maoris, and all half-castes born in Australia. The bogy was not colour prejudice, but cheap labour.

Anyway, as we know, the Chinese problem (plus the problem of the Kanakas working the sugar plantations in the north) resulted, at the turn of the century, in the establishment of the principle of White Australia as a national policy. Complete exclusion was impossible because of the thousands of Chinese already in residence, some naturalised, some with other forms of domicile rights, but all future policy was determined by the Chinese problem, geared to the Chinese problem as it existed then and extended to other Asian groups.

Until World War II we seem to have had an ambivalent attitude towards our Asian residents. There was, on the one hand, something mysterious and deliciously sinister about the thought of opium dens, incense, joss houses, gongs, heathen ritual and such. Brocades and pigtails and long fingernails and oriental inscrutability and Fu Manchu. And on the other something so whimsical about Johnny Chinaman with his market garden, his painted vegetable cart, his fantastic way with the most soiled garments, his cabbalistic laundry tickets, his politeness, his neatness, his baggy pants, his lisp, his deference. But whether whimsical or sinister, superstition clung around him like an almost visible aura. 'You must have crossed a Chinaman.'

But we were British then, and Asia was still the 'Far East' or tea caddies and chinoiserie and mandarins and warlords and silkworms and travellers' tales.

It was not until World War II, when that group of correspondents were posing themselves by the tall eucalypt on the Yunnan plateau (in between getting on with the job of reporting the war effort of the fourth of what were then called the Great Powers), and the Japanese were sweeping down through the islands above us, that Asia was metamorphosed dramatically from the Far East to the Near North. The most alarmingly Near North.

Indeed, our national policy might be dedicated to the proposition that we stay, racially, as we are—98.7 percent European, excluding Aborigines (although it seems doubtful whether the Aborigines are going to go on meekly submitting to exclusion)—but since the end of the war it has been impossible for any one of us, as Europeans, to ignore the fact that two great continents, teeming with the differently coloured skins that comprise half the world's population, lie between us and home base.

One has been very conscious in Europe, over the last decade or so, of the emergent black races, of the problems of Africa, of the American negro, of the race riots in Notting Hill, of the Jamaicans pouring into England.

Coming back to Australia one is even more conscious of Asia. Not as the Far East. Not as the Near North. Not even as Our Neighbours. One is conscious of Asia as the place where one lives.

Asia is in our daily newspapers, in radio broadcasts, in television discussions. Asia is in the minds and mouths of our politicians, economists, churchmen, militarists, moralists, reactionaries and visionaries.

Asia is in faces in the street. Faces at parties. Faces in class photographs at end-of-term at school. Asia abounds in our every crowded place of learning, in schools and universities and hospitals and technological institutes. Young Asia. Eager, absorbent, ardent, enquiring Asia. On quota still, on restricted permit, but here for long enough for us to know them if we will, and for them to know us. Long enough for the exchange of ideas and the reassessment of national values. Long enough, most importantly, for the young to form friendships that might and could endure.

And, anyway, ideas cannot be excluded by immigration laws, and Asia is with us in ideas wherever we look. Look at the cars in the streets, look at your tape-recorder or your camera, observe the trends in entertaining, in daily living, in fashion even. Every chic woman I know has at least one dress of Thai silk. Sukiyaki has taken the place of spaghetti at the clever party. Modern interiors are graced with paper lanterns, or lanterns of filigree brass, screens are a must, and furniture of cane and bamboo. Rock gardens are more stylish than herbaceous borders.

Ideas, like the eucalyptus tree, take root and grow. Watching the young together, Asian and European, I hope profoundly that they are exchanging good souvenirs to plant and proliferate everywhere.

On Living for Love Alone

This morning, as usual, I stirred the breakfast porridge hypnotically to the accompaniment of electric guitars and a continuous wail of vocal groups, in harmony, sobbing and throbbing their belief that if he loves her and she loves him life is eternal spring and ringing bells and birds singing and all that. But if he doesn't or she doesn't, or if either of them prefer somebody else anyway (and with the best of reasons, I should say, just listening) then life is not worth living.

We have this sort of radio program in the mornings to get the time. Besides, the young seem to like it.

The fulfilment of this yearning burning oh my love for yew-hoo-hoo is presumably still marriage. Anyway, if the women's pages of magazines and newspapers are any guide, this week and every week thousands of young couples will go to the altar and promise to love and honour and cherish each other for as long as they both shall live.

And this week and every week the divorce courts will be crammed with petitioners in emotional states that will range through outrage, anger, shock, guilt, dismay, humiliation, cynicism, disillusionment, vindictiveness, defiance, grief, and that terrible sadness that comes when creativeness turns into destruction.

This week some of us will hear, inevitably, on inquiry about some acquaintances not seen for some time: 'Oh, didn't you know? They're splitting up.'

Whatever has happened to marriage? It certainly isn't what it used to be. If indeed, as one cynic says, it ever was.

I have often wondered why brides baulk so stubbornly at promising to obey. Usually, these days, it is cut out of the wedding service altogether. In fact, if you think about it, 'to obey' is about all that a bride can promise. Obedience is at least an act of the will, of self-discipline. Yet radiantly and confidently men and women promise to love and honour each other, emotions that are entirely out of their control. All the self-discipline, all the will in the world, won't keep a woman loving a man or a man loving a woman if he or she proves to be unlovable, or honouring if the other proves to be dishonourable. It won't keep a man cherishing (that lovely word) a woman if, on closer acquaintance—and marriage is very close acquaintance indeed—she turns out to be just not worth it.

Yet every week thousands of credulous couples do make these impossible promises, with sincerity, most of them, I do believe, and go forward into the immense risk and challenge and adventure of marriage, with a touching faith that love alone will see them through.

Until fairly recently (and even now in more primitive societies) marriage was an economic, biological and social contract, valuable and necessary for the consolidation of family property and possessions, the continuation of the race, the solidifying and dignifying of position, insurance against old age. It was a contract into which both parties entered with the full realisation of what they were bringing to it, what they were expected to contribute to it, what their duties were, their responsibilities, and their privileges. Marriage was a state of honour, dignity, and respect, beneficial to the whole community. Love might or might not happen, but incidentally to the main purpose of the contract.

As our social bulwarks have fallen away, or been torn down, and the structure of society has become looser, more fluid—more enlightened if you like—less rigid, anyway—love has assumed a greater and greater importance as the basis for marriage. Ideally, according to our current canons, the only basis for marriage.

It seems to be loading up love with a wearisome burden, to bear the full weight of all the former motives for marrying, and to provide all the answers formerly supplied by social custom and ritual and by the concrete definition of spheres of responsibility and obligation and duty and privilege.

Quite reasonably love usually baulks at being so saddled, and either lies down under the load, leaving marriage to inertia, or bucks it off and gallops away on an irresponsible escapist frolic in the pastures of freedom, with the divorce courts on the side of them.

It doesn't mean that love doesn't exist. Only that we ask too much of it.

I know some very intelligent and thoughtful people who believe that marriage is fast outliving its social usefulness and will soon become obsolete as an institution. I know very many young people who think this too, and express it in their characteristic shrugging-off attitude of, 'Why *bother*?'

Yet the Saturday churches in every suburb and country town are misty with tulle and lace and mothers' tears, and bright with flowers and young hope. Obviously a lot of people believe in marriage still.

Only one wonders, thinking of them, how many are going to find satisfaction, fulfilment, meaning, happiness together, and how many—in more time or less—are going to feel perplexed, cheated, trapped, betrayed by they don't know what. Love, perhaps, which should have answered everything, or life, perhaps, which somewhere got out of hand.

I think the saddest cartoon I have ever seen was one in an American magazine, which shows an elderly couple sitting in silence and obvious boredom, he with his newspaper, she with her knitting, each in a rocking chair on a wide and lonely porch. She is turning to him a face quite poignant in its puzzlement. The caption reads: 'Whatever happened, dear, to the best that was yet to be?'

When everything around us has changed so drastically—morals, manners, attitudes towards just about everything on earth—marriage must surely change too, and not to recognise this seems irrational, if not downright unhealthy.

I think marriage is harder than it has ever been, more risky than it has ever been, more challenging than it has ever been. Risk and challenge are always inherent in creative effort, and marriage in these days must depend more and more on real creative effort than in the days when its rules were fixed and inflexible.

To expect marriage to last on a diet of love alone seems folly, but to marry without love is a greater folly yet. Most of us, fortunately, have proof that love exists, with as many faces as there are people to recognise it, and as unlike that breakfast-time wail from the radio as a diamond is from a piece of tinsel.

I know that in all the marriages I know that have endured and grown into a shared and exciting and rewarding human adventure—and there are so many of them to balance the shattered ones—love has been the third party to the contract. Not as an oracle, though, and not as a whipping boy. But, more gallantly, as a comrade and a conspirator.

Getting with the Forward-Lookers

The building, which is of red brick, is set in bare brown earth which is presently being rolled flat after the gouging of the bulldozers and planted with grass seeds, oleander bushes, rotary clothes hoists and sandstone barbecues.

Every corner bulges with tiers of white iron balconies, of which some have a harbour view and some do not because, while this building was still under construction, it apparently seeded some red bricks on the plot next door, which took root and flourished and are at this moment growing up layer by layer into an identical building (whose balconies, of course, will have a harbour view until another one grows alongside).

Anyway, I don't care about that, because the lowest east bulging balcony does have a harbour view, and that, temporarily (and for reasons which seem to have been mislaid somewhere in the sheer hysteria of moving from one place to another), is mine, and I intend to grow morning glory on it and take very chic public breakfasts and evening aperitifs at a white iron table when I can afford one or acquire one, and I am designing some very forward-looking gowns (or robes) for this purpose.

I have never lived in a new building before, and this one is so new it is still littered with wood shavings and dust from the floor sander. The venetian blinds still have the maker's tags on, the oven of the new cooker is filled with brown paper parcels of intimidating but very forward-looking grill attachments and very complicated books of instruction for the operation of same (I don't think I'll use them because I couldn't bear to get them dirty).

Foreign workmen in shorts and athletic singlets come and go all day long singing lovely foreign songs and fitting forward-looking towel rails and sliding doors and clothes racks and other marvels to which I am totally unaccustomed but find I take to, although somewhat nervously as yet.

Everything smells of lime and mortar and fresh paint, and it is so clean that investigating insects and flies drop dead ten seconds after entry through the aluminium framed picture windows.

The living room (which is going to be my study too, since the children have established squatting rights to the only big bedrooms) has walls that are mushroom-coloured and so flat and matt and unmarked I fear they will need perpetual dry-cleaning, and is furnished with seven tea chests packed with books, one Spanish chest packed with my Greek rugs, two laundry baskets packed with heaven knows what, and a wastepaper basket packed with some unfortunate plastic that my daughter was conned into buying at one of those forward-looking parties that are organised with that very end in view (she is such a con girl herself that I suppose it was just she should be taken once, except that finally she conned me into paying for the horrible things, which is why I can't bear to discard them as I should).

We have some marvellous pictures that would look absolutely gorgeous on the mushroom-coloured walls if only one dared to desecrate them with nails (I don't dare, and intend to woo my nice landlord to dare for me in the name of Culture); a birdcage of fretted wood and stained glass that looks like an Oriental temple and that any bird would go mental in; an ancient amphora that a sponge-diver friend of mine brought me from the bottom of the sea; a shipwright's model of an Aegean trading caique; and a box of things I swept off the mantelpiece for sorting out later when I can face it.

This place, naturally, has no mantelpiece, but I'm sure I can improvise something that will serve to put things on.

There is also a very expensive carpet-shampooing machine that I was conned into buying by a very brisk saleslady who called one day, and of which I am terribly ashamed, since I don't have the sort of carpets that need shampooing and probably never will. Although perhaps it might work on the walls and so justify my lolly.

My predicament lies in the fact that among all these treasures there is nothing one can actually sit on or eat off or drink out of (except the plastic) or cook things in, and I shall have to be very forward-looking indeed to nut out some way of acquiring such practicalities, which should be, ideally, utterly simple and utterly luxurious. I don't want anything that cringes in this forward-looking atmosphere of mushroom walls and built-in cupboards and electric cookers with grill attachments and garbage disposal units.

This, of course, is an exhilarating sort of challenge, and I am reminded of the most forward-looking person I ever knew, who found herself once in a similar, although actually reverse position. I mean, I have a roof over my head (even if it is somebody else's floor) but no things to put under the roof, and she had all the things in the world for sitting on and eating off and sleeping in, but no roof to put them under.

This lady was a Russian aristocrat of classic temperament, beauty, and wit, and was formerly married to the court painter of the Shah of Persia, who was a Scot (the court painter, I mean, not the Shah). She was further distinguished by having only one eye, the other, rumour said, having been scooped out one morning at breakfast by the court painter's grapefruit spoon. But she wore a black patch of distinction and was a very great lady and a very great eccentric (eccentricity I define as being completely natural and poised under all circumstances).

Anyway, when she first came to Greece as a political refugee, she found herself, with her two extremely eccentric children (but without the court painter) bereft of a roof in Athens. She had a grand piano, a four-poster bed, some delicate screens, some Sèvres china and sundry other splendid articles salvaged from times of grandeur.

These she set up in the dry bed of the river Illisos (which isn't what it used to be when Socrates and Plato conversed by its banks) under a convenient viaduct, and sent out invitations to the whole diplomatic corps of Athens to attend a house-warming party. The lady's connections were so impeccable, and her beauty and her fame so great, that a refusal by anybody who was anybody was unthinkable and the cream of the diplomatic corps rolled up in limousines of grey and black and clambered down into the dry river bed at the appointed time, where the lady, blazing with all her jewels (which were something), graciously served them goat's cheese and olives on the Sèvres china and rough retsina in crystal goblets, while her two children (who were prodigies) nibbled on nasturtiums and favoured the guests with duets on the grand piano.

They tell me it was the best diplomatic party (or, indeed, any party) that Athens has ever known, and even when it began to rain and the bed of the Illisos began to run with a real river, and the four-poster bed, complete with diplomats crouched on all fours, began to sail downstream, composure was maintained, toasts were drunk, speeches were completed to the last flowery peroration, and the lady waded out of the Illisos into a fine Ottoman mansion in the most fashionable quarter, which she occupied for many years and where she gave splendid diplomatic parties and occasionally played the balalaika and declaimed Russian poetry.

'My dear,' she said to me once when recounting some of the highlights of this occasion, 'what can one do when one is up the creek without the paddle?'

I don't know but, dear Madame, I think I'm going to cultivate the diplomatic corps.

Living in a Neighbourhood

Practically every popular Greek song I know that doesn't deal with the boy-girl bit, either straight or by way of little cypress trees or spring swallows or white ribbons or some other similar device, has as its subject, nostalgic and yearning, the neighbourhood.

No other neighbourhood is or ever can be the same as the one in which one grew up, or lives now, or will return to after exile, or grow old in, or whatever. No other people could be so friendly, no streets so gay, no corner tavern so lively, no music so enchanting, no girls so pretty, no friends so true. And like that. That is what the song 'Never on Sunday' is all about, whatever the simpering English version says, and when Melina Mercouri sings that song she is singing praise of Piraeus and the harbour and the markets and the football team and the people in the streets and the sailors' dives and her undying loyalty to all this, her neighbourhood, vibrant and squalid and spellbinding.

London, although rather more reticent about putting it to music, has something of that feeling too. Somebody once said that London is less a city than a series of villages, and if you live there for a while you do enter into an emotional relationship with your own village, which might be Chelsea or Soho or Pimlico or Notting Hill Gate or Mayfair or Rotherhithe or Putney or Limehouse or Bloomsbury or Hampstead. Each of these neighbourhoods has its own distinct personality and quality. Each is strongly individual, and its individuality partakes of the people who live in the neighbourhood plus the mixed flavours of its commercial amenities—the bookshops and the barrows and the bakeries and the fishmongers and the gentlemen's hatters and the pubs and the tea shoppes and the espresso bars and the rooms to let and whether the landladies accept coloured gentlemen or not. A neighbourhood is nannies in a square and intense young students and gaudy chieftains in coffee bars and street-corner prophets hurling denunciations and loose ladies being asked to move on and successful actors being seen and decayed and slightly dotty gentlewomen pricing haddock and exquisite women emerging from converted mews to sweep away in silver Jags, and whether a neighbourhood is going down or going up it has a certain intensity in atmosphere and a coherence in spite of its fluidity. The street-corner prophet and the decrepit newsboy and the bird-watcher go on for ever, as does the pub philosopher who knew it when.

I expect this is true of Australia too, or the urban part of it as distinct from the suburban, where I think it would be straining romanticism (even though elastic) just too far to expect anybody to be passionately attached to a service station or a drive-in or a supermarket or a chain store or even a bowling alley or a Leagues Club.

Having just moved into a neighbourhood (the first approximation of one I've lived in since I came back to Australia), I've been loitering about in it this last week or so, idling down streets, mooching in shops, listening in on conversations. Getting acquainted, as it were.

It seems to have a quirky sort of character. A blend of the raffish and the smart, a mixture which I, personally, find piquant and attractive.

There are, naturally, the supermarket and the several service stations, which the neighbourhood wears with the air, at once desperately uncertain and desperately gallant, of somebody trying on a false hairpiece for the first time. The face-lift and the false eyelashes may follow, but there isn't enough confidence for them as yet. The old family grocer is still in business, and many other old family businesses too. The haberdasher does *not* sell textured stockings, and I suspect never will, the florist makes up Victorian posies and also corsages of carnations or orchids, there is a tailor whose window is populated by very ancient dummies clad in tacked half-garments of uncertain period and who will carry out repairs, make ladies' costumes, or convert double-breasted suits into single, with the new narrow lapel. There are two dressmakers who both create formal wear, ladies' own material made up (or created). There is ironmongery and carpentry and shoe-repairing and laundry and electrical goods, and there are a surprising number of other old family businesses boarded up and looking desolate and flyblown, in limbo as it were, until their metamorphosis into smart boutique or pricy antique shop.

There are lots of those, and interior decorators, and glittering pharmacies and purple-draped hairdressing establishments specialising in colour rinses and wiglets, but there are also terribly exciting and cluttered junkshops and an auctioneer's saleroom which is a treasure trove of ancestral discards and very jolly and hectic on auctioneering days. Every greengrocer's and every milk bar is attended by quick and voluble Latins with eyes the colour of Kalamata olives, and there are innumerable delicatessens aromatic with mysterious bundles of sausages and fragrant with cheeses and lovely bread smells and positively vibrating with the hum of foreign conversations, which lack restraint. There are two Chinese restaurants with takeaway meals, which should be very convenient while I am still apprehensive about using my science-fiction electric cooker, and a Spanish one that looks too smart to just drop in on. There is a Polish furniture maker who is a real craftsman, and a folk-singing joint for my adolescent young, and a music hall where I can't afford to go, and a butcher's shop where, to my astonishment and delight, I was served by somebody I went to school with, all dressed up in a blue apron and looking most unlikely.

Then there is a gunsmith whose shop is pure James Bond and who covets my eighteenth-century pistols which I acquired a little dubiously and have entrusted to him for cleaning, and where I have a discreditable but intolerably heady urge to go and practise target shooting. This is closely linked to the wistfulness I feel wandering around the secondhand car dealer's among all the low-slung beauties of decent vintage that I have never owned and have secretly yearned for as much as everybody else with a feeling for style. Perhaps, in this life, one should cultivate frivolity as well as endurance.

And there is the corner pub. Not just a corner pub, although it looks conventionally hideous enough on its street sides. But behind it there is a garden with tables and benches and geraniums blazing away and a wonderful oak tree and it is just about the most civilised public place I've found in a year and I shall have a lot of pleasure there sitting in the sun at a slatted table peeling its paint and drinking very cold beer and making out shopping lists and watching the regulars come and go.

Because the neighbourhood is its inhabitants too, and these are colourful, mixed, not easily slotted into one category. There are the housewives, stopping by to meet after a morning's shopping, and there are the selfconscious weekend customers in carefully careless informal wear with the right accessories of poodles or bull terriers, there are workmen in overalls and foreign wanderers carrying airline bags and nervously suspicious expressions. There are the beautiful young, not yet in one another's arms but working up to it, and there are the oldest of the regulars, stubborn, isolated, and resentful, who knew it when.

There is also, in my street, an old brick cottage with two peppercorn trees in front and a rocking horse on the verandah, and further down there are four small children who say hello to me now as I pass by.

All in all, I have the feeling that I am living in a neighbourhood.

On Waiting for Things to Turn Up

Some weeks ago I wrote a determinedly cheerful piece about living in a brand new bare flat with a lot of young and tea chests. I admit I wrote it in a mood of rampant self-pity, wishing myself to be under an interesting viaduct like my one-eyed Russian friend, with lots and lots of lovely jewels and imperturbably suave diplomatic friends who could conjure up beautiful houses in fashionable quarters.

Obviously I lack the eye-patch and the style, not to mention the viaduct, the jewels, and the necessary diplomatic friends, because after so many weeks I am still living in a bare flat with a lot of young and tea chests. (I hasten to add that not all the young are actually mine, although I sometimes behave as if they were and feel very proprietorial about them, because their conversation is never less than entertaining, their wits are zanily tempered, and their unbridled enthusiasms boundless: I have sometimes thought lately, reading about the smug blunders of complacent old men, that the government of the world should, properly, be put into the hands of intelligent eighteen-year-olds.)

I asked a lady in one of the other flats for drinks the other evening, and she said she would come only if she was permitted to sit in one of the tea chests. I also received a nice letter from another lady who commiserated with me and said that she, too, thought 'in Robinson Crusoe'. That's the stage it's got to. And since I've had a go of pneumonia this last couple of weeks (and a nastier, sweatier, more unromantic complaint I have yet to be afflicted with) and have been, as they say, confined to barracks, I've been pondering on my lot and wondering why I should still be living in a gypsy encampment and not in the order and elegance for which I yearn and to which, in my messy way, I try to aspire.

In the last twenty years I have Started Afresh so many times that I should be used to it, and indeed Starting Afresh has a certain sort of reckless charm, if only in that you can discard all the terrible Mistakes, like the rickety writing desk that proved to be not antique but only secondhand, and the squiggly bentwood table that was short in one leg and inclined to lurch threateningly when a guest set a plate down on it, and all the accumulated tat that obstinately survived when everything pretty and fine had been broken or had worn out.

So, once again, stripped to the few really beautiful and completely unpractical possessions that are dear to me (I left all the rest in Greece) I Started Afresh here with a high heart and a small sum of money which, theoretically, would be adequate for tables and chairs and beds and cups and saucers and cooking pots and brooms and lavatory brushes and all those other items of domestic usage that are obviously necessary but only intended, as far as I am concerned, to provide a sort of comfortable and neutral background for books and paintings and rugs and birdcages and fishing floats and old doorknockers and all the really interesting things.

This time I didn't hurry it either. I wasn't going to buy a single thing that would 'do'. I spent weeks circling the big stores and the smart little ones, pricing, comparing, estimating, adding up columns of figures in a book I bought especially for the purpose, attending auctions, asking very knowledgeable questions about fabrics, and generally acting out the role of a lady hellbent on setting up a classy establishment and not going to be fooled or rushed by anyone. I must say it felt very grand and I enjoyed it enormously while the money lasted.

That was weeks and weeks ago. That was the fun bit. I bought Finnish plates and Czechoslovakian glasses. I bought a nylon broom and a plastic kitchen tidy. I bought inner-spring mattresses for everybody and the sort of refrigerator you walk into. I bought a sofa eight feet long and two chairs that invite philosophic reflections. I bought a teak-topped desk and a filing cabinet, and, deliriously, ordered to be made for me a refectory table and benches for either side (perhaps a little starkly monastic but actually suitable for our way of living, which requires that there be room for people playing chess at one end while others eat down the way and somebody else types up something in the middle, and anyway a wonderful place to put things, like old exam papers and tape-recorders and piles of ironing and the gramophone and keys and reminder notes and unanswered letters and medicine bottles).

Having had my fun I've been sitting around since waiting for things to Turn Up until the waiting seems to have become an end in itself and I cannot at this moment imagine a state of being that wasn't a waiting one.

For every purchase I have made there has been a delivery date expressly and specifically stated, and on that date I have remained at home, whatever my commitments, to see the particular article installed. And not once has delivery been effected on the date stated. No, that isn't true: once delivery was effected on the date stated, but the package was missing two items.

Now every time this happens (or doesn't happen, rather) I must go into town again to the particular store where I bought my goods (for I am waiting for a telephone to Turn Up too) and begin again the laborious and time-consuming business of placating the injured innocence of the salesman or saleslady who originally served me and then tracing the docket through to the warehouse to find out what happened (or didn't happen). And then we start all over again, with many profuse apologies on the part of the retailers, and on mine for bothering them, and mutual professions of goodwill, and I go home and begin the waiting again. And nothing turns up.

Is this a particularly Australian modus operandi? And if so—why? Is it due to laziness, inefficiency, cavalierness, or just plain arrogance? Am I simply disaster-prone? Or doomed, by the inscrutable Fates (who keep their reasons to themselves), to live in tea chests for life everlasting instead of the beautiful houses in fashionable quarters for which I long and where I could be just as disorganised (only more stylishly) as I am in this set-up?

As a matter of fact I think I have a clue to the whole situation, and I came by it while passing my feverish hours sweating liberally all over the books I like, which range from Rabelais through the gloomier Russians to Dickens, whom my children detest and I suppose I was rereading him to find out why.

I didn't find out why my children so revile him, but in *David Copperfield* I was reminded of something I had forgotten, namely, that Mr Micawber and all of Mr Micawber's family, 'done up, like preserved meats, in impervious cases', emigrated to Australia and here prospered.

Which, of course, answers everything. If ever a family Waited for Things to Turn Up it was the Micawbers, and there were so very many of them, Mrs Micawber being so prolific, as well as trusting, that they must have multiplied by this time into thousands, and the generations of the Micawbers are now, obviously, running department stores and repair services and finance companies and telephone allotments and just about everything I'm waiting for (including cheques and galley proofs and medical clearances) on the simple Micawber principle of Sanguine Expectations, at which Mrs Micawber was so brilliant and passed on, as a philosophy, to her numerous progeny.

I think I must be going mad, really. I found myself looking up the telephone directory (which I have in Sanguine Expectation of having a telephone to go with it) and who do you think I found? Mr Micawber. It doesn't say if his Christian name is Wilkins but I know he has an antique shop and the moment I am let out of medical confinement I am going right down to see him and blister his impervious skin with a few imprecations I have invented in my sweaty solitude.

In the meantime, of course, I am waiting for things to Turn Up.

On Being Unable to Write an Article

It has been more than a year now that I have been writing these pieces every week. And this week, as every week, I have come smack bang up against crisis. Annihilation even. Because I know myself to be completely incapable of writing an article. This is the most terrible feeling, of panic and desolation, of terror, of the most awful loss. I have compared notes with other writers about this chronic recurring paralysis of the talent and find that it is common. Everyone gets it. I suppose that ought to help, but in the grip of the paralysis it doesn't seem to be of any consolation at all.

There are, scattered about me at this moment, a litter of—press-*cuttings* I was going to say, only they look like desperate press-*fearings*, any one of which could be elaborated into an article.

There is one, for instance, about the clubs with the poker machines being embarrassed by the difficulty of spending their gains. One could let loose on that. But not today, somehow. There is another that records a 1904 Ford advertisement that boasts with lovely simplicity 'it gets you there and it brings you back'. And that's all it boasts about. Some time or other I would like to base an article on that. But not today. And there is a cute one from Qantas (or about Qantas, rather), who have started up a whole series of advertisements in America in which the Big Sell is an archaic or Sentimental Bloke slang, like 'dekko' and 'bonzer' and 'tucker' and 'shebang' and—God help us—'bobby dazzler'.

I would like to do something on that, but today I think, oh well—they also sponsor the making of some very good films. One wonders. But then one wonders so often.

There is also a perfectly grisly one about the RSL where an official stated (in words that carried the deepest moral conviction, considering the poker machines: the RSL club just up the way from my place covers a whole block and has the squat rich solidity of a Mayan temple) that rather than bring the bodies of dead soldiers home it would be better to spend that money sending more soldiers away. He said that soldiers killed in action should be buried in the nearest war cemetery because bringing them home would 'cause many upsets'.

Well, for goodness sake, let's not upset anybody, and I would have to be very upsetting indeed if I wrote an article on this particular subject.

On the other hand I could write about the current trend in the pop song, which seems to be returning directly to the nursery rhyme. Inky Dinky Spiders and Roses are Red Dilly Dilly and everything. But the very thought of writing about the infantile implications of all this quite honestly makes me sick.

I asked my son, who often helps me out in these recurring crises, what I should write about, and he looked up vaguely from a Ruy Lopez (Steinitz Defence Deferred) involvement which was engaging his attention and said, briefly: 'Chess.'

I thought about this for a while, and indeed some fairly wild ideas began to beat about in my brain, echoes of the sort of delirious and dizzy conversations that are tossed about among the young men who gather around that old chessboard. 'How the Bishop was Rooked'. 'The Blackest Knight in the Castle'. 'How to Identify Losing Gambits, by Napoleon, Hitler, and Barry GoldH20'. But I think it is their subject rather than mine, and I shall leave them to write their chess articles themselves.

The awful thing about having to write an article today is that there are so many other things I should like to be doing.

Like setting off on a trip that would take me to and through all the Australia that I have never seen—the very trip that I have been promising myself ever since I came home, the very trip that in a sort of a way brought me home, since it seemed uncivil, to say the least, to be on such intimate terms with so many other countries when my acquaintance with my own was limited to two cities and one small country town. But like the Steinitz Defence, or Hope, the Trip is always being Deferred—for the most excellent of reasons, naturally (I hate excellent reasons: they ring like the death knell of possibility).

Or, accepting deferment of an introduction to the land I would so very much like to meet, I would like to go shopping. Not desperation shopping (which is my usual type of shopping, because I just have to have stockings or another set of underwear or something suitable to wear to some dinner or lunch or gathering to which I've been invited and although my daughter has Just The Thing, unfortunately I'm bigger than she is and, wiggle and wriggle hopefully as I might, the wretched garment looks as though it belongs to somebody else even if it is Just The Thing: it isn't Just The Thing for me).

No, the sort of shopping I would like to indulge in is the leisurely kind, rather like Nicole and Rosemary in *Tender Is the Night*, who drifted all one afternoon along the boulevards of Paris, and Rosemary bought two dresses and two hats and four pairs of shoes, and Nicole bought coloured beads and a guest bed and a dozen bathing suits and a travelling chess set (how chess does crop up, to be sure) and chamois leather jackets in singing colours and a rubber alligator and lots of other beautiful and impractical things.

I am certain one could do this sort of thing in Australia. I am an avid reader of the shopping columns, which are very enticing, and I know I could drift with the best of them if only I had the money and the time. I don't think one actually needs to buy anything—it's the drifting and looking and trying on that is important, spiritually, I mean.

Or, most of all, I would like to be sitting around that new and splendidly monastic table and benches with George Johnston, talking and talking and talking for hours at a stretch (we talked for thirteen hours straight once and came up with an idea that turned into a novel called *My Brother Jack*) and drinking very cold beer and inventing plots for novels and plays and stories.

We invented a philosopher once and made him acceptable to everybody, and I rather wish now I'd written this article about that, because it is a very moral and instructive story. I will write it one day, only George Johnston has written it already as a short story and it would look as though I was pinching from him (actually, we are allowed to do that between ourselves, but not often, and only from necessity).

Well, then, since I can't sit around the table and talk to George Johnston because George Johnston is in hospital and hospitals aren't conducive to our particular sort of talking and don't have cold beer and wouldn't allow thirteen hours for working out an idea, and since I can't do anything else I want to do today because I have to write this article, I can think about all the things I ought to do, and seek a sort of moral refuge in them.

I ought to take the washing in from the line.

I ought to unpack the groceries.

I ought to have a real archaeological exploration of the midden accumulating in the rooms of my children, since nobody has two socks of the same colour or underwear or students' passes for buses or anything.

I ought to give up smoking, but my doctor knew I had to write this article today and has given me a period of grace which lasts until I go to bed tonight.

At least that gives me something to write about next week (it all reminds me of Laurence Sterne, who was always promising a chapter on 'Chambermaides and Buttonholes': I think my article on Giving Up Smoking might turn out to be one of those—deferred again).

What I should be doing, of course, is writing this article.

News of Earls Court—Fifteen Years Ago

The fog didn't come on little cat's feet exactly. It hung around like bits of dirty drapery, looped up in places, tattered in others, and around the thick ugly pillars that supported the porticoes of soot-stained residentials it trailed streamers sometimes. It smelled something acrid, something lean; not like anything one had ever smelled before, but right, just right, just what a London fog ought to smell like. The streets were soggy with a mulch of leaves, old newspapers, and the evidence of many dogs having been walked. In the Fulham Road there was a shop that sold clowns' masks and joke kits and all the appurtenances of magic.

It was the Festival of Britain that year, and the Australian designer Gordon Andrews was living in Earls Court, and being very involved in the (then) futuristic complex over on the South Bank. His wife, Mary, and I used to roster ourselves for duty chores with our assorted children, like picking them up from school and walking them in parks (Holland Park and Kensington Gardens for preference) and riding them around on those buses so vehemently red in all the grey, or traipsing them through museums. London buildings, the Portland stone ones, looked like bleached bones behind the tracery of bare black branches, and every spring stall was noisily yellow with massed daffodils.

That year, too, I was sitting for a portrait to an Australian painter, Colin Colahan, who lived in Whistler's old house in Tite Street. He had been an expatriate then for more than twenty years and one knew, with certainty, that he would never be going back. His studio windows looked out on the Chelsea Hospital for old military pensioners and he often played Mozart's Requiem Mass while he painted me because he couldn't quite believe that I would always cry at exactly the same point, but I always did. I was filled to bursting with excitement, and I felt very young and very muddled and very choked with being excited and young and muddled, not to mention Mozart and Whistler's house and Nell Gwyn and London London London.

There were a lot of other Australians being excited in London that year. Paul Brickhill had finished *The Great Escape* and was waiting for publication, knowing already, I think, that he was going to crack the best-seller lists. Peter Finch was over in Dolphin Square, not quite yet daring to believe what everybody was saying about his talent, and sometimes needing reassurance. His brother, a test pilot, was obsessed with something called the sound barrier, and at dinners or parties would always be found in a corner, drawing diagrams of leading edges and airflows. Loudon Sainthill hadn't then designed those magical sets and costumes for *The Tempest* that would take us down to Stratford later, in a blizzard, behind a snow-plough, the car waltzing on the iced roads (but worth it to cheer Loudon for a success so spectacular), but he was there, and Cedric Flower was there, doing the rounds of the theatres and painting buses and bridges and guardsmen and the Round Pond and posters for the London Underground, and Pat Flower was there, writing her first thriller, and Albert Arlen was there, talking about the music for *The Sentimental Bloke*, and Sidney Nolan's drought paintings were receiving attention although the buyers weren't stampeding in those days, and more fools they.

I used to think that the most desirable state of being that could be imagined was to be a young and talented Australian in London. Weren't we healthier, more vital, more buoyant? And didn't we have so much enthusiasm, so much talent that it was frustrating to the point of actual discomfort to keep ourselves within decent British bounds? We kept bursting out all over the place. I thought we were like a lot of healthy Antipodean sponges, sopping up everything that touched us, good and bad and smelly and all. The musty smell of the tube stations was in it, and the marvellously comic sight of gentlemen in yachting rig sailing toy boats on the Round Pond, and the prophet with the streaming white beard who held a placard that read 'God Is Going to Get You', and the chars who actually (and unbelievably) called one 'madam', and ration cards and bus queues and Homburg hats and nannies wheeling titled babies in extravagant carriages, as well as theatres and galleries and concerts and all the other intellectual food we were gorging ourselves on. We talked immoderately and played records from clumsy albums of twelve (of which one would invariably be chipped or broken), and collected bits of Victoriana in Church Street and the Portobello Road, as well as funny stories about the English. We were enchanted, amused, excited, indignant, frustrated, discouraged, and sometimes contemptuous.

Australia, which we had left in the jubilee year of Federation, seemed very far away. 'A cultural desert,' we said (but only to other Australians), remembering it as being a distinctly unpleasant place in the immediate postwar years, more prosperous than it had ever been but paralysed by strikes (bathing the babies by candlelight night after night, and never knowing whether there would be a milk delivery or not), cynical with the disillusionment of peace, and the taxi-drivers rapacious and the shop assistants rude and the licensing laws barbarous and creative nourishment scanty.

These memories have been teasing me lately, what with all the passions and vituperations that have been seething and boiling and even exploding (nastily, and with a stench of sulphur) in the cauldron where everybody in the world, it seems, is trying to cook up a brew that will turn out to be an authentic Australian Image.

The Japanese have had a stir in the pot, and the ABC and the Sydney Civic Fathers, and the BBC have added a few toads, and lately the present batch of Australian expatriates—the Australian Londoners—have been articulate in defence of their expatriation.

Australia, they still say, is a cultural desert. They feel themselves to be less expatriates than 'cultural refugees' from the chase after the quid and the GNP. They feel in Australia a sterility, a barrenness, a paucity of ideas, and they make the point that if every creative Australian in London came back it still wouldn't make any difference to Australia's cultural development because Australian society as it is presently constituted couldn't find room for them, and wouldn't even want to anyway.

All this is so hauntingly familiar, echoing fifteen-year-old conversations that must still be palpitating faintly in the fog draped around Earls Court and the Bayswater Road and Notting Hill Gate and Chelsea and innumerable film-set pubs all over London.

Only, what strikes me as curious, in a particularly distressing sort of way, is that fifteen years ago, when we were saying the same things (only not so publicly), radio in Australia was flourishing, writers and actors were as busy as could be, people went to theatres for entertainment as a matter of course, we had a film industry, and a best-selling book—in hard covers too—might sell sixty to eighty thousand copies. There was no TV.

In the fifteen years since we went away the government hasn't changed and neither has much on the cultural scene, except to wither slowly, even to atrophy completely. Most radio is only glorified jukebox, the theatre is struggling more desperately than ever before, the film industry is moribund, and if a hard-cover book sells ten thousand it is a fantastic success. There is TV, which ought to be absorbing all sorts of talents, but—alas—isn't.

A queer business. It is distressing, really, to remember Earls Court fifteen years ago. These days, they tell me, it is known as Kangaroo Valley.

Saturnalias, Resolutions and Other Christmas Wishes

One morning this week (and I'm not saying which one) I woke—as usual—to the raucous shrilling of my demented alarm clock, which sounded more than ever like a chorus of mad seagulls, and just as welcome beside my bed at that sad grey hour of dawn. I was bleary-eyed, very nasty-tasting in the tongue and the throat, and filled with a spiritual mixture—that special blend—compounded of bravado, shame, mental evasion and memory blank, that inevitably follows a party that went on too long and too everything the night before.

To my intense relief I saw (as much as I was capable of seeing anything) that my clothes were neatly folded, there were no cigarette burns in or on my new lace suit, that my beautiful hat—which many people had coveted the night before—had not been given away (I'm inclined to do that), and that my handbag, keys, gloves, chequebook and wallet were by my side (I have been known to have left any or all of them, as well as manuscripts, parcels, urgent copy, passports, incriminating letters, legal documents and important folders, in restaurants, taxis, strange flats, and other people's cars— and I mean perfectly strange other people of whom, the day after, I can remember neither name nor telephone number).

Only, just when I was congratulating myself on having Got Through, as it were, in a ladylike and decorous way I saw my stockings. There they were, carefully folded over the chair, toe to toe and heel to heel.

Except there weren't any toes. And there weren't any heels.

From the brand new and absolutely impeccable legs of the stockings (not a snag, rip, rent or ladder) there dangled a few tatty and extremely dirty shreds on my primitive feet sordid. I didn't need a Sherlock Holmes to discover to me that I had had my shoes off again.

In a way this is perfectly all right.

If anyone is ever personal enough to comment on my primitive feet my husband explains quickly that 'She didn't wear shoes until she was thirteen', which isn't strictly so, but isn't necessarily a lie either just because he made it up. It's just that I would rather be without shoes than with them, and these narrow spike-heeled things we have to wear these days irk my toes, which need dust and rocks and saltwater and wet sand to curl around in. The rest of me has civilised quite surprisingly well, but not my feet. So when I can I take my shoes off.

The awful thing was that I couldn't remember taking them off. When? And with whom?

The soles of the stockings suggested that I had been dancing strenuously. Or walking (or running) on spikily gravelled paths. Or climbing a mountain.

I knew that there had been no mountain, or even gravelled path, around the extremely fashionable place where I had been partying with extremely fashionable people.

That left dancing. And I knew too that I was incapable of the Go-Go stuff (which would have been the sort of dancing if people had been dancing), having never progressed further in that line than the cheek-to-cheek nightclub smooch that dates all too accurately my wooing days, but doesn't wear out the soles of my stockings.

Had I been doing a Zorba-type Greek dance, lace suit, silk hat and all?

All this was so disturbing to a respectably married mother of three that there and then, through the fizz and hiss of the Alka-Seltzer (which sounded, at that moment, like hail on a tin roof) I made another resolution.

If I went to another Christmas party—and I felt like renouncing them all (except that furtively, in the back of my head, I knew I wouldn't, being morally weak about these things)—I resolved not to drink more than the one or two convivial or social ones requisite to the occasion. Or, as my husband warns sometimes (I don't mean to quote him so often but he does make pertinent remarks quite frequently): 'Don't drink between drinks.'

Or, if I went to another Christmas party, I resolved that the moment I felt myself coming over funny and wanting to dance I would call a taxi immediately and come home and dance privately and with the venetians prudently closed.

I know that I am not alone in this or some similar resolution. There must be thousands and thousands, if not millions and millions, of perfectly respectable people gulping down their Alka-Seltzer at this very moment and wondering if they can ever Face Certain People again. This, to me, seems to be the true spirit of Christmas as practised in this fabulous land.

Christmas has reverted to what it was originally. That is to say: the Saturnalia. All the chirping carols and hunks of holly and sweating department-store S. Clauses and Wise Men (or International Children) on tasteful and much too expensive cards are only the flossy decorations around human abandonment, which is what Christmas was—is, rather—all about.

The fact is that nobody really knows when Christ was born. But another fact is that until the fourth century,

December 25 was celebrated as the Winter Solstice, or the Nativity of the Sun.

In Egypt and Syria the celebrants retired into an inner shrine, from which they emerged at midnight, crying: 'The Virgin has brought forth! The light is waxing!' and the Egyptians even represented the newborn sun by the image of an infant which was brought out on this his birthday and displayed.

The Romans, great lovers of pleasure, took up this festival, which they dedicated to Saturn (the equivalent of the Greek Cronos)—a thoroughly nasty deity who ate all his children except Jupiter (air), Neptune (water), and Pluto (the grave), whom Time could not consume—but it was a good enough excuse for a week of unrestrained disorder and misrule, when all schools were closed, no public business could be transacted, no laws passed, and everybody and anybody was entitled to whoop it up according to his taste. No holds barred and no punishments meted out.

Doesn't this seem familiar? Even if we are upside down, and it is summer instead of winter, we drift (or lurch) back to the old custom of things. As sun-worshippers anyway this season suits us. Or perhaps, anywhere in this modern world, a couple of weeks of unrestraint and licence, after a year of pressure and pensions and disciplines, is a necessary catharsis.

And having said all that, and knowing that the Christian fathers didn't take up this festival until the fourth century, and even being cynical about the commercialism that has battened on to this time of year, and agreeing with the Anglican Archbishop of Sydney, Dr H. R. Gough, in everything he has had to say about unnecessary luxuries and office parties and Keeping Up With the Mythical Joneses, I still feel an overwhelming goodwill to everyone (and especially to the lovely people who write to me and whose letters I don't answer because if I did I would never find time to write articles for them to write me letters about) and I am disappearing in a crumpled sea of wrapping paper and getting soggy over carols and stars and Away In A Manger and my own awful brood.

Who cares about an old pair of tattered stockings? You can abandon yourself to love, too.

On Being a Home-Grown Migrant

It is now all of sixteen months ago—on a wild winter night, with the lights of Sydney Harbour blazing away like a festival of coloured candles—that I struggled off a migrant ship with my three children and onto home territory for the first time in nearly fifteen years.

There were more than a thousand of us on that ship, including families of English migrants, Greek proxy brides, be-shawled and bemused grandmothers shrouded in shapeless black and already wailing ritually, and young Greek labourers with the sturdiness and aggressiveness of Cretan bulls. Individually and all together we shoved and jostled and pushed and heaved, and finally hurtled down the gangways like a herd of Gadarene swine into the shrieks and explosions and turbulence and tears of arrival and/or reunion.

For us it was arrival and reunion, my husband George Johnston having come ahead six months before us from Greece, where we had been living for the last ten years, to launch a new novel and scout out the land (fifteen years is a long time to be away from one's country, even if exile has been self-imposed, and we were both dubious about returning to it: we hadn't liked it much at the time we had left it).

It is interesting that we did return to Australia quite literally as migrants, subsidised by the government, whose policy it is to encourage its own nationals to return (I know that most cultural expatriates will challenge this, but I am not talking about cultural encouragement, only passage money) as well as to welcome the two million odd British, Austrian, German, Greek, Hungarian, Italian, Dutch, Polish, Yugoslav, American, Maltese and Stateless (that tragic official word) citizens who have poured into this country, assisted or under their own steam, over the last twenty years.

The first thing of which everybody assured me, with conviction, pride, and even complacency, was that I'd see 'some changes in the old place all right'. And they said: 'It's the migrants that've made the difference. We've got a real Continental way of life now.' (Rather in the manner of a boy scout earning a merit badge, but certainly a pleasant and praiseworthy modulation of the old screeching note of 'bloody reffos'.)

Well now. At the end of sixteen months I am sitting in a brand new, shoddy, and very expensive apartment built by a Yugoslav landlord with foreign labour. My windows look down, at the one corner, onto an enchanting inlet of Sydney Harbour, and up, at the other, to a hill the contours of which remind me of the Mediterranean, except that its curved terraces are planted, not with olive trees, but with red brick bungalows and rotary clothes hoists, all the way up to the high skyline where the home unit blocks are growing taller than the two Norfolk pines and three cabbage palms that have sometimes given me solace.

Change there is, certainly, and certainly a European influence that is obvious in shop signs, in flavoursome scraps of conversation overheard on buses and street corners, in the Polish furniture maker around the corner, the Dutch framer, the Austrian hairdresser down the street who is a whiz at cutting, and in eating and drinking habits which have improved out of mind. All this adds piquancy to what used to be a fairly dull and conventional dish as a Way of Life.

And there is change too in the look of the city itself. I always thought Sydney beautiful (that is to say the foreshores of the harbour), but now, coming over the bridge from the north side, or across the water by ferry, it looks as romantic in its way as San Gimignano of the Towers. Sometimes I ache with it, and think I would like to live here forever. It is aspiring now, soaring up from the sea, with the intoxicating geometry of angled cranes dizzily high against the hazy Sydney sky (and the climate is awful, incidentally, whatever they say) and the tall skeletons of steel and concrete swarming with ant-sized figures that are marked by the vehement red and yellow dots of safety helmets.

Most of those ant figures will speak English with a foreign accent, and if you came across by taxi it is ten to one your driver spoke with a foreign accent too. If you are coming into town for lunch you will probably be going to a foreign restaurant (small, civilised, and densely patronised at midday by paunchy males in executive-type suits—whatever happened to the lean Australian type?—and groups of ladies in extraordinary hats vying for the attention of the social photographer).

All this is exciting and stimulating, and one has the sense of being in a real city, a big city by world standards, vibrant with the urgencies of busy commercial life, growing at a breathtaking pace. But once the commercial day is over the city empties, and the tide of human activity that has surged and crashed through it in the working hours rushes out at full ebb to the suburbs, where Sydney domestic life is lived—if you call it living.

Returning to our muttons, or the view from my window, I have often thought, with a sort of fascinated horror, of this view multiplied by thousands and minus the harbour inlet, to the south and the west and the north, the red brick and tile going on and on and on and away in a nightmare grid of what must be the most hideous domestic architecture in the world. One feels that the zestful and piquant influences of the Old World have been rejected here, or beaten back, or perhaps have not yet got so far. Except for the shopping centres, where the milk bar, the delicatessen, and the greengrocery will almost certainly be run by Greeks or Italians, there is no evidence of a 'Continental way of life'. Sydney suburbia appears to be as stupefyingly dull as it was fifteen years ago, only more prosperous and therefore more smug.

For all that, and for all the terrifying cost of living, which sometimes causes me to break out in a sweat of sheer panic, I think I am glad we came back, and I am only qualifying that statement because I fancy it takes longer than sixteen months for a migrant to adjust—even a home-grown one like me.

It is a queerly tentative place, lacking real definition yet. Perhaps that is what is so exciting about it really. It is a place still becoming, a place where anything might happen, a place—and one feels this with a desperate, wishful eagerness—where one might even be able to *make* things happen if one tries hard enough. Heaven knows there's scope.

It is true that the live theatre is struggling for survival, it is true that the television channels are clogged with the crummiest of the American West, it is true that there is a general political and public apathy toward anything more creative than chasing a quid (dollar now, of course), it is true that young talent is fleeing Europewards by the boatload and older talent already there is refusing to come home, thank you very much.

Yet there are other boatloads coming in from Europe all the time, bringing all sorts of talents. If they continue to come in at their present rate this country might even have a population of twenty-three or twenty-four million by the year 2000 (always provided, of course, that we survive that long). Enough population and enough talent to make anything possible, even a cultural revolution, or suburbia blossoming into exciting life.

Anyway, as a migrant, I think it is worthwhile sticking around for a bit just to see.

On a Lowering Sky in the East

One of the kids, who has been experimenting in ceramics, came up with a gimmick that the rest of the mob acclaim as the sharpest sartorial idea of the season—His and Hers cufflinks ornamented with the Nuclear Disarmament symbol. Special wear for protest marches. The dedicated protestants are clamouring for her to go into full production—Youth Against Conscription cufflinks, Racial Equality cufflinks, and so on. Most of the group are presently pretty dedicated protestants.

They are against the Bomb and they are against the White Australia Policy and they are against censorship and they are against conscription and they are against the war in Vietnam. They are against America fairly generally, excepting for Pete Seeger and Bob Dylan and Joan Baez and the rest of the message singers and Freedom Riders, and Martin Luther King, who they are emphatically for, as they are for Civil Rights, Equality for Aborigines, Understanding Asia, et cetera (I don't think it is necessary for me to expand that 'et cetera', although it warms me very much that they are for more things than they are against).

For their age grouping and intellectual rating and the state of the world they live in they seem to be properly and healthily insurgent. At an equivalent stage of development I was a fairly fervent protestant myself, albeit a rather woolly one, never having had the right sort of head for political thinking, but only a passionate instinct for justice.

Still, I remember well enough and understand well enough and sympathise well enough. It is right for youth to protest against what it believes to be intolerance, oppression, injustice. Many of these young people, even perhaps most of them, will compromise later under the pressures of society and the pull of their own personal ambitions, just as their elders did before them. There is nothing like time and tradesmen's bills to curb headlong idealism. But they won't compromise yet. Peace and freedom and the equality of man are noble human concepts. There are even some stubborn elders left around (thank God) who still believe the concepts to be realisable, in spite of what is happening in the world at the beginning of this brand new year of 1966.

It looms ahead portentous as years go, dark in colour as a lowering sky, shot with ominous flickers that might presage real lightning bolts, uneasy with rumours of economic recessions, readjustments, restrictions, sanctions, deepening military commitments, grave predictions, hints from high places that things might have to get worse before they get better.

And the slaughter continuing.

I remember as a child seeing a newspaper photograph that shocked the world as well as me—a photograph taken after the bombing of Shanghai—and the photograph showed one Chinese baby, face contorted in terror and desolation, quite alone in the waste that had been the Shanghai railway yards. That one photograph was enough to jolt the whole world into some sort of moral attitude about the Sino-Japanese war; it became quite famous and long years later was included in the exhibition called (and one weeps at the hope of such a title) 'The Family of Man'.

We see such photographs in our newspapers any day of the week now. Babies not only abandoned but burned with napalm, fleeing women bloodied and torn, screaming faces, young boys bound under viciously kicking boots or smashing rifle butts: the horror is blunted by such constant repetition that we turn to the sport or the gossip concerning television celebrities or the social pages. And read the stars.

My two elder children were born in that little lull between the end of the Second World War and the beginning of the Korean one. In their lifetimes the world has staggered through crisis after crisis—the Berlin Air Lift, the Berlin Wall, Suez, Cuba, Cyprus (when my youngest child was born), the Hungarian Revolt, as well as the continuing attrition of the Cold War, and innumerable military coups, assassinations, race riots, atrocities, and abominations.

What is interesting is that in all that time the anxiety of the world has been focused on Europe. I can remember reading an article in *Esquire* magazine which listed, with true American efficiency, the relative safety—in the event of nuclear attack or nuclear accident (and accidents seemed likely)—of all the countries of the world in terms of survival. And Australia then was right up on top of the list. The novel, and later the film made from the novel, *On the Beach*, was a fictional rendition of this same premise, that Australia would survive longer than any place else.

That premise doesn't hold good any longer. The cockpit of the world has shifted from Europe to Asia, and not on Spengler's theory of the Decline of the West either. It is improbable that the Horde will sweep through Europe again to the gates of Kiev. But we Australians are sitting right on the rim of the cockpit, and my children aren't safe and your children aren't safe, and in my mind I have this haunting gallery of newspaper photographs showing burned babies and screaming women and young boys bound under the boots and the rifle butts, boys of about the same age as (or even younger than) this group of well-fed, well-educated, well-housed and presently dedicated protestants, who believe—at least in this time of their youth—in the concepts of peace and freedom and the equality of man, and intend, some of them, to take Asiatic studies as a better way towards living harmoniously with their neighbours than bombs and bullets.

I don't like the beginning of this year much. The portents are too dark. And what is so awful is that what will come about in this year is not so important to us elders, who have brought this state of things to pass by our own ignorance and apathy and the compromises we made for the sake of tradesmen's bills and our own personal ambitions, but to these same young people, who might find in a couple of years' time that they are forced to exchange their Asiatic studies for the rifles they don't want.

And yet, as always, I find my hope for the future in the young.

Not just my own group of protestants, but young protestants all over the world. Perhaps if they have the will and the passion to keep on protesting, perhaps if they are stubborn and tenacious enough to stick to their belief that peace and freedom and the equality of man are realisable concepts, they might bring the whole world a little closer to the possibility of such a state.

At any rate, they are at least trying.

On Being Middle-Aged

I remember, when I was fourteen years old and just beginning to be conscious of my own body, the shape of it, its possibilities, seeing a middle-aged woman naked in the changing rooms of the local swimming baths. I remember my outrage, horror, and disbelief. I remember the violence and vehemence of the 'No' I said then. 'Never,' I said. I said, 'I'd rather be dead.'

At about this time too, I remember that one evening my mother put her hand—brown, blotched, swollen-knuckled, tobacco-stained and ripped and ragged at the nails (she worked hard in those Depression years—as a matter of fact she always worked hard)—beside the young firm smooth hand of my sister, who was polishing her nails with French chalk and a chamois pad. And my mother grinned a certain wry lopsided grin I came to know very well later when I was a little more perceptive and began to realise her and recognise her as the incredible person she was.

The other day, scrabbling over the breakfast table in that early-morning panic that always grips our lot, I saw my own hand next to the hand of my seventeen-year-old daughter. And I saw it in horror, outrage, and disbelief.

One goes around for so long believing that every little physical setback or deterioration is temporary, can be retrieved—the torn nail, the grey hair, the loose tooth, the muscle that sags on the bone, the broken vein, the laughter lines and the worry lines. 'When I get time,' one says. Or: 'I must do something about that.' 'Later,' one says.

Cyril Connolly writes that inside every fat man there is a thin one screaming to be let out. I swear that inside every forty-year-old and fifty-year-old there is still a twenty-year-old, and this double identity makes for all sorts of confusions.

We are forever excusing young people their follies and errors on account of their youth. 'Forgive them because they are young.' 'Try to understand them because they are young.' 'Yes, it is wrong, but after all they are only young.' But being young, in fact, is much easier and more pleasurable than being middle-aged. The young have health, energy, alertness, resilience. The harder you bounce them the higher they soar. Their reflexes work like lovely, precision instruments, they have great reserves and banks and dams of unused strength to call on, they have no need to spend time or ingenuity on camouflaging the unpleasant little scars of time that, with the middle-aged, accumulate at a faster rate than they can possibly repair. Best of all, the young have in front of them seemingly limitless vistas of years—time to keep and time to lose and time to play with and time to squander and time to experiment.

Whereas the middle-aged drag time around with them like a long chain of fetters, all the years that they cannot escape, the mistakes that can never be undone, the stupidities that can never be uncommitted now, the shames and humiliations and treacheries and betrayals as well as the prides and accomplishments and happinesses and brief moments of wonder. This is called experience and is supposed to be the recompense for youth and beauty and health and energy (which is all still there, somewhere, if one could only find the trick of releasing it—the loss of it has never been more than temporary—it has just been mislaid, or put aside for a time).

I often think that middle-aged people have two lives, the one they've lived, and a parallel life, as it were, that walks around with them like a cast shadow and lies down with them when they go to sleep, and this is the life they might have lived if they had made different choices in that time when time was so abundant and the choices were so many. And sometimes it still seems possible to live this other life: all that is necessary is to shift to the parallel tracks; perhaps, in some queer way, one has been living it all along.

Of course there are people who refuse to be middle-aged. I don't know whether they are brave or only sad. There are those desperately healthy men, bald perhaps but determinedly hearty, who bound around the squash courts and gymnasiums, relentlessly pursue the weekend suntan, the weight-watchers, the wide-smilers with their bellies sucked in and their shoulders held square and only a hint of panic in their clear frank eyes. It must be terrible keeping it up. I've seen some of them who have got to the point where there isn't anything left but their suntans, but they've still been trying, and I've thought of all that time that might have been spent pursuing some other end than youth.

And those women who spend hours of every week with masseuse, hairdresser, manicurist, skin specialist, dressmaker. Their dressing tables and medicine cabinets are stocked with a library of little fears, and their conversation is inclined to centre around the compliments of strangers who mistook them for their daughters. It seems like such terribly hard work, although I understand the motivation. Who really wants to relinquish beauty, which is a joy and a delight and should not be so fragile and perishable?

Then there are the ones who give in early, who 'let themselves go', the saggers and floppers who seem to parade their physical deterioration, even to flaunt it deliberately as an insult—or perhaps a warning—to the young and beautiful and careless.

I think being middle-aged is really a rather nasty joke and in fact nasty jokes are made of it. 'Mutton dressed up as lamb.' 'The sere and yellow.' 'Of a certain age.' 'She (or he) is no chicken.' I think that there is very little that is consolatory about it excepting that, if one has been lucky, or even brave once or twice, there might be a small score of accomplishments, a couple of notches marked firmly, and even if one is disconsolate one is no longer afraid—at least, not of the same things; one has faced most of them by this time.

Middle-age becomes a familiar territory. One begins to move about in it with confidence, to accept the limitations of its horizons and the fact that time is now calculable.

Only—perhaps it is time for a little reverse in understanding.

It would be nice if the beautiful, energetic, careless young could bring themselves to say: 'Forgive them—because they are middle-aged.' Or: 'Try to understand them because they are middle-aged.' 'Yes, it is wrong but after all they are only middle-aged.'

They'll get there too one day.

Taking the Wrong Road

It used to be said, by Victorian novelists, that the black sheep of the family, the young man who had ignored (or disdained, or rejected) the dignities, the duties, the responsibilities, and the good name of the family, and had whooped it up in undesirable company and high living, or hooked off to sea, or joined the French Foreign Legion, or taken to wife a chorus girl or an opera singer, had 'taken the wrong road'. (Vicars were always terribly good at pronouncing this, mournfully, over tea and very thin cucumber sandwiches.)

Young women were also prone to taking the wrong road, which led them to carriages, boxes at the opera, furs and velvets, bouquets of camellias, suave gentlemen in cloaks and top hats, champagne suppers at midnight, boudoirs hung (I love that word in reference to interior decoration) with satin, muslin, or lace (or Eastern shawls, which are even better). All of which was the prelude to maternity, disgrace, and stumbling around in the snow with a pitiable bundle wrapped up in a shawl (cashmere). From this condition they usually went to a watery grave (Thames, Seine, Danube, or Volga). Or humble penitence and good works. Or even positive saintliness in plain black rep, by which time the poor offender had become wan and pale and glided rather than walked.

It is interesting, I think, that the young men who took the wrong road were always from the most aristocratic families, while the young women who took the wrong road were always from the most humble. Now East might be East and

West might be West, but it is nothing short of marvellous that the poor little Nells and the wicked Rodneys always managed to meet up somewhere on the wrong road and have a ball, which perhaps consoled them a little in the time of retribution, which followed as inevitably as the Hound of Heaven.

Personally, I have always been attracted by wrong roads (I mean literally rather than morally) and have wandered off down one whenever I could, on the principle that you never know where it might lead, and while, quite often, it has led to some nasty shocks, on the other hand it has sometimes led to the most pleasurable and delightful experiences. (I was going to write 'surprises' there, but then, of course, one is never surprised by the unprecedented. That's what ought to happen. Every day of the week.)

Once, driving into Freiburg in torrential rain and with the windscreen wipers out of action (one of our children used to call them 'skweepers' and I'm sure it is a very good name for them, but whatever they were called they didn't work), we went through our Michelin Guide from one-star hotels to (desperately) three-star ones, and there was no room for us anywhere. Freiburg was having a festival. So we drove out again, and because of the rain and our skweepers we took a wrong road. This wrong road led us (crawling and cursing) to a railway track and a small, melancholy sort of inn, dripping with rain and budding vines, and it turned out to be an inn where Goethe had lived for many years, so we stayed there and ate the most delicious food and drank the most delicious wine and slept on feather mattresses about six feet deep, and all night long trains hooted and wailed like Woody Guthrie (as a matter of fact I don't think that there is all that much difference between Goethe and Woody Guthrie; they would have got along famously: I remember thinking that in my bed of feathers). As another matter of fact I don't quite know why I think that story is romantic, but I do—experience is so unique, and nothing, nothing in the world can be imagined beforehand. Everything is made up of particulars.

Once too, when I was young, and out with my rifle on a Saturday (my brother's rifle actually, which he used to lend me sometimes, our father having some queer notion that girls ought not to own guns although they should be able to use them; he was the same about fishing rods and pocketknives: it used to make me spit), I didn't take the same old quarry track through the lantana and the blackberries, but a different one—a wrong one. And this led me up a hill to a group of Moreton Bay figs, where I was attacked by a whole gaggle of enraged crows, who must have been nesting. They darted and swooped and dive-bombed, trying, I thought, for my eyes. It was a purple, growly sort of day, the way you get them sometimes on the south coast of New South Wales—thunder and lightning and blasts of wind and rain (rather like the beginning of the film version of *Oliver Twist*)—and I didn't even try to shoot the crows, but I ran and ran and ran, screaming. So that wrong road led me to the first real fear I had ever felt in all my life. I have been afraid of birds ever since.

There was another wrong road that led me to six cypress trees and some shards and blocks of marble that are all that is left of the oldest temple in Greece, and some prickly pear fruit offered on a fresh-cut vine leaf, and the most profound statement I have ever heard, from an old man, villainously moustached and dressed in faded blue, patched and pieced and darned in a way that Mondrian could never have invented.

And he said: 'Nothing worth knowing ever happens beyond the distance of a mule ride.' I have often thought of that since, and if we could all get back to mules, and town criers instead of newspapers, we might settle ourselves in our various states a little more comfortably than we do at present. I don't think that this idea is blinkering oneself: it is Confucian, rather: cultivate your own garden and let the others cultivate theirs. I am certain that we all agitate ourselves much too much about what is happening beyond the distance of a mule ride, which we can't do anything about anyway. Confucius said, 'The good man makes the good family. The good family makes the good neighbour. The good neighbour makes the good village. The good village makes the good community. The good community makes the good state. The good state makes the good country.' I suppose the good country makes the good world.

It is an interesting thought, anyway.

When I was sixteen I took a wrong road (a track rather, fern and bracken and scrubby sort of trees) that led me to an armful of wild peach blossom, which I will never forget: no flowers have ever been so beautiful since.

When I was seventeen I took a wrong road (asphalt) that led me to a couple of crazy painters and an introduction to poetry (I mean, I knew *The Lady of the Lake* before and 'Roll on thou deep and dark blue ocean' and 'Pippa Passes' and all that, but I had never really met Carl Sandburg or Mr Eliot or John Donne or Robert Frost or lots of others I have been in love with ever since—Marvell and Suckling and those gents).

When I was eighteen I took a wrong road through great Norfolk pines, that led me to disaster.

When I was twenty-one I took a wrong road (only a stairway, actually, and deeply carpeted) that led me to love, and poverty, and three children, and great times.

I think all I mean is that the straight and narrow is terribly straight and narrow, and that there are so many interesting tracks branching off, and winding away, and we don't have to be poor little Nells or even wicked Rodneys to be brave enough, or curious enough, or devious enough, to go exploring every now and again. You never know what might happen.

The Show Behind the Show

Virginia Woolf (of whom I am not all that much afraid—I mean, only a bit because she did write deliciously) said that no person aspiring to be a writer should even contemplate a literary career without the prerequisites of five hundred pounds a year and 'a room of her own'.

The five hundred a year is a bit of a hoot these days, but I wish I could recall her distinguished shade to tell her how fervently I agree with her dictum about the room of one's own. I wish this, not in anger or rage or frustration (having used up all those emotions years ago and not wanting to exhaust myself further and to no purpose, because anger and rage and frustration have availed me nothing), but quite wistfully, really (although not with complete resignation—I'm not that far gone yet).

Just a little while ago I overheard one of the chess players down at the other end of the room (that is to say, about ten feet away from where I am working) ask of my son, with a quite interested glance in my direction: 'What is your mother writing about?'

'I don't know,' said my son, and of course there was no earthly reason why he should, because he is not a clairvoyant and in any case his mother didn't know either.

At that moment a sports car roared up outside the block of flats, and another herd of young swept in as boisterously as an equinoctial gale to sweep my daughter off to some jollity or other, and suddenly the living room (which is the only place I can put my desk) was seething with ebullience, and the girls were clattering backwards and forwards down the hall to put on different clothes, or to exchange the ones they were wearing (I don't know why; I thought they looked very nice in their own), and so the boys had to wait while the girls shrieked and giggled in the bedroom, and because they had to wait they obviously thought it polite to make conversation with me, and while this was going on the landlord called to see me about a cleaning lady he had heard of (and whose ministrations I await with the ardour of a girl longing for love), a blast of rain spattered against the windows and I remembered that there was washing on the line and had to tear downstairs to retrieve it because there wouldn't have been any towels for anybody otherwise, or clean shirts, or pyjamas for my hospital-incarcerated husband, and while I was pelting upstairs again (they were yelling down at me that I was wanted on the telephone) I thought wildly of Virginia Woolf, and also of something somebody said to me only the week before:

'You must live such an interesting life,' she said, 'and meet so many interesting people.'

One of the interesting people I know is a television producer, who maintains that one should never permit the public to even peep behind the scenes of a performance. He says that mystery and illusion must be maintained. The curtain parts, the show is played, the curtain closes again, and that's all the audience should be allowed to know about it. It makes me think of a gully-gully man producing chickens from the most unlikely places and beaming as blandly as a heathen idol.

Actually I have always thought the show behind the show to be as interesting—if not more so—than the show itself, and in this respect I do indeed live a very interesting life, although not quite in the way my acquaintance of last week imagined, and certainly not according to Virginia Woolf.

The show behind the show, as far as my own little performance is concerned, is high comedy with Heath Robinson devices in the way of stage machinery.

To begin with I live in a flat, and in the second place I share it with two teenagers (the third child being boarded out for the period of crisis). Theoretically this is all quite sound, since the flat has three bedrooms, and is agreeable enough and convenient enough as flats go, being so modern as to be fresh from the builders' trowels, and the teenagers of sufficient years to make the whole arrangement tenable—three people living, as it were, communally, but you in your small corner and I in mine and all that.

Practically, it works out quite differently. (And I am for teenagers rather than against them so this is not a particular grizzle or whine: as a matter of fact I am quite inordinately fond of my own, and agree that this is their temporary home just as much as it is my temporary home and they are entitled to bring their friends also.)

However. This is the sort of thing that happens. Last week I had to go to Melbourne on a business trip, and having been pressed rather hard by circumstances (and weather, over which I have no organisational powers) I left the flat rather messy, and with the washing (which I had got up early to do—I mean five o'clock in the morning early) in a laundry basket, with instructions that it should be put out on the line as soon as the rain stopped, and further instructions and directions relating to kitchen refuse, old tins and bottles, hospital visiting, and all the rest.

Two and a half days later I arrived back, glowing with the pleasure of unaccustomed luxury, and bearing a sheaf of flowers gorgeous enough for Joan Sutherland. Also a guest from the south.

This is what greeted me:

Twelve dirty milk bottles, and two half-empty ones growing penicillin. Four unmade beds. One kitchen of which the sink and every available service was stacked and heaped with unwashed plates and cups and glasses. One laundry basket exactly where I had left it but with the damp washing gone mouldy. One ironing basket tipped up across a floor. Four cartons of bottles and tins that had been added to rather than taken away (and too late too late: garbage collection had been and gone). One filthy bathroom. One living room littered with discarded newspapers, articles of clothing, piles of records, coffee cups, punched cans of lemon drink, and a perfectly strange teenager lolling on the sofa and conducting a conversation on the telephone. One desk from which the typewriter (which is my livelihood) was missing, but to which had been added innumerable lists of chess scores and other esoteric data, while my mail and documents had been shifted to the floor. One refrigerator and a whole set of cupboards empty of any sort of provisions for the weekend (and too late to buy any) excepting for a dozen eggs and two pounds of butter (it is extraordinary what little purchasing power ten dollars has, although my daughter had, I noticed, a jazzy new slack suit).

Two horror-stricken faces. And two voices crying in dismayed unison: 'But we didn't think you were coming back until *tomorrow*! We were just going to start cleaning up.'

'Well, why don't you?'

A giggle from my daughter. 'Because you're back now.'

Banners, Causes and Convictions

Going through files the other day in an attempt to sort out a messy accumulation of bits of paper, I came across a whole bundle of letters that my husband had written to me two years ago when he was newly back in Australia and I was still in Greece.

One letter, commenting on Australian youth, said that he thought the young comely, but mentally flabby. I suppose, he wrote, that everything is really too easy. They lack the stimulation of causes.

This was like the echo of discussions we had had ten years before, when we had been trying to come to some sort of understanding of the young Americans who were invading Europe then. Strange, we found them, with a curiously unformed chrysalis quality inside their lavish cocoons of education. The only cause they believed in was the utter futility of all causes, and they expounded this theme monotonously in their flat, sad voices. Kerouac and Ginsberg were their prophets. Inaction was their creed. When they were not turned on with pot they seemed soft, somehow, and defenceless. The angst of their young European contemporaries was of a different order: it had the veracity of real cynicism, of observed—and sometimes experienced—anguish.

I found such ennui, such a reduction of the human qualities of hope and desire and passion, as mystifying as their jargon. What extraordinarily long and esoteric words they used to express ... what? Not failure, because they had never tried.

Not even perplexity. They were incurious, and it always seemed to me to be odd that they travelled about so much: there seemed to be no real reason why they should be in one place rather than another.

One of them, I remember, was a near fatality that summer at the cave where we used to swim. After he had been fished out and resuscitated and dried off someone asked him what had been his last thought before he lost consciousness. With a perfect earnestness he said that he had thought of all that education wasted.

I am sure that they found our enthusiasms naive, our indignations a useless squandering of mental energy, our more cherished beliefs and convictions childlike.

'You get so worked up about things,' they said.

I suppose that until complacency sets in, a generation brought up in a Depression and then plunged into a war is bound to fall into the habit of getting worked up about things.

As a child I remember the fervour of politics that affected whole family relationships, shattered lifelong friendships, split up young lovers and ostracised schoolchildren. Voices rose high and vehement on street corners where men in flannel undershirts gathered in the evenings, watched from verandahs or behind curtains by tight-faced wives who were tired of the dole.

And at the time of the Spanish Civil War my father used to pace around the house at night, restless, bitter, impotent of action. It was all so far away, he was no longer young, there was nothing he could do. He was a liberal humanist, his passion for justice was intense, his rages against persecution and oppression were monumental, his condemnations absolute and unalterable. We were conscious through all our childhood of vast forces working for good and evil and that such forces directly concerned us: at the time of Munich my father wept.

My husband says that in those years he had two young journalist friends in Melbourne who paid their passage money in reichmarks on a German ship and sailed off to Spain to fight, the one for the government and the other for Franco. They shared a cabin all the way over and argued the right of their different causes until they separated to fight for them. One of them was killed quite soon so it is impossible to know now whether their friendship would have survived.

The young Americans we knew (or failed to know, rather) a decade ago in Europe were as ignorant of the Spanish Civil War as if it had happened on an evening star. So soon does time blur great events.

Thinking about all this I have been interested to read a number of recent articles in American magazines and periodicals that report in some detail on the activities of the present crop of American youth. Their causes, at this moment in time, are legion. In a country convulsed by violence and communal eruptions, where hatred and terror can explode even from the formless and the inexplicable, platitudes no longer satisfy, or even soothe. It is necessary to choose sides. The social rebels are active and vocal, and the kids are setting up new icons of their own choosing. Protest singers are rewarded, as one article points out, by a grateful America with riches in return for being their whipping boy.

Is something like this happening here? Certainly attitudes have changed considerably since my husband wrote me that letter only two years ago.

The list of action committees grows. The slogans multiply and surely beget their opposing slogans. More and more people are positively for or positively against bureaucratic policies. Students meet and march. Banners are snatched and torn like battle trophies. Political rallies are stormy and even physically violent. Mothers of sons march for one cause and outraged architects for another while another group vigorously demands racial equality. Dissension spreads. Hostility also. Vigils, protests, sit-ins, teach-ins and even freedom rides are becoming usual. Debates are passionate with opposing convictions, and television cameras record some fairly startling scenes as meetings are broken up officially.

Postwar apathy of the complacent affluent society has exploded into drama suddenly. Emotions run high, if not riot.

I believe this to be a far healthier state of affairs than that curious formlessness and lack of belief or definition that was so apparent even eighteen months or a year ago. Lack of interest. Lack of purpose in other than immediate material gains. Non-involvement.

One thing is certain. No state of affairs was ever bettered by putting up with it, no wrongs ever righted by passively accepting them. A cause, a purpose, a goal, a creed, an idea, a cherished attachment is the stuff all human evolution is made of. Without some belief most passionately held we would expire for want of vitality.

The great reptiles, that most stable society, died out because they could not adapt themselves to changed circumstances. The lotus-eaters dreamed their way into oblivion. I think we, who are still young as societies go, ought to put out more flags.

The Magic of Mornings

By breakfast time the complexion of the day had turned sallow and rather muddy-looking. 'You'd never believe,' I said, 'how gorgeous it was at dawn.' And they all groaned and accused me of being smug as well as masochistic.

I don't care. It *was* gorgeous at that. Crisp as a stalk of fresh celery, and as the earth rolled over to the sun the night unpeeled along the horizon behind sleeping silhouettes of houses and church spires. All the yellow studs of municipal lights snapped out, and for a moment there was a wonderful giddying roller-coaster feeling of hurtling towards the narrow chink of revealed day. Between darkness and darkness it was the coolest, palest green, a sea-colour rather than a sky-colour, and as if to prove that fair exchange is always possible, the inlet of the harbour down below blushed suddenly and quite modestly pink.

I like this mysterious still time before reality is quite declared. Before shapes really emerge, when everything floats nebulously in that queer drowned light that makes one think, atavistically, of the beginnings of things. Before the milkman clatters furiously up the steps and the daily quota of world folly comes sailing over front fences and the garbage men try out fiendish variations on a theme of tins and bottles (shunning all cardboard cartons) and neighbours' alarm clocks begin shrilling dementedly and the rollerdoors of garages go groaning and thunking and the efficiency of the plumbing throughout this building is put noisily to the test and the world reveals itself to be, after all, pretty much what it was yesterday.

Overindulgence in sunrises leads, I know, to some fairly grandiose and unrealistic thinking, especially if one has a taste for the gaudy and spectacular.

Sunrises, like sunsets, are pretty pompous affairs on the whole. I have even heard people dismiss them as vulgar, and carp about the inexpertness of the stage machinery that jerks that huge glittering bauble up over the hill or out of the sea: it isn't a smooth performance at all. I expect that it is sour grapes on the part of the critics, because all that splendour makes one feel rather seedy by comparison. I suppose that's what the Druids were really doing prowling and chanting among the sarsen stones, convincing themselves that they were an integral part of the whole extravagant ritual: such elaborate capers, like the flowing beards, made them feel a bit more significant.

I am becoming addicted to sunrises. I suspect I always was, only these days I get up for them instead of staying up for them. Staying up needs stamina I don't have any more, although I remember with pleasure those more romantic and reckless days when it was usual for revelries to end at dawn in early morning markets, all-night cafés or railway refreshment rooms, with breakfasts of meat pies and hot dogs and big thick mugs of tea, or—in other countries—croissants and cafés au lait, bowls of tripe and onion soup, skewered bits of lamb wrapped in a pancake with herbs and yoghurt, in the company of truckers and gypsies and sailors and street sweepers and wharf labourers and crumpled ladies with smeary mascara: it is amazing how many people and of what a rich variety belong to that indeterminate dawn time. Real enjoyment of this sort of thing depends, probably, on a sense of drama, the resilience of youth, and whether you can get in a decent kip after.

In the military period of my life dawn was always the time that the battery major—an eager and conscientious man—staged sneak raids on the gun-emplacements. To keep the guards, he said, on their toes. As if one could keep on one's toes in those great clumping boots, besides being weighed down with the full panoply of war, including tin hat and rifle. Thus ludicrously arrayed we sleepy Amazons patrolled the perimeter of barbed wire that fenced off our guns and igloos from the rest of the peaceful and pretty golf course, peering into the paling light for the cunning major and his crew, who were out there somewhere crawling on all fours through the frost-spiked grass. These exercises proved to be invigorating and mirth-provoking as far as the girls were concerned, and, I regret to say, brought out some pretty sadistic instincts in otherwise well-behaved young women before the battery major, discomfited and dishevelled, gave up. Dawn is traditionally a time for the hunter and the hunted—for going around the traps, as it were—and no man in his right senses should involve women in such an atavistic business ... not if he wants to get out of it whole, that is.

I don't know whether it is true that dawn is also the time that the majority of people choose to enter the world or to leave it, but it does seem to be a suitable hour either to slip out with the last of the night or make an entrance as the day breaks. In the Cotswolds we used to help out with the lambing, and there were many many dawns when we felt exultant and good and fulfilled, walking home from the fields through lingering crunchy snow, and often carrying one of those absurd trembling creatures to the warmth and benison of the kitchen fire. It's good to be present at birth. Even the sardonic farmhands, inured to wonder, you would think, blazed with flickering excitements during lambing time, and would rather sit in the kitchen, sipping at a rum and ginger wine and telling tales in the dawn, than go home to their beds after the long night's vigil in the freezing fields. I think I'm lucky to have had that.

And I'm lucky to have seen dawns from fishing boats and shepherds' huts and mountain slopes, and I shall never forget waking in the dawn at Delphi, with the goat bells tinkling on Parnassus and the olive groves a shining river of silver all the way down to the Corinthian sea: it was possible to believe anything, anything beyond the world then.

And there was that first May Day in the Dodecanese Islands, which was not marked by labour processions but by the whole town rising before dawn to fetch fresh water from the wells, and then to clamber up the dark mountainside to watch the sun shoot up all jazzy orange out of Turkey over a sea as white and thick and still as milk. And that must have been as weird a sight as the Druids among the heathen stones ... all those hundreds of twentieth-century people rising up among the mist-wreathed mountain rocks, with their faces turned to the sun.

Afterwards we all gathered mountain flowers and made them into wreaths to hang on our doors, and that is a charming thing to do and I have kept it up as part of family ritual, although the month is wrong here and the flowers more civilised around town and you don't have to climb a mountain to pick them, or watch the sun come up either.

Nobody could ever tell me why it was necessary to watch the sun come up on May Day. It was. It had always been so. Perhaps it was a collective affirmation of life and warmth and continuity, like examining one's safe deposit on a certain day every year.

I only know that I go on doing it, and watching dawns. Immoderately. And that, my family tell me sententiously, is why I am so hopeless in the afternoons.

On Turning Slightly Sepia

The photograph isn't sepia really—more a sort of reproduction gruel colour in the commemorative booklet to mark the fiftieth anniversary of the school's founding—but you feel that in its place in the family album the edges are probably curling.

The group is of ten fifth-year students in the year 1937, five boys and five girls, formally posed with the boys lined up behind the girls and their hands resting on the girls' shoulders. The girls are wearing clumsy tunics practically down to their black-stockinged ankles, and assorted white blouses that look crumpled. One girl wears a skirt and white blouse instead of a tunic. Their hair is short, and frizzy at the ends in the fashion of that time when permanent waving was still a crude business and curling tongs were often used instead. The boys are all clipped short-back-and-sides. Their necks are stalky and their protruding ears poignant. They wear various wide-lapelled suitings, not uniforms.

Every one of those young faces, frowning, smiling, staring sternly front, squinting into the sun—caught that long ago summer day all unwittingly 'in period'—is a face still hauntingly familiar to me, because they were seniors while I was still a junior and as seniors they were august, individualistic, and forever memorable. So I can still see one of those girls arched in a perfect swallow dive, and remember precisely a collar of little pearl buttons on a blue crepe dress that another of them wore to an end-of-term dance that year. They are associated with prefects' badges and house colours, cheering, strange war cries, trophies, speeches, prize-givings, and all the high-hearted accomplishment and hopefulness of eager youth about to attack the world.

The faces are only vulnerable in retrospect, now that 1937 is period in fact, and it is already twenty years and more since the name of that serious boy second from the left was inscribed on the school's honour roll under the draped flags among all the other names of students who never came back from the war.

It is probably only hindsight that makes me see Depression stamped all over that grey group photograph—hindsight and a formal visit to the city of Wollongong, where for some years, and before it was a city, I went to school.

There are high schools all up and down the Illawarra coast now, but in those days Wollongong High School was the only one for fifty miles. From the sweetly pastoral dairy country to the south and the harsh grandeur of the coal cliffs to the north, where the mountains slide straight down into the sea, boys and girls travelled each day to Wollongong in ancient uncomfortable railway carriages that were hitched behind the normal passenger coaches: waterless, toiletless, segregated strictly as to sexes, we clattered and hooted to school, and there were many who walked or cycled miles to a country station before the journey even began.

It seemed ordinary enough then, just as it seemed ordinary that many fathers were out of work, and ordinary that senior students might repeat their leaving year once or twice because there were no jobs for them to go to, and ordinary that other students dropped out at fourteen if there was the least chance of a job or a trade apprenticeship offering.

That was the climate of our time and because we knew no other we accepted it blithely and even felt privileged, I think, to be able to go to a high school at all. And well we might have done. Most of us were familiar with the official forms our parents filled out to state that the family income was less than £250 a year and therefore claiming exemption from examination fees and other school dues. But without that high school—for us in the country towns and hamlets, anyway— there was no future beyond working behind a counter for the girls, and for the boys an alternative of helping out on a farm, delivering groceries, getting acquainted with a pick and shovel, or joining the queues of shabby desperate men who turned up each day at Port Kembla for the chance of a day's work on the coke ovens or in the steel mills. All along the coast, in colliery, quarry, smelting works, and mill, men were taking wage cuts or being laid off altogether. To a man in a dole line-up, or a man in a gang uselessly shifting sand from one end of a beach to the other, it must at times have seemed unimportant that his son or daughter was penetrating the mysteries of French and Latin, of physics and chemistry, of algebra and geometry, all unaware then that even their teachers were sometimes uncertain of the next salary cheque.

It's an old story now, the bitterness and the humiliation, but I thought of it facing the massed ladies of the club which had asked me to luncheon—ladies of Depression vintage most of them, my vintage, pressed in the pages of a photograph album. And I thought of it clutching my safety helmet and gasping and gaping in proper awe at the Dante's Inferno of blast furnaces, slag heaps, flickering blue fire, rivers of molten prosperity rushing to the moulding: all the vast industrial complex of the Port Kembla Steelworks that has now eaten up the old Tom Thumb lagoon and the miles of wild sandhills and the swamps and the marshes. Thousands of degrees, millions of tons, miles of metal, production figures, employment figures, expansion figures, safety figures, consumption figures, so many full-time training scholarships, so many part-time training scholarships.

My brother's first job, at sixteen and with an honours pass, was turning men away there every morning.

And I thought of it driving with one of my hostesses up into the newest residential areas terraced into the mountains, where the houses are architect-designed and the views are stupendous, and where still, anachronistically, there remain a few little ramshackle weatherboard cottages as a reminder, and all the weatherboard cottages are curling at the edges like the photographs in the albums. The coast below, farmlands and wastelands alike, has disappeared under a solid crust of houses. The town has become a city indeed, and over it the great chimneys of Port Kembla dominate, pluming further prosperity. Nothing there to mourn. The mountains are still noble, and I expect that men still hunt there, but for sport now and not to eke out the dole ration. The immensity of the sea—so blue, so vast, so hugely glittering—is untainted, and the beaches curl in dazzling scallops of clean sand still, free to executive, steelworker, shopkeeper, migrant, academic, farm labourer, housewife, student. For an industrial city it is singularly fortunate in its setting.

Between the ocean and the mountains there is a complex of modern, well-designed buildings set in acres of green space that I heard many residents refer to as 'Education Valley'. The University College is there, the Teachers' Training College, the Technical College, and the new-look Wollongong High School, which ten years ago grew out of the old jumble of buildings and temporary classrooms that I once knew.

It was a queer business to face the whole assembly of those boys and girls, so smartly, neatly, and precisely uniformed now, so confident of well-appointed classrooms, splendid playing fields, up-to-date sporting equipment, music rooms, libraries, so confident in their right to secondary education and tertiary education beyond it, and beyond that careers of their own choosing, so amused by stories of educational makeshifts and student misdemeanours and absurd travellers' tales dating from that impossible-to-imagine time before they were born.

And I wonder if they realised that standing up there before them I knew myself to be curling at the edges and turning slightly sepia.

Read Any Good Books Lately?

So many people have written to ask me what ten books have most influenced my life, or what ten books I have most enjoyed, or what ten books I would choose to be stranded on a desert island with, that I began making lists the other day—idly enough in the beginning, to be sure, but then with considerable interest. What a very intriguing exercise it is.

Because of course the books that actually and positively influence your life are not necessarily the books you enjoy most, and the most enjoyable books are not always the most prudent choice for a lengthy sojourn on a desert island, where something more practical might be required, such as an illustrated handbook on simple raft construction, the boy scouts' manual (for signals, bushcraft, knot-tying, first aid and so on), some comprehensive works on botany, zoology and marine biology (for purposeful recreation when you got bored with lolling about with a hibiscus behind your ear), and a book of instruction on the working of bark (there must *be* one somewhere). And pottery? Brick-making? Just compiling a list involves you in endless ramifications of speculation and challenge: for a Walter Mitty moment I was actually there, with my selected list of books and a couple of king-sized notebooks with thousands of beautifully blank pages for Observations and Conclusions. Also the Heinemann edition of the *Bible Designed To Be Read as Literature*, which would provide in one volume all the stories, songs, poems, history, philosophy, and enigmatic questions that any person could ever possibly require in the way of intellectual nourishment.

As an afterthought a book on yoga might be quite desirable too, because there would be lots and lots of time for contemplation and no one about to jeer or giggle if you got tangled up in all those complicated positions. Apart from keeping fit you might in time train yourself to do something really spectacular, like levitating right off the island altogether, or going into a cataleptic trance for a couple of hundred years and waking up in a different world (no, on second thoughts, no trances).

As for books I've enjoyed, I couldn't for the life of me niggle down to ten the hundreds and thousands I have devoured in my life. If I say Conrad I have to say Joyce Cary, but which Conrad and which Cary, and which William Faulkner and which of Dostoyevsky, and if Dostoyevsky how about the other Russian giants, and the English and French ones too, and I have been reading E.M. Forster again with more delight than ever, and I have always loved Jane Austen, and Emily Bronte too. And how about Sartre and Camus and Kafka? And Alejo Carpentier? And Richard Hughes? And Thomas Mann? And Rose Macaulay? And Trollope and Dickens and Fielding and Stendhal and Proust and Scott Fitzgerald and Nathanael West? And all the poetry in the world?

No. It's impossible. In fact I have enjoyed, in one way or another, every book I have ever read, because my reading has been largely unselective, erratic, omnivorous, and rather in the nature of an addiction. I mean I will read labels, and advertising, and tracts, and bus tickets, and school textbooks, and even dunning letters if there is nothing else to read, and I have a weakness (if not a passion) for long, bad novels that my family regards as a sort of secret vice of mine and tries to hush up or, intermittently, to cure by hiding Ayn Rand and her ilk and presenting me with lovely exciting batches of new books which, naturally, I enjoy very much indeed.

Confessing that little peculiarity makes me wonder if this particular (and, to my family, perverse) taste of mine doesn't have its origins in childhood, when I was force-fed on Cervantes, Rabelais, Montaigne, Gibbon, Homer, Johnson, Sterne, Ruskin, and all that push, before I was fairly out of Henny Penny or even into Tanglewood Tales.

I don't say that these eminent authors are necessarily unsuitable reading for the under-twelves, and indeed to this day *Tristram Shandy* is far and away my favourite novel, but I do think my father was taking great risks by recommending (and often insisting on) certain works, which proved to be influential in a way he never dreamed.

For instance, by galloping through *Tristram Shandy* at the age of ten I was enabled to recognise that my father was, in fact, actually modelling himself on Mr Shandy, filching Shandyisms and using them as his own, expounding Shandy philosophies every day of the week with never a word of acknowledgement. This precocious perception of mine subtly altered my relationship with my (to then) infallible parent. I knew he was play-acting, and that he play-acted as often as I play-acted, but the difference was that he didn't know I knew. In a way it was saddening. It made him vulnerable.

Also, I would now question the wisdom of encouraging normally coarse and piggy-minded children to gorge themselves on Rabelais. We could think up plenty of vulgarities of our own without Gargantua's refinements, and the fact of the matter was, of course, that the crudest bits were the only bits we actually understood. We were inclined to trot them out with deadpan devastation in company, secure in our father's approving bellow of laughter and callous of our mother's discomfiture. The pity of it was that for years we went on confusing vulgarity with funniness, and were naturally thrown off course when the reaction to our Rabelaisian sallies was outrage instead of applause.

But the book that influenced my childhood and subsequent life most was the volume of Montaigne's *Essays*, and this simply by not reading them. Perhaps I was reading a normal child's book at that time and enjoying it, but I remember that the more my father insisted that I read Montaigne, the more he called Heaven to witness what a botch had been made of my mental capabilities, the more he derided my doltishness, the more recalcitrant I became, until one day I went further than I had intended and swore to him a solemn oath that I would never read Montaigne as long as I lived. And, sheepishly, I must say here that I kept my oath. I have read wonderful appreciations of Montaigne, and biographical notes on Montaigne. I have even been to the house near Bordeaux where Montaigne lived. I have had a copy of the essays on my bookshelves for longer than I can remember. But every time I open it I gag. So that Montaigne was instrumental in revealing and developing early in life a terrible mulishness in my nature. I can be led gently anywhere, I can be encouraged into attempting things far beyond my capacities. But from Montaigne on I have resisted force, insistence, and all moral pressures.

Now, having used so much space on my skeleton closets, there is practically none left for the books that most influenced me after childhood, like the *Rubaiyat of Omar Khayyam* (sorry, but it's true), Huxley's *Brave New World*, a collection of fantasy stories called *Presenting Moonshine* (author forgotten), a popular science anthology with an essay by Donald Culross Peattie called 'Flowering Earth', James Frazer's *Golden Bough*, the collected poems of John Donne, the short stories of Katherine Mansfield, and, even more, the short stories of D.H. Lawrence, the *Reader's Encyclopaedia*, W. MacNeil Dixon's *Human Situation*, Robert Graves' *Greek Myths*, Isak Dinesen's *Gothic Tales*, Pepys' Diary, W. Grey Walter's *Living Brain*, *The Second Sex* of Simone de Beauvoir, and a set of cookbooks put out by the Wine and Food Society, edited by André Simon, and called *A Concise Encyclopaedia of Gastronomy*.

And if you can make anything whatever of that lot, you are more than welcome. Personally, I am steeling myself for another try at Montaigne.

The Jungle at the Bottom
of the Street

On the last day of school holidays, when it was finally my turn to have our two small visitors—my ten-year-old son Jason and his younger cousin Terry—to myself for a whole afternoon, we considered plans with a very proper deliberation and gravity.

At least I did, because in this last year I have been separated from my youngest for school-term periods and so when I see him I am inclined to marvel at the perfectly natural evidences of growth and change: he has put on new layers of fresh bark while I was not watching and is becoming, I suppose, something else. Also, it was their last day, and I was formal with a sense of occasion. I must say they were very graceful about my suggestions, possibly out of that grave and beautiful courtesy which children sometimes surprisingly display towards their elders, or possibly because they had been just about everywhere already and were so gorged with treats that they couldn't have cared less where we went.

What is curious is that I have been looking down from my balcony for a whole year now at an inlet of the harbour below and for a whole year I have noted and catalogued mentally the mood and the colour and the light on the water against the monotonous darkish scrub of bush that fringes it and the unhealed scars of the new developments— although at dawn and dusk these new developments take on a queer oriental quality with brush-flicks of light angled along their tiled roofs and the stark planes of their geometry softened by wreaths of harbour mist. And for a whole year I have said to myself that one day I must walk down there and explore a bit.

Agreeably the children said they would like to do that too if I would—and I was humbled slightly by realising that they knew perfectly well that they were giving me the treat—and so on a spring afternoon we loitered, the three of us, down the suburban hill along the ordinary bus route between the solid brick bungalows set in their groomed spring shrubberies and the not-so-solid blocks of new units set in bare clay just tufting here and there with lawn grass and spindly labelled sticks that will no doubt turn into shrubberies eventually, and we looked over fences and into windows when we could and I noted that the bungalows had frilly curtains and the units straight 'contemporary' ones and I thought how neatly boxed people are these days and then I thought of Rilke walking through the streets of Paris and writing such memorable and moving words about one decayed house that had called to him with such persistent melancholy, and then I shrugged mentally and thought that if there was nothing romantic about these streets there was solidity and prosperity and order and man had established himself quite well and decently on these hills against some fairly terrific odds and was here to stay.

And it was just then, still high high above the harbour inlet that was our goal, that we crossed the main road (observing our traffic drill) and through a flame of coral trees and walked into a jungle.

I have never been familiar with the real bush. I grew up in pastoral country and have lived my adult life in cities mostly, so the bush mystique has never touched me. Until now, that is, because it seems a very strange and magic thing to have a jungle at the bottom of the street and to have had it there all along and not to have known about it.

It is a vertiginous jungle, and it plummets in a deep hoop from the busy road down and down and down to a shaved oval of grass that I suppose is used for sport, although how people get down to it is a mystery. Indeed, how the grass is kept so velvet smooth is a mystery. We couldn't find any tracks at all, and that was all the more exciting because we had to slither and slip and slide down precipitous slopes of ancient sandstone, clutching creepers and branches to brake our headlong descent, and there was no sky any more and no sound of traffic and we were plunging down through a primeval world that could not have filled me with more wonder if I had been Alice falling down the rabbit hole.

I have been in forests, great forests, Sherwood and Burnham Beeches, and the Black Forest where the wolves still prowl, and the spruce forests that press in on the Fern Pass in Austria, and I have been awed and made sombre by so much majesty.

But this was something else. Older. More poignant in some way. And more formidable because so indifferent. It was dark and cool and quiet as all leafy places are, but dry with a curious dryness of air and scent that was bitter and aromatic and the leafiness was harsh and spiky and even inimical and the forms of tree and bush and plant and leaf were primitive forms and the flowers that sparked so palely ragged among the grey down-drooping sickled leaves or the malevolent spikes that were not even leaves were like the first tentative sketches of flowers, not flowers at all yet but strange little desperate sparkings and explosions of something not yet desire but poignant beyond all telling because the desire was there. And once the children, trying to brake me, tumbled us all together into a bed of leaves dried as hard and fine as razors and smelling of ants, and at eye level, erect and triumphant on a sandstone outcrop, a spike of saffron rock-lily glimmered victorious.

At the very bottom we plunged out of the jungle into a wall, and this was the wall of a building in ruin with around it a series of strange concrete ramps like fortifications pierced regularly with circular shafts and grown over with more wild nasturtiums than I have ever seen together in my life before. There were millions of nasturtiums. Billions of nasturtiums. Cascades and carpets of nasturtiums shouting their noisy brilliance among the silk-fine circles of their veined leaves, succulent green and as big as dinner plates. As though the nasturtiums had decided to take over the whole world, in spite of that shaved oval of grass below them, and beyond it, still a long way away, the harbour inlet and the civilised motor cruisers and the pretty painted yachts rocking on a diamond dusting of sunlight.

Terry said, over armfuls of orange and gold and blazing scarlet: 'There's a waterfall.' And of course there was, but very high, on the opposite side of the hoop which we had descended. So we had to climb to it, they like the wild healthy young animals they are in great bounds and leaps, laughing down at me through the spikes and thorns and sparking bush flowers from huge gold buttresses of rock where they stood poised for flight, spilling all around them wilting nasturtiums that glowed on the golden rock like scraps of torn and brilliant silk.

And I looked for ... what? Fossils and wings and delicate bones embedded in the ancient rocks. Casts of worm burrows, tracks of crawling things, marks of a raindrop, a sun-crack, a footprint so old that its origin could not even be surmised. And yet I needed none of these proofs and evidence to tell me how old this place was. I sat very still in that primeval stillness and I knew all right.

We found the waterfall, and it might well have been a sewer outlet, just as the magical ruin down below might well have been the heart of some sewerage system.

But walking up the suburban street again, scratched and bruised and scarred and scored with our adventure and still quiet with the spell on us, I looked again at the bungalows and the crust of asphalt and brick and I knew that it was only that—a crust. In the immensity of time the works of our hands are the most transient of all.

The Right of Dissent

Well, it's over now. The balloons have all burst. The children's flags have been lost or broken or have just disintegrated. The disconsolate marching girls have recovered from disappointment and are dreaming of the next big chance to display their stuff. The demonstrators have pinned up their torn banners like battle trophies. In pubs and clubs and lounge rooms and over morning tea friends and neighbours are becoming bored with hearing Len and Alice recount the story of the mystic moment of touching the lifelike flesh of the great man himself. Chagrined ladies, thwarted of the actual laying on of hands in the National Art Gallery, have probably become philosophical and decided that the new Thai silk outfit will do very well for the Cup Day party. A handful of rebellious young, probably a bit scared by now, have been bailed out by desperately concerned parents. The garbage has been swept up from the streets of Sydney.

It is over, over, over. Pipes, timbrels, tumult and shouting. Apart from the Lens and the Alices they say some other fortunate few caught a glimpse of the President, although most waved at the wrong car and everything went so fast anyway and there was all that paper confusing vision so you couldn't really see anything and on the whole it might have been better to have stayed at home and watched it on the television. And apart from the disappointment of the marching girls who didn't get a chance to march, wasn't it a shame about the pigeons, and the koalas and kangaroos and wallabies? So much trouble for nothing.

It is over. But is it? I wonder if we'll ever be the same again. Can we possibly go back to being what we were—whatever that was, because nobody seems to be certain—or have we, by surrendering to hysteria, changed already into something else?

Certainly the whole affair was a tolerably accurate reproduction of an American reproduction of a Roman triumph, organised to a degree that has never been attempted here before, from the strategically placed claques of little children to the cheer leaders to the ticker tape to the inane slogans to the formidable security measures, which might be common enough on the other side of the world but are alien here and sinister and thrilling as a gripping gangster movie. Who will ever forget those tough anonymous men in sunglasses swarming the bulletproof bubbletop and the following convertible? Their impact value even survived their obvious fallibility—the Melbourne bombs were only paint but they hit the car for all that, and made headlines all over the United States. One wonders, with a chill, who had to accept that buck afterwards.

Watching the Progress on the television screen one had a sense of unreality and of familiarity too. Familiar because it was happening on the television screen and we have all watched such processions on the television screen before. Unreal, because it was happening here, and nothing like it has ever happened here. What was difficult to accept was that the Australian people rushed into role with such alacrity, and acted out hysteria as convincingly as ever their more practised American cousins did. Perhaps we've all been secretly feeling deprived of the Great Public Figure we've never managed to produce ourselves. Somebody to be hysterical about.

I suppose the security men, and the American people generally, were quite right to be so apprehensive about the safety of their First Executive. The Australians are a friendly people, but a mob is a mob, and while sports heroes, pop idols, film stars, politicians, Heads of State, and other symbol figures cannot do without a mob—if only to reassure themselves that they are really symbols—a mob is ungovernable, capricious, ultimately unreasonable. Particularly if the mob is, in the main, ignorant of the real issues behind the occasion. And, in the main, mobs are. The Romans placated the mob with bread and circuses, but Caligula was reputed to have said privately that if the mob had one neck he would cut it. Coriolanus hated and feared the mob: 'What would you have, you curs, that like not peace or war? The one affrights you, the other makes you proud.' Joyce Cary's Gully Jimson felt rather the same: 'For the people is just as big a danger as the government. I mean, if you let it get on your mind. Because there's more of it. More and worse and bigger and emptier and stupider.'

Harsh sentiments indeed. But anyone who has ever been in a mob will know the terrifying virulence of mass emotion, epidemic emotion, unreasoning emotion. Happily for official Australian–American relations the Sydney mob was dangerous only in the violence of its enthusiasm for the President of the United States. Its antipathy was reserved for the demonstrators, who were certainly a minority but extremely well organised, and on the whole much better informed and with more sense of the purpose of their presence there. Long before the motorcade whizzed through at high speed, feelings were running high between all-the-wayers and none-of-the-wayers, insults and provocation were being exchanged, and physical jostling. The all-the-wayers seemed to be outraged, but were not articulate in argument. They had come to cheer and were not going to be thwarted by a bunch of dirty, long-haired peacemongers. (I don't quite know why, when the public opinion of student demonstrators is invariably couched in these or more derogatory terms, so many ordinary citizens move heaven and earth to get their children into universities.)

'Why don't you grow up?' one enraged all-the-way gentleman demanded furiously.

'Sir,' said the long-haired boy with the banner, 'we are trying to. That is why we are here.'

Not all of the exchanges were so polite. One young girl told me afterwards that the most amazing part of the demonstration as far as she was concerned was the revelation that so many neatly dressed suburban matrons have such an astonishing command of obscenity and abuse.

And so violence, real violence, erupted in the Sydney streets. Violence of the documentary kind too, the sort of violence that the rest of the world—torn by racial dissension, civil liberties riots, bitter bigotries, passionate political factions, isms and ideologies—is accustomed to, but startling here where complacency and apathy have reigned for such a very long time. Passions have not been vented so wholeheartedly since the thirties.

Afterwards one commentator tried to get a poll of opinion on the demonstrations from among the crowd at Mascot. As individuals, separated from the mob, every person canvassed expressed the opinion that there should not have been any demonstrations, although not one of them could say why. Vaguely they felt it had been in bad taste. It had 'spoiled' the day. They felt cheated because of the haste of the official proceedings.

Yet the President of the United States has himself upheld the right of dissent. And the right of dissent is something that we Australian people used to hold dear, all the way back to the Eureka Stockade and back beyond that too. Although the

President mentioned our cattle and sheep in his speeches, one assumes that it was not human cattle or sheep that he came to see. And the dissension in our community, as well as the hysteria, may be an indication that we are moving out of apathy at last. In any case, even though it's over, I don't think we'll ever be the same again.

Goodbye to a Skyline

The skyline is a mile and more away, and high, and all sorts of roads ascend to it, or descend from it, both straight and deviously winding, and the roads divide the bricks and gables and the unfunctional chimneypots and the shrubs and the fences and the lawns into dense dull blocks of red geometry with a bit of matchbox blue here and there for relief and the dark green blobs of foliage like lumps of teased and dyed kapok.

It isn't very interesting as a vista, but at least it is a vista and I always try to get some interest out of it, seeing I have to look at it most of the time.

The skyline is something else, though. Perhaps because it is so high, and so far away, and there is so very much of it—miles and miles and miles—and so very much sky too, and all the shapes on the skyline are delineated as precisely against this enormous sky as paper cutouts. All that prodigality of space and light is rich bounty in a city—the tender blues and the soft greys and the cotton-wool lumps of clouds drifting about the lightning flashes and thunderheads and rainbows and dawn greens and dusk gentians. In London in winter the sky was as thick and murky as stockpot and the sun swam in it sluggishly, a squashy crimson blob that never struggled higher than the rows of grimy rooftops. I admit that I thought it incredibly romantic at the time, but I can breathe here.

One of the charms of my skyline is its variety. It was wild country once, that's for certain. All these hills were wild.

Sandstone. Scrub. Jungle. Up there, miles away, like upturned mops drying out above the domestic rooftops, there are three cabbage palms in a row. I like them so much better than the poplars beyond, perhaps because they have this grim little air of defiance. They've held out against the taming of these hills. And that's good, because they are a kind of symbol. Convicts wove cabbage-tree fronds into hats for protection against the fierceness of a cruel and alien sun, their children, the currency lads and lasses, adopted the fashion—defiantly too, perhaps— and by the time of the gold rushes the cabbage-tree hat had become the cult emblem of colonial independence, of swagger, of spiritual freedom, of anti-imperialism, of individuality. Men would pay as much as ten pounds for a cabbage-tree hat, so prized had they become. Henry Lawson writes of men in the nineties wearing cabbage hats black with age, hats that had been handed down like heirlooms.

Queer how an article of wearing apparel can become a cult symbol. Black leather jackets or bludger caps or faded jeans or gear or bowler hats. In Greece we wore unblocked woven straw hats and dipped them in the sea and rolled them up to work them into a floppy mushroom shape, and that was a cult too. I imagine a cabbage-tree hat might have looked something like that.

Among neat red peaks of rooftops serrating the skyline there are some slate ones too—older, broader, with many more chimneys—and of course the blocks of home units towering up between, isolated yet and rawly new, but flying flags to announce readiness for inspection; their bare jutting balconies give them the look of tall ransacked chests of drawers. Every one of them has been built in the year I've lived here. I wonder how long the few broad slate roofs can last. And I wonder too about the huge concrete building that presents to me a threequarter back-view of great blank uncompromisingly ugly planes. Ventilators squat along its irregular rooflines like rows of unpleasant fungoids; triffids perhaps, or something similar. I think it might be an old cinema but if it is then it must be on the arterial road that runs along that high ridge, and I have to travel along there frequently and I've never placed the cinema from the front. Perhaps it only exists from the back, or perhaps the front is now disguised as something else entirely. So many suburban cinemas have been turned into something else, or just closed up sadly. That's the end of an era too. Saturday night at the movies, new dress, newly set hair, best blue suit, brilliantine, box of chocolates, clumsy fumbling in the fly-toxed dark. 'He says I am the living image of Myrna Loy.' I've seen women all over the world who must have been told once that they were the living image of Myrna Loy, or Hedy Lamarr or Greer Garson or Ingrid Bergman or Veronica Lake. They were bravely keeping up the style and the eyebrows and the make-up all those years after. Poignant in a way, the gallantry of blood-red nails and black-red mouths and the dresses draped in sarong style and a glitter of sequins on the shoulder straps.

When so much is changing—as it should, because change is life and growth and a city is a live thing—it is still comforting, reassuring in some way, to have a church on the skyline too. Not a very beautiful church, rather heavy Lutheran in character, but its spire and its little bell tower are classically aspiring and sometimes the moon at the full jerks up theatrically behind the cabbage palms and seems to pause a moment to frame the spindly cross in a perfect halo of gold, and on Sunday the chimes are real bells, not electric. I love bells, and this church reminds me of Feldkirch in the Vorarlberg which I first saw on a Sunday morning in the snow and there were such neat plain heavy churches and sober Sunday congregations plain and black against the white, and big black open umbrellas clustered in repetitive curves and bells and bells and bells wild in the cold clean air. And once on a summer holiday in Cornwall I was initiated into the dangerous art of bell-ringing at the Mermaid Church at Zennor and shot up on the sally rope ignominiously and had to be hauled down by a hysterical vicar. Bells all over the world have told time, have summoned the faithful to prayer, have signalled birth and mating and death, and war and peril as well as rejoicing, and sanctuary as well as catastrophe.

I am looking at my skyline rather intently and in detail just now because I will be leaving it soon. We are moving over that high hill to the other side. There is always a lovely anticipation about going over a hill. Even though one really knows that one is just moving into another dense dull block of red geometry relieved by some blobby green clumps of foliage the skyline is going to be different again. On this one the towers will keep rising. By the time the little girls in their bright uniforms have passed out forever from the exclusive school up the way, the ridges and hills may look medieval. But I hope the bells still ring on Sundays through the blond brick canyons, and I hope those three cabbage palms still stream against a windy sky. One needs some continuity as well as change.

Where My Caravan Has Rested

The card, which is salmon pink bordered in green and blotched with age and liquor rings, is made out in my husband's name as a vice-president and director of the Rio Grande Steamship and Navigation Company (Whaling and Blubber) and entitles him to transportation, life-preserver, and boots and spurs when needed, on 'all vessels operated by the company over the entire system'.

It is only one of a number of similar wartime whimsies, like the Burma Road Jeeping and Marching Association, and the Short Snorter Club, and I came across it in the portable attic, which is a rusted tin trunk that has accompanied us on our perpetual odyssey and which I turn out every time we make another move in the vain hope that some of the accumulation of all the years can be discarded. None of the accumulation can. Never. Not ever. Not a bit of memorabilia, not the discarded beginnings of a manuscript, not a faded photograph, not a creased and tattered document, not a yellowed newspaper clipping. Not even though the portable attic is only opened at moving times. Perhaps we've really been hoarding all this stuff to form the nucleus of a permanent attic for the amusement, edification—and possibly the mystification—of our grandchildren and great-grandchildren, who might reasonably be expected to have some small interest in their forebears. Romantic fiction is filled with verbena-scented ghosts flushed out from attic cobwebs at the first crackle of an old love letter or the discovery of a pressed dog-rose between the pages of *Sesame and Lilies* or something similar. I would quite like to be a verbena-scented ghost, although I think 'Ma Griffe' is actually more me and would be racier and more intriguing generally.

Apart from the egotistical calculation of this posthumous attention-seeking, my household moves have always been characterised by an incurable and quite unwarranted optimism. I go on believing in Fresh Starts. This time, I say to myself, it is going to be different. I am not quite sure what I mean by 'it', but the places we have occupied in these nomadic shiftings of abode have always seemed to me to be like a series of staging posts on a fairly rugged journey. One is always galloping madly and at breakneck pace to get to the next one, convinced that the prospect beyond will open up pleasant and fair. And by the time one realises that the prospect is pretty much what it was before, one is, of necessity, galloping on again.

This particular staging post is pretty close ahead now, and pretty inviting, and this time, this time for certain, surely the reaching of it will mean that life will become gracious and orderly, that everybody will be struck—as with a blinding revelation—with the unutterable beauty of tidiness. There will be a place for everything and everything will be returned to its place after use. Towels will be hung on rails instead of dropped on the bathroom floor, socks will stay in pairs and books on shelves and records in sleeves and clothes on hangers and cups on saucers, caps will be screwed back on to shampoo bottles and toothpaste tubes, papers will be filed in appropriate folders, letters will be answered, appointments entered into the book provided for them, and the kitchen reminder pad will be used for kitchen remindering and not for chess scores, mysterious and unidentifiable telephone numbers, illegible messages, or plain and fancy doodling. Dressmaking scissors will be used for dressmaking, haircutting scissors for haircutting, and kitchen scissors for the kitchen, and from now on wire will be cut with wire-cutters instead—which reminds me that I had better try to find all those scissors and have them sharpened in anticipation of this happy state of affairs. Also the screwdriver, which I feel answers its function better than the best knives or my nail file, although I've not yet been able to persuade anybody else of this.

In the meantime, in preparation for the placidity and harmony that will undoubtedly surround me after the move is made, I am vigorously and determinedly tidying up this camping place where my caravan has rested for the last year or so. Of course I was confident of achieving grace and order when we came to rest here too. I admit that events proved such confidence to have been misplaced, but then there were certain unforeseen circumstances.

As a matter of fact it does seem to be a little extraordinary now that we moved in here such a short time ago with only a bed apiece and a desk and four chairs and not enough personal possessions to even half-fill the cupboard space. How did we manage to acquire so many things? And what on earth is one to do with them all? How did so many things, once acquired, wear out so quickly? For certainly all our possessions have a terribly used look. There is a heap of garments that I had earmarked for the collection bags which are left on our doormat several times a week, but which, on examination, might more decently be shoved into the incinerator. Is it worthwhile packing sheets that look as if they might shred in the next wash anyway? And the blankets that the dog chewed up the move before last? Will the handleless cups come in handy as receptacles for something or other or is it better to pitch them out now? Cupless saucers also. Will it be possible this time to find a sponge that fits the squeegee or should one leave it with the other squeegee handles that proved to be the wrong shape or size or brand for any sponges I could find? If a new broom is to sweep clean I would like the broom to really be new and not moulting. And there is something terribly disheartening about packing old dusters, even though one knows one will need dusters. Not to mention old tea towels. What does one do with bent safety pins, odd earrings, elastic bands, spare suspenders, assorted buttons, saucers filled with one-cent pieces, ends of string, torn packets of paper clips, old birthday cards, and all the other miscellaneous small items that have collected on shelves?

The furniture, I think, might just fit in the new house, but what a pity that a bottle of nail polish should have been spilled on the coffee table and the filing cabinet scratched so badly and the sofa arms looking so greasy where people have been sitting on them and the gilt screws lost from one leather chair strap and the refectory table scored with so many rings and spillings and burns and general crud and the metal bed frames out of alignment and the mattresses gone rather lumpy and the bathroom towels, while still in good order, quite unsuitable in colour for the new bathrooms.

I mean, it would be nice to start all fresh and new. There's one thing, though, and I think of this as I sort out papers and documents and newspaper clippings and pages of unfinished manuscript and photographs that have no conceivable use but that I cannot bear to throw away. There's still some room in the portable attic, and I have every chance of fooling my grandchildren and my great-grandchildren yet.

Other People's Houses

The first other person's house which really impressed me profoundly—indelibly, as it turned out—was a weatherboard cottage just up the hill from our own similar one. Three bedrooms, living-dining room, kitchen, tin shed tacked on the back for ablutions and laundry, sentry-box style lavatory at the end of the yard, and all painted that grim colour called, I think, 'builders' stone', and topped by a roof of sun-faded red corrugated iron.

So everything about this cottage was familiar to me, as the home base of any of the kids who played around with us would have been, but it happened that I called when the family was preparing for the evening meal, and unlike us, who ate in the main room, they were eating in the kitchen. The father, a small meek anonymous man, was sitting in shirtsleeves at a table covered with lino. The children were putting away their homework. The mother, a large woman without upper teeth and shapeless from the recent birth of a baby, was serving food onto plates at the iron range; she had a towel tucked into the bodice of her print dress and held the baby against one hip.

The kitchen smelled of cabbage steam, damp baby, and boiled corned beef. It was crowded with unnecessary furniture, cheap and ugly, and family photographs, and simpering religious prints, and inexplicably I wanted to cry, wanted to be part of it, wanted to eat corned beef off lino and live in that steamy kitchen for ever and ever. I have been hooked on other people's houses ever since, or perhaps hooked on other people's lives, because people live inside their houses in a way they do not publicly. The very arrangement of a chair and a table is intimate, almost shockingly personal. All objects in daily use are revealing. And I have felt this sharp, stinging sense of recognition that I felt in the cottage kitchen as a child in other houses too—in a little French château on the Loire once, in a shepherd's hut on the high Greek mountains, and in a lovely old house in Tite Street in London that was owned, when I knew it, by a painter who had plundered Europe to fill it with treasures. But it doesn't matter whether the house is great or small; a set of blue saucepans on a whitewashed wall can be as poignant as the four-poster bed hung with tapestries where generations have been born and died or a child's highchair drawn up to a table.

A very curious thing happens, though, if you actually live in another person's house, no matter how desirable that house may be. And of course I am not talking about renting a furnished holiday house or flat, but taking over a habitation that has been lived in for a long time by people with intensely personal tastes and quirks and idiosyncrasies.

It happened to us once that we exchanged houses with an English family for a period of six months. They took over our island house, and we took over their Tudor farmhouse in the Cotswolds. Each of us had children. We had the same tastes in reading and music and living generally. We were simple or sophisticated to about the same degree. It should have been ideal.

But what actually happened was that we found, by living in their house, that we began living their lives. We began playing at landed gentry and hobnobbing around with other landed gentry and our conversation became knowledgeable about sheep and lambing and crops and point-to-point meetings and field labour and their friends became our friends and their retainers became our retainers and their problems became our problems. While on the island they became islanders to the manner born and took on our role as completely as we were taking on theirs.

It all ended badly, as these things are bound to do. In both cases personal possessions were damaged, things were lost or mislaid, books were missing, and some sadly querulous correspondence ensued in which a very real friendship suffered traumatically, never really to recover.

Because of course you can't turn into somebody else by living in somebody else's house and using somebody else's personal things and following somebody else's life pattern. It is all make-believe. Because you didn't choose the things, nor will you use them in precisely the same way. I know, for instance, that my bentwood table with the slate top is rickety and mustn't be leaned on, and that the lamp with the porcelain hood must always be taken off the ledge before the shutter is closed because the iron bar swings. What I didn't know, in the Tudor farmhouse in the Cotswolds, was that the writing desk that was always shedding its handles was sacred and not meant to be actually used, or that the dog, if locked in, had a habit of chewing the curtains, or that the pretty little carved chair in the corner was spavined and was there for ornamental purposes only.

I've known other people since who have also lived in other people's houses and their experiences have been much the same. Never once has it turned out successfully. Other people's houses obviously are entrancing only if you don't try to live in them.

Still, I will, I suppose, go on peering into windows, and being emotionally moved by glimpses seen through open doors and hankering after lace balconies and half-seen courtyards where vines hang and rooms that are exciting, probably, only because they are different to my own rooms, and seem, momentarily, more desirable.

My newspapers are absolutely crammed these days with drawings and photographs of brick veneers and textures and fibros and timbers called Winston and Pamela and Madeira and Tudor which you can buy in so many squares already packaged and ready to set down on one of the new housing estates, itself bulldozed flat and cleared of anything growing. None of these habitations looks to be permanent nor can one imagine being moved in any way at all by anything that could possibly take place in them once they are occupied. I could be wrong about this. Perhaps people will make them interesting.

Anyway, there are still a lot of other people's houses to be curious about, and I would rather write about them than about state visits or invasions of bluebottles, and go on being rather excited at living in my own house.

A Room of One's Own

The prerequisites for anybody aspiring to be a writer, said Virginia Woolf (of whom I am not all that much afraid, and remembering anyway that Albee got his title from a bit of graffiti scrawled on a wall), are five hundred pounds a year and a room of one's own.

The five hundred a year is patently ridiculous these days in this sort of society—the dry-cleaner, the greengrocer, and the daily bus will eat up that much without you even noticing—but the room of your own, I agree, is highly desirable. There are others besides Virginia Woolf who would say it is absolutely necessary.

And so I have achieved it. After twenty years of belting somebody else's cast-off typewriter in corridors and corners or in my lap for the want of better work space I not only have a typewriter of my own, but actually a room of my own.

The door mouldings are picked out in gold ('antique gold', the architect called it and wouldn't let me rub it back to something more discreet; he said I would get used to it) and the door handle is solid brass and on the door are the decorations and warnings that have been somewhere about my workplaces for the last ten years. A scrawled chalk Icarus, pink and white, that was sent me once when I was feeling low; the publishers' trade announcement of my first novel— 'On the way', it says, 'on the way'; and a mad little man with an umbrella and a finger to his mouth saying 'Do not disturb' ...this last a bit cute for my tastes but I inherited it from a Norwegian writer who was soaring just then and cared about my chronic disturbances and he gave it with such good heart and goodwill and lack of understanding that I have grown to think of it as a talisman.

The room of my own is quite small and monastic. Painted white, with a sloping wood ceiling and a sash window that looks obliquely into the sash window next door (but we are very polite about this) and a wall of bookshelves and a floor of vinyl tiles that look almost real (I am snobbish about tiles, but so grateful to have this room of my own that I don't really care).

But what is most interesting about my cubbyhole is the wall of bookshelves. Queensland maple, and the two bottom shelves built extra deep for reference books and encyclopaedias, and not a book to be seen, or, at least, not for more than a day at a time. Because in this house everybody has walls of bookshelves, and for the first time in this mad community we call a family there aren't enough books to go round. This is one of the penalties you pay for being a nomad. Something always has to be left behind, and often—alas—it has to be books. So we have set up young women with circulating libraries (that was when we were reviewing and had lots and lots of mediocre novels and bad biographies). And then, at the next shift of domicile, there was a friend going into the flat-letting business who was glad to take a thousand books or so to furnish out his fancy bookshelves and justify his rents. And when I was coming back to Australia and wondering what on earth to do with the walls and walls of books that had accumulated in all those years—not being able to afford to freight them and not being able to discard them—there was an offer from a very rich and aristocratic gentleman who had just married his third young wife and had a quixotic fancy to give her an

English library. We hauled the books up the mountain to his mansion in wooden carts borrowed from the wharf labourers and nearly busted our innards in the hauling and I have sometimes wondered since whether that third young wife derived any benefit from them. There is a fourth wife, now, French, and even younger, and one doubts that she would be interested in the sort of random grab-bag of English literature that makes up writers' personal libraries.

What we do currently is to sneak around in the dead of night and filch books from each other's shelves. Temporarily, of course, and with no malice. At one o'clock or two in the morning (and I have been robbed as late as four) there is usually somebody on the prowl, upstairs or down, quietly making away with a swatch of poetry or philosophy or Australiana or university textbooks or Folio Society specials. I seem to come out worst in this. They promised me I could have all the long bad novels that nobody else wants but in fact my son's English course this year demands more long bad novels than even I can supply, and I wonder a little at what the university is coming to.

They promised me I could have the poetry too, but it has all been whisked off to adorn other shelves in other rooms. What they have left me is a dictionary, because nobody trusts my spelling, a tatty copy of *The Sunburnt Country*, W. Grey Walter's *Living Brain* (because nobody else shares my passion for this), and *Everybody's Book of Epitaphs*.

But if I am a bit down on books in this room of my own, I am well furnished with other items of interest and sentiment. Like the carved Skyros chair that fell to pieces on the voyage. And all the pieces of the bentwood rocker awaiting reassembly. And four brass lamps requiring solder and leads and plugs. And the offcuts of the vinyl and the leftover bits of carpet. And a discarded typewriter that we can't think what to do with. And boxes and boxes of photographs and photograph albums and files of memorabilia and old manuscripts and old correspondence and old documents (I don't think I will ever need my marriage lines, still less my commission in the Armed Services, or a school report dating from 1937, or a lifesaving certificate, or a petition to the Queen, or even The Order of Dress for the Coronation, but you never know). And I have hundreds of colour transparencies stuck together and thousands of negatives dating back twenty years, and an old blanket that the man who was laying vinyl used to mop up the adhesive, and swatches of wallpaper I am keeping to match up bedspreads and curtains when we can afford bedspreads and curtains. And I have sheaves of impressive contracts that didn't prove to be worth all that thick paper and lovely script and whacking great seals and bold signatures. And a French mirror that went with the French bed I carted all the way back to Australia and had to give away because although everybody loved it nobody wanted to sleep on it. And I have an enormous Spanish chest filled with rugs that can't be mended in this country and can't be used in this house anyway because they are too big or the wrong colours or the wrong shapes or something. And I have twelve framed prints of bewhiskered Greek heroes of the War of Independence stacked around with watercolour sketches, bad oil-paintings, good etchings, a dubious portrait, two small Nolans, and other works of art awaiting reframing or allocation to other rooms. I have a huge cardboard box packed with the shattered pieces of an ancient amphora that survived 2700 years, a sea journey in the Spanish chest padded with the useless rugs, and lasted two minutes at my welcome-home party.

And, most ironic of all, I have boxes and boxes and boxes of the do-it-yourself bookshelves that I bought for the flat we had before this house, and the boxes and boxes of do-it-yourself bookshelves are stacked on my built-in shelves of Queensland maple and take up so much room that even if I had brought home all the books instead of selling them to the third wife of the rich aristocrat and left French beds and mirrors and bentwood chairs and Turkish stoves and bad paintings and Spanish chests and useless rugs and all the rest of this junk, I wouldn't, at the moment, have anywhere to put books anyway.

What I really need is another room. One of my own, I mean.

Report from a Migrant, Three Years After

Actually it is still a month off three years since we migrated here, but time has played its usual trick and we are startled that such a quantity of the elusive stuff is already the past. Three years! we say to each other in wonder, and mentally start totting up a balance sheet of profit and loss … so much material gain, so much experience, so much happiness, so much dissatisfaction, so many mistakes, so much uncertainty, so much frustration, so many disappointments … obviously we are not millionaires in goods or achievement, but the company seems sound and we are not regretful about setting it up in this country.

It is interesting now to look back on the things we wrote three years ago. The words 'challenge', 'excitement', 'vigour', 'vitality', 'opportunity' occur often. Also 'a sense of imminence'. I wonder whatever happened to that? Or were we, with bridges burned behind us, doing a desperate bit of wishful thinking? All migrants, I think, are optimistic, or, anyway, hoping like blazes that they've really done the right thing. And we were odd sorts of migrants, in that we were migrating to home, which from fifteen years and half a world away could be distorted—by the curve of the earth, memory, and couriers' reports—into Utopia or Hicksville.

Patently it is neither. But it is a curious sort of country, so catastrophically excessive in elemental drama—drought, flood, fire—so prodigal in opportunity (I still think so), and yet so unheroic, bland, and even meek in the character of its people. There is so little anger here. I suppose, as Bernard Shaw said, nobody will trouble themselves about anything that doesn't trouble them.

And, mostly, Australians seem to be untroubled. Most Australians, that is. Far from being anti-authoritarian, as I had always believed, they actually seem to derive a sense of comfort and ease from unquestioning submission.

I was thinking of the things that have happened in the last three years, the things that have become acceptable just by the acceptance of them. Like the commitment of our young men, by lottery, to a war that most of the world agrees is extremely nasty and strictly none of our business anyway. Once this would have been inconceivable. Now their protesting mothers scarcely rate a news picture. As long as one is not personally affected the lottery becomes acceptable. Acceptable too are higher and higher prices, increased fees here and fees there, shoddier standards, worse public transport, further despoliation of natural places, present curtailment of educational facilities and unpleasant hints of future curtailment of civil liberties. The most puritanical and piously paternal censorship is not only acceptable, but actually helped along by timid and sycophantic self-censorship.

It is not just the banning of films and books. We finally get to see *Till Death Us Do Part* (with episodes deleted). But it is not within the realms of possibility that we could make an Australian version of such a theme, although heaven knows we have our own Alf Garnetts in plenty, equally bigoted, equally dogmatic, and there are plenty of targets just asking to be shied at. On the other hand, in spite of the postmaster general's complete lack of confidence in the ability of Australians to write, direct or produce television, a few brash or audacious or stubborn people have gone ahead and done it anyway—not enough of it yet, but enough to prove that it is time Big Daddy treated us as grown-ups. Those of us who want to be treated as grown-ups.

Obviously there are many who don't. If the mass media are a reflection of mass thought, real controversy is only aroused by trivia. The length of girls' skirts or boys' hair is of much more passionate moment than the tragedy of the Sydney Opera House or the departure of Dean Dixon or the mean and threadbare state of education. Massage parlours are more shocking than the insidious encroachment of foreign capital and foreign ownership; we've been told soothingly and smilingly not to worry about that, and Big Daddy knows best.

I know that there is protest. But it seems to be spasmodic protest, and not sustained, excepting by the few with the conviction, courage, tenacity, and sheer endurance to go on battling through the cotton-wool suffocation of public indifference. Sometimes a fight is won, such as recognition of the Aborigines as quasi-citizens, but then emotion subsides, and only the people who are personally and vitally interested are prepared to carry on. The rest of us have proved that we're decent blokes and ready to give the Abo a fair go and now we can relax again into our customary desultory hedonism with easy consciences. We've given the government the power to act, but action is Big Daddy's business now and we needn't bother any more about it.

Nor does protest ever become a whole new mass movement, as in America, where thousands and thousands of youngsters, rightly or wrongly, have created an entirely new way of life and seem to be prepared to live it. Whether they are right or wrong is arguable, but not the point. They are original. They have the courage to act upon their convictions. And we are not original. We will, in time, borrow hippyism as a fashion as we borrow all our fashions, usually long after the rest of the world has passed on to new ones.

I don't know whether it is distance that produces this curiously out-of-date, lagging-behind sort of atmosphere, or mental flabbiness that explains our lack of invention and our inability to evolve manners, modes and fashions of our own. Certainly it is almost impossible, if we limit ourselves to local sources, to keep up with intellectual trends and developments elsewhere. News of them comes to us late and flyblown: without constant attention to overseas periodicals it seems doubtful at times if we would ever learn of certain movements at all.

I could think that this lack of interest might well spring from deep self-satisfaction, excepting that there does persist an Emperor's New Clothes attitude towards all imports. We neglect our own talent so shamefully that it has to leave to live, and unquestioningly accept imported third- and fourth-raters at their own, or their publicity agent's, valuation.

As a migrant, three years on the way to adjustment, or acclimatisation or whatever, I begin to wonder when I too will stop asking questions, meekly heed authority, and settle for the adequate, the pretty and the approximate instead of demanding the good, the true and the beautiful. It is so easy to give in.

Three years out I wonder why I like the damn place so much.

On Trouble in Lotus Land

A few weeks ago I wrote in this column my impressions as a migrant three years settled (or unsettled?) in this my country. I said Australia seemed to me to be an untroubled place. I said there was little anger here. I said that most people appeared to be content to leave decisions to Big Daddy. I said other things too of a critical kind, and thought I might be sticking my neck out too far.

I thought that I might get a spate of letters on the old theme of 'Well if you don't like it why don't you go back to where you came from?'

In fact I did get a spate of letters, but not one of them was on that theme at all. Actually, my mail has been so overwhelming and so positive that it is evident that there are a great many citizens who are both angry and troubled, and this concern is spread through a more varied strata of society than I had ever supposed. There are a lot of people who are finding that a steady diet of lotus becomes sickly and dissatisfying. Even distasteful. There are other people who haven't managed yet to get more than a nibble at the delectable bud, and would like to know why.

There are people who advocate a return to old spartan simplicities to get ourselves toughened up again. There are people raging to smash what I can only call The Indifference Barrier and push on with creeds, policies and convictions that range from mysticism and meditation to active political participation. There are puzzled people who feel guilty but don't quite know why. There are poets who accuse. There are

Uncle Tobys charging away like knights-errant on their favourite hobbyhorses—Diet, Exercise, Youth, Age, Finance, Women's Rights, Aboriginal Rights, Pensions, Unmarried Mothers, Delinquent Girls, Education, Marriage, Foreign Capital, Homosexuality, The Brain Drain, Development of the North, Litter, Immigration, Urban Pollution, Defence, Censorship, Retarded Children, Slum Clearance, Noise, Conscription, Housing, Harold Holt, Gough Whitlam, Jim Cairns, and Gordon Barton. And of course The Elizabethan Trust and the Sydney Opera House. Not to mention Her Majesty the Queen.

On my desk at the moment are more tracts, pamphlets, invitations, explanations and exhortations (also more questions) than I have ever had at the one time.

'There is sweet music here that softer falls than petals from blown roses on the grass ... '? Well, there might have been once, but I am delighted, invigorated, and greatly greatly heartened, to hear some discordant notes in the Lotus Eaters' Song.

I always enjoy my mail, even if I can't always answer all of it. I suppose all that any writer asks, apart from a labourer's wage, is the knowledge that he is in communication with responsive people. In the time that I have been writing this column I have been aware that there are a vast number of intelligent, responsive women, with their antennae alert and questing. Concerned women. Women who appear to be more interested in ideas than in gossip.

I am not a crusading feminist, and I enjoy the letters I get from men too, although sometimes these are sheepish or patronising, and agreement or response is often tempered by a note of surprise or gallant chiding, as though it is impertinent or pushing of me, as a woman, to think such thoughts, let alone publish them. It is the attitude that still publicly refers to wives as their husbands' 'good ladies'. It is an attitude that makes me spit nails, razor blades, and green venom. It is an attitude that also makes me chew hard sometimes and swallow toads, nasty or not.

Anyway, there is a male letter (only faintly patronising) that states categorically that the Australians were a mighty race until forty-five years ago, when the First World War drained us of our best offspring. The Second World War again 'seriously reduced the men of courage, pride and initiative'. He goes on to state that the most constant and insidious factor in our retrogression for thirty-five years has been the influence of the 'inferior and un-Australian way of life'. He writes of the men with picks and shovels who made the railway tracks, the tunnels, the embankments, the canals and channels, the men 'endowed with pride and unbounding energy'. He agrees that we have become a tame, regimented and compliant race, and traces it from the top down (surely, I thought, our Prime Minister could never have actually said: 'Bolte and Holtie are a good combination'?). Anyway, it doesn't seem to me that the men with the picks and the shovels are going to help us much now, unless they be un-Australian picks and shovels.

My female correspondents are more positive. One lists for me, with sudden and urgent horror, the contents of her refrigerator. Half a cooked rabbit, an uncooked one, leftovers like stew, bacon, eggs, cheese, liverwurst, milk, a crisper of vegetables (six varieties and a garden full of ditto), a miscellaneous assortment of other foods. In her cupboard was salmon and fruit and baked beans and much more. 'To feed,' she wrote, 'a middle-aged man and his wife'. She goes on to write about the hungry of the world, and her dreadful consciousness of them:

'The biggest (and most scoffed at) idea I have been able to produce is the naive, "Yes we should be in Vietnam with the same number of men and amount of money, all dedicated to preserving life and land, not destroying it". I would be interested to know your opinion of that angle. If you, or even one other person agrees, I cherish a dream of Utopian spontaneous combustion across the country to tell Big Daddy so.'

Another writes: 'Couldn't we march to South Australia and have a chat with swinging Mr Dunstan? Perhaps we could start a Women's Crusade to finish this madness. Or do a Lysistrata act and go on strike (everybody else is) until our all-male leaders come to their senses?'

Another: 'Sometimes it frustrates me—being a migrant of fourteen years—and I also wonder "Why do I like it so much?" Because I do not think I have reached the apathetic state of most Australians yet.'

And another. 'It's hard to be brave and speak up for what you believe in when everyone else seems to be behaving differently. Maybe if the parents were not so worried about conforming all the time, whether they really approved or not, then the youngsters would not be afraid to say so when they do not wish to do something they feel is wrong.'

Another: 'Migrant or not—I'm third/fourth generation Australian myself—it is not hard to see that some kind of psychological or spiritual "smog" has got Australia bogged down.'

Another: 'I am a voice crying in the wilderness too. I am fifty and have just in the last year started a writers' course. Not much one can do with it in Australia ... most magazines only use American stories. Wish you would write an article on the lack of markets for stories here. My last cry is the futility of war, for surely we have outgrown this stupid practice.'

Well, then. I haven't room for more, but thank you for reassuring me about my own people. We might, even as our husbands' 'good ladies', have news for Big Daddy yet.

Uncrating Mr Nolan

Mr Nolan looked thinner than when I had last seen him. I thought he looked smaller too. But that might have been only in contrast with Hal Missingham, the Director of the Art Gallery of New South Wales, who is sizeable. Or, more likely, the fact that the packing crates were so large.

The vaults of the gallery were stacked with crates, opened and unopened. The uncrated paintings leaned against still-crated ones and walls and posts and pillars, backs outward, revealing nothing but masonite, nails, fluff, brass hooks, numbers, gallery stickers (Redfern, Marlborough, Tate, Museum of Modern Art) and chalk-scrawled identifications—Collection of So-and-So. I thought if I had been So-and-So I would have been a bit leery of relinquishing a piece of my collection, even temporarily, by lending it out to the other side of the world, even to the painter himself, even for a great retrospective exhibition, as this was to be. Too many things could happen between here and there.

Hal Missingham said that once a whole exhibition of French paintings had run aground on the Tasmanian coast. But it had turned out all right, he said, because that particular hold hadn't been waterlogged. He'd been able to mount the exhibition, complete and undamaged. And, thankful to the Fates, he'd be able to mount this one too, although he confessed his great relief at having it all assembled finally. He had had a bad scare with the closing of the Suez Canal. Mr Nolan said he had had a bit of a scare too. He had thought of Burke and Wills on the Bitter Lakes, but this time they had been paddling the painting.

They had a great thick swatch of numbered slips between them on the deal table. Hal Missingham said it had been hell trying to get the paintings into chronological order. The exhibition covered a span of thirty years, and Mr Nolan's memory, although better than good, was not absolutely reliable on actual dates. When you paint as prolifically as he does I suppose some confusion is inevitable. It seemed that he had dated two paintings, ten days apart, the wrong way round. There were letters he had written twenty years ago, referring to the paintings in the right order.

I thought it must be a queer thing to be fifty years old and sitting there at a deal table in the cold vaults surrounded by thirty years of yourself, crated and uncrated, bits of yourself gathered from all over the world, cut up into uncompromising oblongs and stacked enigmatically, backs outward, like random packs of playing cards waiting for the magician's trick.

You could cut the stacks anywhere and come up with anything—the pier at St Kilda, Mrs Fraser in a tropical forest, an African monkey, Leda and the Swan, a drought carcass. Hal Missingham cut a stack and came up with a painting still in wraps. The fact that it was still in wraps was mysterious and exciting, and I had one of those strange flashbacks that everyone has some time, to a hot, dusty workaday street in the Piraeus in 1959. There was a big trench dug in the street, and shovels leaning everywhere, and out of the trench, reverently raised by a team of men and with his beautiful green-bronze flesh still wrapped in Piraeus clay, came an archaic Apollo, lost for two thousand years.

It wasn't Apollo who came out of these wraps, though, but Sergeant Kennedy, dead at Stringybark Creek. Mr Nolan looked surprised, as though that wasn't what he had expected. He said the pink hill had got a lot pinker in the twenty-one years since he'd seen the painting last. He ran his fingers exploratively over Sergeant Kennedy's spilt blood and suddenly grinned and said: 'Still fresh.' There was a clump of what looked like snowdrops growing in the blood. He said: 'Yes, yes, Adonis and the flowers springing up eternally.'

After a while of looking he nodded a couple of times— acceptance? confirmation?—and Hal Missingham staggered out of the stacks with a huge Wimmera landscape which Mr Nolan had painted only last year, so that shouldn't have surprised him at all, particularly as it belongs in his own collection anyway. But he looked at that one for as long as he had looked at the other, and touched it, and he said what was interesting was that he had painted two paintings of this same landscape, from exactly the same viewpoint, but the paintings were twenty-five years apart.

So the early one was brought out from another stack and placed alongside, and it was just as if the magician had brought off his card trick, because the effect was startling. You could see that there was twenty-five years between them, and in that twenty-five years nothing had happened to the landscape but a great deal had happened to Mr Nolan. He looked as pleased as if he had won a bet. You knew that those two paintings were terribly important to him, spiritually important, I mean. A sort of touchstone. Hal Missingham said that they were both very very good paintings. Mr Nolan said that the Australian landscape became beautiful when you couldn't farm it. He said the key to Australian landscape was the light—it had an incandescence, he said—he said the sky was more important than the landscape itself. He said that the earlier Wimmera painting was the first time he had managed to tilt the landscape, but he couldn't make the lakes stay flat. Hal Missingham said he still couldn't—all the water was still running out, twenty-five years later.

After that he asked to see the Trojan Women, or what had begun as the Trojan Women, stacked like firewood in the sacked city of Troy, but had turned into the Inferno, where their dead white flesh, blooming with wounds like flowers, spiralled and floated as a flock of white birds might, loosed into eternity. There were three panels of this major work uncrated, six still in crates. When it is assembled and hung it will measure forty feet. I thought that Hippocrates had stated categorically that art is long, and wondered if he could possibly have had Mr Nolan in mind.

But art was pretty long in Hippocrates' day too, and I thought, shivering a bit there in the cold vaults among the crates and the protective wraps and the enigmatic stacks of thirty years of a man's life assembled piecemeal from all over the world, that the longest thing about art is that it goes on working through time. Hippocrates could say with confidence: 'Life is short but art is long.' Pericles could say with confidence: 'Future ages will wonder at us, as the present age wonders at us now.' And Mr Nolan could say, running his fingers exploratively over Sergeant Kennedy's spilt blood: 'Still fresh.'

I kept on thinking of the archaic bronze Apollo, smiling his archaic smile through the protective wrapping of two thousand years of Piraeus clay.

The Centre

If you come to the Centre, as I did, by air from Adelaide, the surprise of it is infinitely more surprising than you are prepared for, even though you have prepared yourself by much industrious homework on the geology of the place, its flora and fauna, climate, characters, myths, legends, yarns and tall tales.

You get there already visually bruised and aching, tender in the sensibilities with the effort of belief in the awful innocence of your country so exposed to your inspection, drinking cold beer and eating more airline chicken and advancing your watch a half-hour. You are a little shamed and uneasy, as though you have taken an unfair advantage, and you think of the explorers crawling like maddened lice across that vast wrinkled anatomy, crazed by thirst and dreams and the radiantly tender pink blush on beckoning hills. From twenty thousand feet the hills are like fat squishy tumours, or dried-out scabby ones. Benign compared with the incurable acid-wound of Lake Eyre, steaming corrosive white and vitriolic after placid Torrens, where, all unknowing, Swift set the longitude and latitude of Lilliput. Gulliver sprawls defenceless for your microscopic examination. Pitted pores. Dried-out capillaries of watercourses. Culture slides of viridian clotting thick creamy yellow. Wind ridges raised like old scars, and beyond them the even, arid serrations of the Simpson Desert, dead tissue, beyond regeneration.

And yet, the tenderness of the pinks, the soft glow of the reds, the dulcet beige, and violet seeping in. The landscape, after all, is alluring beyond reason. Voluptuous, even. You could abandon yourself to it and die in a dream, like those savages of whom Kafka speaks, who have so great a longing for death that they do not even abandon themselves, but fall in the sand and never get up again. Such unearthly beauty, one knows—and still yearns—is fatal. It is a landscape for saints and mystics and madmen.

And after that the vibrant shock of being terrestrial again, bucketing in toward the Alice in a Landrover with the air singing clear and thin and sweet and your lap filled with the strange flat-podded pink flowers that are clumped beside the road and under the ghost gums and the wattle. You could not have foreseen that, nor, with all your homework on the history and geology of the MacDonnell Ranges, could you have foreseen the lilac beyond the red and the gold, floating in a boundless clarity where perspective is meaningless. You accept that the mountains are as old as the convulsions of the earth. They had suffered a sea-change before life crawled on the land. They were old, very old already, when life was new. They were worn down and weathered before such as we were even heralded by creeping things. To see them is to know that they could not possibly be less ancient than that. A thousand million years at least it takes to make something so rich and strange, so profound, so unbearably potent with dreams.

It takes less time to make an Alice. Contemporary Alice, that is. They say it was different before the tourist boom. Old hands mourn, bitterly. It was nearly evening when we reached it, and the mountains were moving in close about hotels and motels and gem shops and rock shops, banks, garages, milk bars, tourist agencies, boutiques, galleries and the Old Timers' Home. Is it Persian lilac that lines the main street? The scent in the evening air is enough to bowl you over.

Fronded trees sparking delicately with little starry clusters, and between them a desecration of imbecile Op lighting, great lozenges of red and blue and green and yellow clownishly colouring the tourists stepping eager for bargains, souvenirs, and drinks before dinner. And through the tourists, the lilac-scented air, the hectic funfair illumination, the slow lurching drift and black shadow-weave of the disinherited, stripped of ancient dignity, degraded, subservient, aimlessly drunk on a Friday night.

A lady inheritor, sensible in drip-dry, shoulder-bag bulging—rocks? gems? berry necklaces? mission grass-weaving? bad bark paintings?—postcards poised ready for the slot, pounces on a tall black trio teetering in the most curiously graceful progression. Cheap boomerangs, she wants. The real thing. Not the junk in the tourist shops. She is loud and articulate. Imperious. (I think of the last Afghan and the last camel train, also imperious, stepping out slow slow from the Alice and disappearing into the vast distance.) The black trio, thus accosted, are soft, slurred, incomprehensible and perhaps uncomprehending. They sway away and back again, surprisingly regrouped under the ghastly green of the street light, awaiting the lady's exasperated dismissal. Two barefooted women scuttle under the Persian lilac and across the street to their men on the opposite corner. They are high in the haunches, long in the heels. Their legs are like thin crumpled brown ribbons flying, their hair pale straw. Drysdale has drawn them often and compassionately, by tin huts and shanties, patient with the heavy burden of life. Now they are patient on the street corner, movement arrested, patiently waiting as if waiting was an end in itself.

But the hotel bar is air-conditioned, clean, contemporary, anonymous. Around the small plastic-topped tables there are tourists in holiday gear and every degree of age and sunburn. The girls behind the bar—and this is to be true of most hotels, motels and restaurants in the Centre—are European or from the south. Girls on a working holiday. Transient population. But there is to be a cattle sale the next day, and among the clean white shirts ranked against the bar there are some of the men who brought the cattle in, so authentically themselves in jeans and battered drovers' hats, so weathered, leathered, creased and sun-cured, so thirsty, exuberant, excited and vocal that you can't quite believe in them, not even when one of them takes a guitar that is leaning against the bar and they all begin to sing. Cattle songs. Outback songs. Melancholy or ironic. They are probably film extras, togged up for another cheap outback drama. And the black one, confidently harmonising, must be in make-up, because he cannot possibly be of the same race as the frieze moving on the other side of the plate glass, although the frieze is also costumed in jeans and slouch hats, but out of step and coordination, somehow terribly vulnerable. Occasionally a figure detaches and pastes itself against the plate glass, looking in.

'The Aryans,' one of my companions says. 'Looking at the Huns and wondering whatever happened.'

So this is the Alice. And the Alice is thriving and putting on sophistication, although a little uneasily, like finery to which it is not yet accustomed. Selfishly, I am glad of the comfort of the new motel where our working party makes base. Glad of the good bed, the air-conditioning, the hot water, the private shower, the swimming pool, the excellent food and wine and service in the restaurant. It is good enough to satisfy the most fastidious traveller. In the days ahead we are going to see many exciting places, talk with many unique people. There will be much discussion and instruction on the Question. The Problem. Let them die out. Assimilate them. Put them on reserves. Forget them. Wait. Keep out the do-gooders. And in all our comings and goings, reeling, all of us, with the revelation of wonders, I will be haunted by that daily frieze impasted on banks and tourist agencies and galleries and gem shops and rock shops. Patient. Waiting. Moving, if at all, from one side of the street to the other. The women and girls squatting in ripply black silk circles around groomed trees in a groomed park. Looking on.

I want to say, 'I'm sorry.' Apologise. Absolve myself. I want to tell them that I was not one of those maddened lice of explorers crawling to the discovery of their magic tribal place. I did not personally dispossess them of the ranges and the gorges and the waterholes and the caves where the Huns leave beer cans now, and crumpled paper tissues, and dubious identities chipped into the ancient rock. I did not personally disinherit them of the most sophisticated, ethereal concept of origin that ever a people dreamed. Their blood, for all I know, might be bluer than our heaven.

But here in the thriving Alice the guilt hurts intolerably. What are the dreaming people dreaming now?

The Rock

Between the ancient MacDonnell Ranges to the north and the even more ancient Musgraves to the south there spreads a great flat plain, apparently featureless and certainly without perspective. It is, in fact, more like a sea than a plain, which should not be surprising because very long ago it was.

It is not Moby Dick who heaves up over the horizon, however, but three extraordinary, isolated rocks, tors, mountains—there is nothing to compare them with to give you any sense of scale; they could be the gigantic eggs of the greatest auk that ever was. Away over to the left the flat-topped mesa of Mt Conner. In the centre the rounded hump of Ayers Rock. And further to the west, across miles of sand ridges and scrub the completely improbable monoliths of Mt Olga, lifting their stately domes into the morning as fragile and insubstantial as a dream. In the distance the tors are misty lilac, floating: it is not until you are close that the red begins to burn and glow and you shrink to your own insignificant human size. Ayers Rock, where you land on the strip if you are lucky enough to fly in as we did, is six miles in circumference and 1100 feet high. It is a prolonged and momentous event in time about which one might well walk warily and with due humility, pondering on the brevity of one's own existence. It is a place for silence.

Perhaps it is some such oppression of the spirit in the face of majesty that incites inadequate, uneasy, or defiant human beings to acts of desecration. From the air you could not miss the heliographs of the empty beer cans. At the base you identify the oddly fringed foliage as torn paper tissues. Among the last lot of campers was one who dipped the soles of his shoes in wet paint in a madly pathetic attempt to register a despairing identity on that huge red indifferent surface. If he can be traced he will be asked politely to return to the Rock at his own expense and scrub out his footprints.

To police the monolith adequately against such vandalism would require, one imagines, a staff of permanent guards. The custodian of the reserve has one assistant.

I suppose it was inevitable that such a fantastic phenomenon of nature would have to become a mecca for tourists. Half the world is presently engaged in rushing from the familiar to the unfamiliar—perhaps for instruction and enlightenment, but more likely for new colour slides, or something to do in the holidays, or because somebody else did it last year. Tourism is big business, and important to the Centre, which might well flourish exceedingly on nomadic traffic of such economic consequence.

And yet you could weep for the desecration of nobility, for the shoddiness of buildings thrown together too hurriedly and too cheaply to accommodate the floodtide of the eager and the curious, coachload after coachload determined to be gay, to have a good time, to get their money's worth. You could weep for the wire fences hung with campers' washing, the concrete latrine blocks, the Keep Out notices, the shanty-town atmosphere that prevails under the breathtaking scarps and buttresses which are spiked and chained now for easier climbing. The ants who crawl up the chains from dawn until dark say it is thrilling beyond belief, and the more thrilling for the notice that warns them of difficulty, danger, the possibility of injury, and even death. There are memorial plaques set in the rock to reinforce the validity of this warning.

Perhaps we are too inexperienced, too new at tourism yet. A little more thought and deliberation would surely have suggested that the reserve be left inviolate. Since nobody can come to the Rock without transport, motels and chalets and camping areas might well have been located some miles away, quite outside the reserve itself and designed to sit more harmoniously in the landscape than this aggressively ugly clutter that looks more like a refugee camp than anything else I can think of. The United Nations building would be tolerable, but anything with less authority should be so reticent as to play chameleon among the mulga and not even try to compete with the natural grandeurs. Such consideration of landscape costs money, I know, but I can't believe that the present disrespect of it is going to pay off eventually. It is too short-term and short-sighted.

For one thing I doubt whether overseas visitors can be entirely satisfied with the sort of service that was meted out grudgingly in the motel where our party put up for the night. If you are being adventurous you do not complain of discomfort or lack of civilised niceties. But this, after all, was not real adventure country. It was a thriving tourist outpost, and for myself I can see no reason why such a profitable outpost should be run on the disciplinary lines of a corrective institution. The staff was undoubtedly insufficient, and undoubtedly tired and abraded after a long, busy season. Undoubtedly, also, the arrival of our party was an unexpected nuisance to an establishment that is organised mainly for job lots and package deals. But surely it would be good policy to invest a little more money in extra staff and better working conditions? A contented staff would do much to change the resentful and grudging atmosphere into one of friendliness and cooperation. If it is really necessary for the generator to cut out at eleven o'clock at night, is it entirely unreasonable to expect candles to be supplied? Suppose someone was sick in the night? And should one have to feel like Oliver Twist if one is hungry out of regulation hours? To be early or late was to invite not short shrift, but no shrift whatever. Sometimes I think Australians will put up with anything.

Perhaps they put up with it because they have come a long way and spent a lot of money and cannot bear to confess any disappointment. This theory was borne out by the air of frenzied gaiety that prevailed in the frontier-style pub half a mile away through the scrub. Rival coach parties shouted witticisms or wrote them on the weatherboard walls among the thousands and thousands of names and messages already recorded there. Even the pursuit of romance was being conducted with a sort of shrieking desperation, as if time might run out before any encounter could be really clarified: love on the run, dependent upon tour schedules. A fun-time place this, a hectic, transitory Dance-in, Drink-in, Shout-in, Laugh-in, Write-in. A Holiday Happening that must surely convince you that you are having a wonderful time.

And yet, in the aftermath of revelry and the cutting out of the generator the silence was profound, the majesty of the place awesome. If the culmination of desperate encounters took place in myth-haunted cave or on legend-haunted rock it would have been fitting. From the scufflings in the darkened encampment one gathered that this was not the case.

Our windows do not face the Rock—curiously enough, only four in the whole motel do, which seems a queer oversight on the part of the designers—so we are up and dressed in half-light to wait for dawn to strike the soaring surfaces. Also to cringe to the cook for an early breakfast, because two of us are scheduled to climb one of the Olgas this morning, while the others involve themselves in some tricky and rather dangerous aerial photography above us.

Celestial lighting arrangements are perfect. At a given signal from a tree whose rustling foliage turns out to be green and gold budgerigars, Prometheus Chained puts on incandescent glory. It is more than enough. Even to see such a thing through wire and washing. Nature's pure forms are, after all, triumphant over contemporary man's brutish lack of any form whatever.

And between Ayers Rock and the dreaming Olgas there is no habitation at all. After the Sunset Strips swathed into the vegetation for the convenience of evening photographers there are only the miles of red sand dunes quilted with tufts of white grass and fragile formal posies of flowers, stunted mulga, grevillea branching yellow candles, rolling buckweed, jewelled finches and parakeets that escort us as playfully as dolphins. You would not do more than blink at a unicorn.

Is it too late already to hope that this will be left unspoiled by further tourist speculation? Or will the shoddy caravanserai creep out from behind Ayers Rock and advance across the flowered plain in the wake of the coaches that are limited to day trips now? If there is someone in authority who has foresight and even a rudimentary sense of aesthetics it is just possible, even now, to preserve at least part of this immemorial paradise, as a heritage for the generations to come. Perhaps they will be more sensitive to beauty than this one, more finely attuned to the nobility of elemental places, less uneasy, simpler in natural reverence.

You wouldn't, after all, leave beer cans or the evidence of natural functions in Chartres Cathedral, would you?

The Olgas

At the mouth of the gorge the ranger makes billy tea expertly, and we drink it with corned-beef sandwiches that are curling at the edges and taste like every childhood picnic one ever had. The temperature is in the low eighties, the breeze is gentle, above us the sheer smooth stately domes glitter a soft and brilliant red. I am still weak and foolish with relief that I am not after all expected to climb Mt Olga itself, jointless, seamless, polished from the silvery-green mulga at its base to the rounded summit reared 1500 feet up. Deadpan outback humour is frighteningly convincing. But the ranger has relented and promised an easy scarp further on.

These must surely be the strangest mountains in the world. Probably fragments of the Musgraves to the south, torn by surf from the high rocky coast of the oldest land of all, Yilgarnia, and rounded through ages by rolling seas and fine sands, cemented together, polished smooth, and finally left exposed as a series of monoliths rising abruptly from the plain and slashed by chasms and gorges so deep and vertical and narrow that the sky is only a thin blue ribbon and the vegetation is lush with trapped moisture.

We have just been exploring one of these gorges where the silicious cemented conglomerate of boulders appears as the most intricate mosaic, finely honed and polished and looking slippery. All our faces are dyed bright salmon pink with the reflection of so much dazzling red. We have the wrong sort of complexions for this unearthly light, and the wrong sort of bodies for this sort of terrain: we are soft and white and flabby and overcivilised and know it and are ashamed. If I could turn myself into a bronze Henry Moore figure I would and sit deep in the gorge for ever and ever, grown over with lianas and crowned with nesting birds. I am obviously not proofed against immortal longings. I suspect the others aren't either, because wordlessly we all fan out and each one walks alone, mysteriously, a tiny recession of Chirico figures moving deeper and deeper into the red slopes and verticals, listening to silence.

Neither do we talk about it much afterwards. We eat our sandwiches and drink our scalding tea, watch the territorial principle in action as a butcherbird routs a crow from its individual tree, meticulously erase all traces of our alien presence in this grave and solemn place, and get the expedition under way before the coach lumbering up through the scrub in a cloud of red dust can disgorge its passengers and break the spell. Nothing less sturdy than a small tank could follow on the track we are taking, which leads us in a jolting, lurching, bone-rattling, muscle-wrenching half-circle over the sand dunes and through the flowers—purple and white and yellow circular clumps two feet and three feet across, like no flowers you ever saw in your life before—skirting the bases of the glistening domes until we round them and pull up, shattered, under the scarp which we are to climb.

I think at first that this is another joke. Unseemly, because there is a slope to this buttress and it might be just possible for somebody young and fit and utterly fearless to actually scramble up the ridges and the polished red planes to the top. Not me, of course. I know film people are mostly insane, but not as insane as that. They are unloading the gear, checking and correcting each delicate piece for possible damage during the jolting. My shoulder-bag is being loaded with tapes and film and binoculars. The ranger cheerfully points out the easiest route of ascent, along the stream-bed, diagonally up and across the scrub to the watercourse streaked dark on the red at a dizzying angle. He will wait at the dead tree to guide us up the steeper planes.

Before we are out of the scrub my bare legs are lacerated with thorns and my sneakers are filled with bindies and I have given up smoking for good and all. By the time we are at the watercourse I realise that the conglomerate rock of this particular monolith hasn't been cemented properly: pebbles and boulders roll and slip alarmingly under agonised ankles; there is not an even surface anywhere and everything goes up. By the time I have reached the dead tree where the real climb begins, I know I am a stranger in paradise, unfit, unworthy, with my immortal longings reduced to the overriding problem of keeping my lungs working: they seem to be sticking to my ribs and tearing at every breath. Only the sight of the men bowed and staggering across the mountain face under the weight of cameras, tripods, sound equipment, lumpy duffel-bags of accessories keeps me going. I am no longer a feminist: I am fiendishly glad to have been let off with the lightest load.

The ranger, older than any of us, is two planes higher, and going up with the lithe agility of a mountain goat. I wish I was a mountain goat. I dare not look up any more and I dare not look down. I look at my feet scrabbling for purchase. I listen to my breath screaming and whistling. I feel hysterical with pain and fear. I am a coward and a weakling and a sissy and I don't care. I want to sit down and blubber. I seem to think that thought for eternity, willing my jelly-legs to work, and then the breeze is cool on my face and the rock is level, and there is the ranger sitting on a cairn of stones in the middle of what looks like an Elizabethan herb garden, rolling a cigarette and grinning at me. The others lurch up over the rise one by one, faces suffused and eyes bulging. We all collapse in mad, gasping triumph.

'The only bloody Sherpa film unit in the world,' one says.

There are formal bunches of sweet-smelling spiky grass, posies of the most exquisitely delicate flowers, lavender in colour and flannel soft to touch, green butterflies. The birds are flying below us and one is a shining unbelievable blue. We can see a hundred miles over the plain that is more like a sea than ever, its detail lost from this height and the vegetation swirled in weed patterns. Around us and still above us the pure bubble domes glisten. Kubla Khan never decreed anything at Xanadu more strange or more beautiful.

I don't think I want to write about it at all really. I would like to keep it to myself and never tell a soul. Afterwards, not then, I thought about what Kafka had written of paradise ... that we were fashioned to live there, and paradise was destined to serve us. Our destiny has been altered, but that this has also happened with the destiny of paradise is not stated.

I see the altered destiny of the people who lived in this paradise in the Alice. I see the altered destiny of paradise in this coach far below us, pulling up at the bottom of the creek-bed. What has happened to paradise is being stated, loud and clear. We presumptuous people, making a film in this paradisiacal herb garden, are part of the statement, no matter how carefully we erase our traces. Only the ranger belongs here, by right of love and knowledge. I hope, desperately, sadly, that he is able to preserve it.

The Gulf

Karumba is a name on the map of Australia, a dot on the mouth of the Norman River where it flows into the Gulf of Carpentaria and the hawks hang over the mangroves and the sandflies are murder. Thousands of jellyfish pulse on the tide, and the opaque, oily-looking water harbours huge coarse repellent fish, mud-crabs as big as large platters, sharks by the hundred, and still, they tell me, a few old and sagacious crocodiles.

It is sinister country. Evil to me since I react violently to landscape and am repelled utterly by this one that seems to be saturated with a sort of thick grey heat. The river here is broad, sluggish, yellow-grey in colour. The mangroves are green-grey, dense and heavy. And the blue-grey sky seems to have a tangible skin of heat on it. From the river the baking saltpans and the sparse grey scrub recede into forever. It is not, one would think, a desirable residential area. Still, I suppose frontier towns never did spring up because of residential qualifications. A frontier is pushed forward because of the commercial possibilities of the terrain— because of gold or minerals or gems or hides or seals or ships or apes or ebony or peacocks.

This frontier community of Karumba has mushroomed up in a few months because of prawns. Thousands of prawns, millions of prawns, the whole Gulf apparently teeming with prawns, banana prawns, tiger prawns, endeavour prawns, king prawns. A prawn bonanza the extent of which isn't even known yet, although the CSIRO is working up here methodically and patiently, weighing, measuring, examining, recording, tabulating, tracking down the breeding grounds and the habits of every variety of prawn hauled in. Among the prawn-fishers who have been first in on the bonanza there is a certain scepticism tingeing present jubilation. Prawning grounds have been fished out before. Exmouth Gulf in the west might be booming, but the east coast is giving only skimpy pickings, and Moreton Bay has been closed to all prawn-fishers. How long will this one last?

Presently there are only fourteen boats working out into the Gulf from Karumba—*Cindy*, *Kotuku*, *Audrey June*, *Rama*, *Toowoon Bay*, *Sea Marie*, *Santa Maria*, *Ulitarra*, *Sea Fever*, *Clan Nellie*, *Sea Tang*, *Vixen Star*, *Troubadour*, *Silhouette*—boats ranging from thirty-six to sixty-eight feet, privately owned and operated by skippers who were willing and game to pioneer this enterprise, but all of them (except for *Kotuku*, which is known as the rebel boat) dependent upon the commercial plant which the firm of Craig Mostyn has set up on the riverbank to receive and process the hauls, to fuel, water and provision the boats, to supply the ice to preserve the catch at sea and, importantly, to provide the spotter plane that is used when the banana prawns run from March to July to pick up the mud boils and direct the boats in.

So the boats on the river and the plant on the bank of it are the heart of the matter. Reason enough for a frontier town. Although perhaps you could not call Karumba a town yet. There is the plant—utilitarian, ugly, looking a bit rushed-up and straining at the tin seams, although it is evident that extensions are under way. On either side of the plant, up the riverbank and down the riverbank, are the caravans where the fishermen's wives and children are living, at least those wives who were game enough or optimistic enough or gypsy-blooded enough to brave the Gulf to be with their men. Probably more will come later. Behind the plant is a new building to house the male company employees. The women who work in the plant (other than fishermen's wives) live temporarily in a long metal caravan divided into cabins. There is a bungalow for the manager, who also has his wife with him, and a very young baby.

But along the bank from all this hurriedly assembled caravan town straggling through scrub and sand, there are raked shell paths, borders of Japanese balsam, hibiscus, poinsettias, bougainvillea, tall feathery white cedars, docked bushes of prince's crown, bird-of-paradise, young coconut palms, and though this vegetation looks parched it is extraordinary in the setting, and the more extraordinary in that it surrounds an oasis of elegance known as The Lodge. The Lodge is a complex that includes a big guest bungalow, cool and airy and polished, with a private shower and lavatory to every clean curtained room, and cherry-red counterpanes. Beside the guest bungalow is a chlorinated swimming pool, and on the other side of the swimming pool a long, high block on stilts that has living quarters, a big dining room with cane and bamboo furniture, and a completely modern and rather sophisticated bar. There are storerooms behind, as well as the generating plant, a bungalow for the licensee, and another for the domestic staff. It is so anachronistic that you could believe it to be a set run up for a film adaptation of a Somerset Maugham story. In fact The Lodge came first, long ago, as a Qantas refuelling base, and through the war was taken over as a base for the Catalinas and Sunderlands. After the war it was shut up for years and years, until Ansett took it over in 1959, and presumably restored it. The Craig Mostyn company bought it later.

Unless you count the pilot station and fauna reserve, or the Pawlowskis' crocodile farm away over the saltpan by the airstrip, that is the extent of Karumba. Frontier new-style. Part shambles, part luxury. There are more than one hundred and fifty people living here now. Next year, if the bonanza holds and the company can increase the water supply, there will be more. And the next year more still. In a few years there might even be a real town, kerbed and guttered around separate bungalows.

At the moment water is a nightmarish problem. There is only the original well to supply all the needs of the community and the even more urgent needs of the processing plant. Prawns have to be processed cold and frozen fast. The boats which are still unrefrigerated might need as much as seventy baskets of ice every trip. If the place is to expand to capacity there will need to be bores sunk, or a pipeline run from Normanton, the old port, forty miles away up the river.

In spite of the bonus of bar and swimming pool I suspect that life is tough enough on this frontier. The caravans have power supplied, and the wives have fitted them out as ingeniously and comfortably as possible, but they must be cramped quarters at best, and lonely living when the men are at sea. Also expensive living. As with any frontier town, everything—from frozen meat to razor-blades to soft drink for the kids—costs more here than it does anywhere else. And there is only the company store to buy from.

Company employees mess very well at the plant, but there is no canteen, no recreation hall, no newspapers, magazines, books, radio, or TV, and nothing to do out of working hours and nowhere to go but up through the scrub and along the riverbank to The Lodge, where drinks are expensive too, but at least there you can sit for hours at the bar under the shells and the turtle carapaces and talk about prawns and prawns again and fishing grounds and boats and engines and the latest gossip. Inevitably there is much gossip, but good-natured rather than malicious. A live-and-let-live attitude prevails.

This community, as a community, has only been in existence for a few months. In a place that has sprung up so quickly it is not surprising that amenities have failed to keep pace with commercial growth and consolidation. For instance there is no school for the children. There are no medical facilities. The school is not absolutely urgent yet since the married group is surprisingly young on the whole, and most of the kids haven't reached school age. The few that have are struggling, rebelliously, with intermittent correspondence lessons. But the medical position is worrying. The Flying Doctor comes in once a month, and if any health worry crops up in between there is Normanton, forty-odd miles away.

In fact all the children look very healthy, rampagingly healthy actually, far too healthy and bouncing for good order and discipline in such boring surroundings: their young mothers look wan and tired, sometimes, coping with their devils, and they must worry quite a lot. The women and girls grading and packing the prawns in the processing plant complain of constant brine rash. Sandfly bites infect easily and turn into pussy sores. So does the slightest scratch. Many of the adults have sores bandaged or healing. And none of the women has been through a wet season yet. The heat is building up now, sticky and enervating in spite of the deceptive breeze off the river. The palms of your hands sweat, and the roots of your hair, and after you have been sitting for a while your clothes stick to your skin. When the wet comes the community will be cut off even from Normanton by flooded saltpans, and only the plane will be able to get in.

The twice-weekly arrival of the old DC3 is the lifeline to civilisation away across the saltpans and the bleak cattle country and the abandoned gold-diggings and the Atherton Tableland to lush green Cairns on the east coast. One feels a great respect and affection for the old Dakotas that are still flying the wildest, toughest runs after so many years of service. And there is something gallant about the arrival of the DC3 here, bringing stores and mail and sometimes a stranger to enliven monotony. On Fridays the crew stays overnight, old friends now to everybody, and The Lodge is very gay and lively with news and gossip, and people sing spontaneously, as at an old-fashioned country social.

For there is, evidently, a very real feeling of community here. These are the pioneers, and they know it and have a sense of pride in accomplishment. Even when they complain it is without real rancour. The boats have had a marvellous season with the banana prawns—one hauled 96 000 pounds, working only two or three days every fortnight when the double tides were running. Others hauled 40 000 pounds in the five months. At twenty-five cents a pound this is good money, even with deckhands to be paid, food and fuel to be discounted, and ice at thirty-six cents a basket. This first year of bonanza has only been restricted by the lack of storage capacity and refrigeration in boats accustomed to working on the east coast for skimpy hauls, and by the processing capacity of the plant. Presently the quarry is tiger prawns, which are being hauled in at the rate of 500–600 pounds a night, and sold to the company at thirty-six cents a pound.

Most of the season's profits are being invested in more storage capacity, refrigeration to hold the catch longer, better gear, stronger masts and tackle, because many boats suffered such an embarrassment of riches that they could not haul in their catches without breaking their masts and gear, or store the prawns if they could.

So there is, in spite of boredom and monotony and heat and sandflies, an air of high excitement about this place. The company's investment and the years of patient survey and exploration have paid off. So has the risk of the boats in coming up here. So far, that is. Now there is constant speculation. Will next season be as good? How many boats will head for the Gulf? Will there be other companies setting up competitive processing plants? Is this bonanza rich enough to be shared out among all the people who will want to be in on it? Next year. What will happen next year?

I expect next year will tell. But beside this inimical river, with the heat rising and the sandflies biting, and the hawks and the gulls swooping down on their bonanza of prawn heads, and the weathered boats fitting out for sea or steaming triumphantly in-river with their storage tanks loaded, there is an atmosphere of challenge and adventure and high hope and endeavour that is about the most refreshing and exciting thing I have struck in Australia. In this most unlikely place a town called Karumba is away to a flying start. And Australia is a more exciting country than I ever dreamed.

Karumba Observed

In the high cool damp packing shed Linda is grading prawns. Linda is very young and darkly handsome. Thick black Stuart eyebrows. Thick dark glossy Stuart curls. A Restoration wench. Or Hogarth's Shrimp Girl.

Over her old shorts and shirt she wears a big black rubber apron. On her feet gumboots. A rubber glove is on her right hand—the left is bare and looks red and soggy, but at the moment she doesn't have brine rash. (Her mother does, and shows me later the tormenting blisters between her fingers and the red rash spots running up the insides of her arms.)

All the women are incensed at a newspaper report which has them earning $120 a week. They assure me that $60 is really good, and very much dependent on their skill and speed.

The metal grading tables form an L. There are three women, Linda's mother Evelyn among them, grading at the lower table, Linda and another girl at this one. A bladed fan clicks and whirrs over their heads, and a hose streams shells and heads away from their feet. They stand on rubber mats, and at the bottom table there is a tray of iced water to soothe burning hands. From the row of great vats at the bottom of the shed one of the men scoops netting ladles of prawns into trays and tips one tray onto the table in front of each grader; she shells and heads the prawns and sorts them into a series of flat trays according to size and quality. Linda's hands are young and quick and competent. A rip and a flick and the prawn is decapitated, denuded of its thin, clever, outside skeleton, and there it lies in the tray, naked except for its pretty fan tail, which now looks flippant and irrelevant.

The catch is from *Rama* and the prawns are tigers, so named for their stripes, which are a beautiful translucent green and blue, barred with rose pink which carries into the leathery rose legs and whiskers. There are also some endeavour prawns, a thick deep creamy colour with turquoise tails.

I suggest to Graham of the CSIRO that the raw prawn is surely one of nature's most peculiar experiments. Graham, who is wearing nothing except a pair of racy checked Bermudas, points out gravely that the experiment has obviously been most successful. His position is at the top of the L of the grading tables. He has a large board on the table in front of him, marked into numbered squares. He has callipers and a micrometer gauge and a finicky little set of kitchen scales. He is sexing the prawns, measuring and weighing them—a sample from every vat—and recording the information of sexes, weights, sizes, number of females impregnated, onto a sheet which is divided into columns and marked with *Rama*. This is computer fodder, part of the long investigation into the life cycles and breeding habits of every type of prawn caught in the Gulf. Graham is generous with information and most explicit, and by the time foreman Tom is free to show me the rest of the plant I am mentally boggling with the extraordinary visual images evoked by the facts of a prawn's love life. What wonders occur in the deeps, to be sure. I suspect that behind my back Graham is grinning.

Tom takes me on a tour of machine rooms, ice-making plant, freezing rooms, company store, and so on. When we get back to the workroom Linda has been shifted from grading to packing, which she is doing with incredible speed, flipping them two by two into position on the cellophane lining of the box, each nestling cosily into the curve of its neighbour, with tails fanned in a straight line like a precision chorus.

Later I talk to Linda's mother, who turns out to be an ex-Flight Mechanic Aero Engines, RAF, ex-fisherwoman working out from San Remo. There is little about engines and fish that she does not know. I wonder (but strictly to myself) what on earth a woman of such specialised skills is doing grading prawns on the steamy Gulf. I wonder about many of the people here, particularly the itinerant women workers. I suspect that this is one of the places where one does not ask too many personal questions.

Cindy came in this morning, to the relief of the whole camp. They had thought her lost, and were preparing to send out a rescue fleet. In fact she had been in trouble, but not catastrophically, although she has limped in with only 800 pounds of prawns in her tanks. Now she is moored to the ramp in front of the processing plant, unloading. The hawks and the gulls are screeching down through the hazy heat on the mountain of heads and shells pouring like a great pile of crumpled cellophane, down the chute from the plant to the river. The jellyfish are palpitating by with their streamers trailing. On the *Cindy* the storage containers are open and filled with sloshy iced water and floating prawns, which are ladled up to us in scoops. We sort into wicker baskets—tigers, endeavours, and those curious repulsive-looking blunt-nosed crays that are called 'bugs' here. I think again of the experiments of nature—the prawn and the jellyfish and this ugly armoured creature. How very prodigal and diverse life is. It seems miraculous to be human, sorting prawns on the deck of the *Cindy* when, with a quirk of evolutionary luck, one might well have been a prawn oneself, being sorted.

Tuppence from *Ulitarra*, who has come alongside in an outboard on his way up to the shower block, says *Ulitarra* is fitting out and I can come on board if I like. I do like. *Ulitarra* is in midstream, and when Tuppence comes back from the showers we go out with Laurie, the skipper. It is my first time out on the river, which is even broader and more repellent than it appears from the shore. The great grey greasy Limpopo, all right, set about with fever-trees and all. But the *Ulitarra* is sturdy and workmanlike and reassuring, and reminds me of Greek sponging boats I have known. Upriver the government survey vessel looks sleek and white and elegant and utterly alien.

Tuppence lengthens cables with chain. Laurie is mending a prawning net. I like watching these quick, dexterous, simple movements with needle and twine, and in my overconfidence ask if I might try a bit. I might have known. All my skill as a needlewoman is of no use to me here. I am clumsy and awkward and loop the twine in every knot but the right one, but I am stubborn too, and Laurie patient beyond the call of hostliness, so the mending of the nets takes twice as long as it should, and looks, alas, botched. I feel guiltily responsible, and am troubled by the fear that that particular net might break at the crucial moment in a haul, but afterwards it occurs to me that Laurie, in his courtesy and generosity, probably undid my botches quietly when I had gone, and sewed the net up again properly.

Later, when *Ulitarra* takes *Cindy*'s place at the ramp, I go with Tuppence to the store to provision for the trip. In the store shed we buy frozen steak and chops and sausages, frozen vegetables, potatoes, bread, tinned fruit and cream, tinned soups, flour and tea and sugar, and—inevitably— tomato sauce. The tiger grounds are from eight to fifteen hours steaming, and the prawns can only be hauled at night, so *Ulitarra* will be out for quite a few days. After we stow the stores in the galley, and while Laurie is fuelling and watering, they give me a pair of boots and a jacket and we go into the icehouse with a load of baskets to fill. The cold is visibly vaporous—I've always thought that hell might turn out to be cold instead of hot. We all skate and slither and slide through the curling white mists to the dimly discerned barrier behind which the ice flakes are chinking down the chute. My only job is to position baskets to the shovel and when a basket is full to skid it through my legs to Tuppence at the door. It is a little like playing tunnel-ball in hell. Later my muscles shriek the information that actually it was quite strenuous work.

But later is later. Between the plant and The Lodge the caravans are dull, dusty silver, shimmering with heat. The women are herding their kids, getting their washing in, fixing dinners. Laurie's wife Marion has a wire fence set up around her caravan to restrain little Stevie, who wanders. There are women coming from the shower block, wet hair turbaned in towels. And in the sand at the bottom of the slip, where the *Silhouette* is moored, the huge and hideous corpse of a giant groper lies bloating. They caught three this morning, not one of them under 200 pounds. There is a groper hole just out there somewhere. Looking at this dirty-white repulsive predator I feel like throwing up. I will never venture even a toe in this river.

In the guest bungalow, showered and changed from filthy jeans and shirt, I contemplate my own legs with dismay. It seems to me that in these last weeks' wanderings they have become quite poignant. The scratches I got from thorns in the Centre have not yet healed. Now there are sandfly bites, and barked shins, and my knees are decorated with purple and yellow bruises where I crashed in an enthusiastic leap from the deckhouse of *Ulitarra* to that of *Santa Maria*. My ankles are swollen with heat. I would disown my legs altogether if I didn't feel sorry for the poor things.

Even after the shower I am sticky and hot. The river breeze has dropped. The heat is heavy, thick, oppressive. Between bungalow and bar, Bill the gardener is doling out precious water to the wilting plants. The swimming pool looks soupy. For dinner in the big polished dining room, proliferating plastic flowers from shell-encrusted containers, there is the usual soup, entree, choice of roast lamb roast pork roast beef, with junkets and jellies and other nursery desserts to follow. It seems odd that no seafood is ever served. Some of the unattached fishermen are eating in The Lodge tonight instead of on their boats. At $2.50 a meal they don't do it often. There are other guests too. A honeymoon couple—I think this is a peculiar place for a honeymoon, but perhaps they don't see it that way—a party of sportsmen up from Julia Creek for the fishing and shooting, a nice old pair of grandparents who have come on adventuring after seeing their daughter at Mt Isa, a family from Normanton dining out (and that's curious too when one considers that Normanton was once the crowded busy thriving prosperous Gulf port).

And the bar is packed. *Rama* is celebrating a good catch, *Cindy* is celebrating homecoming (and, perhaps, deliverance), *Ulitarra* is celebrating last shore night for a while. There are beards and tattooed arms ranked and double-ranked piratically along the bar, where Kath deals with orders and jests and gossip and racy suggestions with tolerant and amused efficiency. (She says, incidentally, that the wild pigs were in again last night, looking for water.) Evelyn is here, and Linda, and June, and Billy who is going back to head office in a few days, and Beverley and little Kay and Laurie's wife Marion, and Pat, and Tom the foreman, and Tassy with the labrador bitch Kim faithfully under foot, and the rebels off *Kotuku*, with the skipper Ken telling a marvellous story about a harelipped Greek, and little Georgie nodding and slipping and righting himself on a bar stool.

Behind the bar the crocodile head that mysterious Mrs Pawlowska over the saltpan mounted, and the baby crocodile that Mrs Pawlowska stuffed, the long jagged saws from saw sharks foolish enough to have tangled with prawning nets, the curious shells, the huge turtle carapaces on the wall, have taken on familiarity. This is the way a bar should look, and the faces around the bar look the way faces should look. (Excepting that I would add a few single gold earrings, but I know I am inclined to overdo things.) Tonight nobody is wearing a disguise of any sort. Perhaps up here nobody wears disguises at all. And that, heaven knows, is an odd thought.

The jukebox, fortunately, is broken, so it will be a night for singing. Young Ernie hasn't yet got around to proposing to any of the girls, but he has progressed as far as 'The Wild Colonial Boy', which everybody assures me is a sign. And, anyway, you can tell it is going to be a night by the frequency of shattering impact as the empty bottles hurtle down the chute and crash into the truck waiting to receive them. The borogroves are going to be mimsy as all get-out later, and the slithy toves will be gyring and gimballing in a positive dementia of activity. Most of the people here will fall or be pushed or willingly jump into the swimming pool before the night is through.

And later still one will come back to the consciousness of the vast scale of the night, and its silence, and think of poor

Burke and Wills, and mad Ludwig Leichhardt, and Flinders patiently charting these waters, and not one of them foretelling this encampment, with a last torch wavering through it, a last burst of laughter fading down the bank, a last splash of a dinghy's oars receding across the river to the dim white boats. The porch light still shines over the guesthouse door, and will shine all through the night. A symbol. Or a challenge. I like it anyway. Human beings have dug in here. And will stay. But the rest is a great deep stillness.

The Island

The one certain thing about going north in Australia is that the further north you get the further north you want to go. And so I have fared north until I have fared right off the tip of the northward-pointing finger of Cape York and find myself, intrigued at the very least, on Thursday Island in the Torres Strait, a place which has been of some public interest lately because of certain medical revelations concerning the incidence of what is nicely called 'social disease'. It is a place, also, of which Somerset Maugham wrote a long time ago that there was nothing there but goats, and that the wind blew for six months of the year from one direction and then turned round and blew for six months from the opposite.

There are no goats any more, but the wind still blows. Presently from the southeast, a buffeting bouncing lively wind that clashes around in the coconut palms and tosses a waxy storm of cream and pink around the frangipani trees, stirs even the dark heavy mangoes and figs to turbulence, and raises such a storm of dust in the unpaved streets that you are nearly blinded. Your hair streams backwards, your clothes belly out like sails, your skin is coated with a layer of fine dust and your mouth is permanently gritty, but at night it is blessedly cool under the billowing mosquito net and the palm shadows dance on your flimsy walls and the crepitant coconut fronds make a soft scraping rhythm to counterpoint the monotonous thrum thrum thrum of the power plant, which, with typical official cunning, has been built slap-bang on the waterfront immediately in front of the main hotel.

Obviously there is no scheme afoot to develop this as a tourist island. But you sleep well here and dream strange dreams.

It is not a lovely island. It is barren, dusty, the stony soil is completely uncultivated, the streets are, for the most part, unpaved, the beaches are scungy with oozy weed, rusting tin, and a million broken bottles, the habitations are ugly and utilitarian—even wood and roofing tin have to be brought up from the south. Everything has to be brought up from the south—meat and eggs and fresh fruit and vegetables and milk—what you eat and what you wear and what you drink and the very roof over your head. The only pastures are in the sea, and it is only the sea that is really beautiful, the sea and the near distances filled with the sensuous undulations of islands—Horn and Prince of Wales—which have an illusory enchantment. I say illusory because Horn is where you land on the airstrip, and at close quarters it is just as stony and barren and uninviting as Thursday Island itself.

But the flavour of Thursday is authentically tropical. If you have read enough Somerset Maugham and Graham Greene you will recognise it instantly—the heat, the dust, the rusting tin, the decaying jetties, the verandahed hotels, the rhetorical customs house, the mangy dogs, the anchored luggers, the visual impact of black flesh. The old hands stamped with the tired inescapable stamp of too many years and too much tropical knowledge, the bums washed up by freakish currents and beached here, the merchants—Chinese and Sinhalese and Philippine and European and every possible combination of race as well—officialdom pink and superior and aloof, twisting decorously with the hospital sisters at the three consecutive 'cabaret' nights, Thursday at the Grand, Friday at the Torres, Saturday at the Federal. At the Royal every night is cabaret, and every day too if it comes to that, black jellying joyful spontaneous cabaret to a jukebox blasting full-belt under flyblown posters of Esther Williams and Gene Kelly. The Royal is a gold-rush pub from Cooktown, freighted up here holus-bolus long ago and re-erected. Now it has reached the last stages of decay: the stairs have collapsed entirely, the top floor is reduced to a few gappy slats which reveal old intimacies of wardrobes and chests of drawers, and Heaven knows whether the bar and the couple of decrepit rooms which are all that is left of the ground floor can hold out under the exuberance of nightly gaiety until December, when the new Royal, presently only girders on the lot next door, is scheduled for completion.

The native population is now free to drink what and where and when it chooses, and mostly it chooses the wreck of the Royal and draught beer in great jugs and an absence of inhibition.

An old-timer who was good enough to give me a couple of hours of reminiscence regretted bitterly the passing of the protectorate, segregation, European supremacy, and the no-drinks-for-natives rule. What he was mourning, I think, was paternalism. He said that the native population was happier in the old days, and that their present freedom was only debauching them, and debauching the European population with them. He quoted rates of illegitimacy and venereal disease, mixed alliances, crossbreeding, and the somewhat forward behaviour of certain young women.

It is terribly difficult for a stranger to assess the complexities of the social structure of Thursday Island. I suppose it is presumptuous of me even to try.

To begin with Thursday Islanders aren't necessarily born on Thursday Island. They come, most of them, from other islands in the Strait—Murray, Darnley, Mabuiag, Badu, Saibai, Boigu, Dauan—to this trading post, administrative centre, and clearing house for labour. Here there is a hospital, schools for the children, hotels and shops and taxis, work in the town or on the pearling luggers, which still—in spite of all one has heard about the bottom having dropped out of the market—go out for commercial shell, although these days the main and profitable catch is live shell to feed the cultured-pearl farms on Friday Island and Horn and Possession and Good's, on Albany and Darnley and Boigu, at Poid on Moa, and the Escape River. Out of a native population of between 1500 and 1700, about 600 men are engaged directly in pearling.

From here too the enterprising or adventurous or ambitious Islander can move south to swell the labour force on the mainland. The Torres Strait Islanders are a big race, tall, and physically strong: they can earn good money labouring on roads and railways, in quarries and canefields. Education here is improving; there are schools up to the seventh grade on Darnley, Murray, York, Mabuiag, and Badu, and on Thursday Island itself a high school up to junior standard where children from the outer islands are brought in and housed in a hostel if their potential warrants it (only boys yet, which is a bit sad: the Australian attitude towards women carries through even in this fresh and exciting field of social experiment).

What is evident is that here the educated young have no avenues open to them in which they might profitably use their education. A few can be absorbed into the Department of Native Affairs, which still administers the Strait's islands, but the majority have to move south, often through Bamaga on the Cape, a settlement which has training facilities and operates as a launching pad to the south, economic and spiritual independence, and—one desperately hopes—eventual integration. It is a time of tribal movement: Thursday Island drains the outer islands of the young, the clever, the hopeful, the ambitious, and the south drains Thursday Island. One could, I suppose, foresee a time when the outer islands will become twilight homes for the aged, and, when the aged die, revert to nature and silence, which is a fairly spooky thing to contemplate.

In this movement of population inevitably—and I suppose unfortunately—much of custom and tradition is left behind as unnecessary baggage. On the outer islands there is still feasting and singing and dancing, but here on Thursday there is little evidence of any indigenous culture. No crafts are practised, except for the crafts of the sea, feasts of turtle meat and turtle eggs are not usual, and apart from All Souls' Cathedral ('... erected to the Glory of God and in memory of those lost in the wreck of the B.I. s.s. Quetta 3,484 tons, which about 9.14 p.m. on Friday 28th February 1890, struck an uncharted rock in the Adolphus Channel, whilst outward bound from Brisbane to London, and although in calm water & bright moonlight sank within three minutes with the loss of 133 lives out of a total of 293 on board'), where services are very High Church and hymns are sung in the native language to the accompaniment of a drum (and this is a breathtaking experience for a stranger), songs are likely to be pop, and dancing European.

And yet. And yet. This place tastes exotic, like strange warm fruit. The trades blow, the palms stream, the dust swirls in clouds and coats ugly houses, tropical trees, rolling children, and hurtling taxis filled with grinning black faces. The days of Assemblies, China boats, shell traders, pearl buyers, and the reign of Burns Philp, might be gone, but something lingers, a smell and a taste and an essence, half squalid and half romantic, something indolent, excessive, irresponsible, shameless and happy. One responds instinctively, and I suppose primitively.

Of course one should deplore drunkenness and promiscuity, illegitimate babies of uncertain fatherhood, and disease apparently spreading like the plague. But the drink and the disease are a white gift, and the illegitimate babies are beautiful and happy and adored. People laugh here, and wear flowers in their hair, and go fishing and get drunk and make babies and grow fat without concern or regret.

I cannot see that law or even incentive will alter this pattern in this generation which, consciously or unconsciously, still pulses to old rhythms. Freedom is only a word until its meaning is deciphered; it needs time and the right key and constant usage.

But the children of this generation will understand it. Or some of them will. Their children's children will consider freedom, equality, independence to be a birthright. As it should be. Legally the Torres Strait Islanders are now Australian citizens, with all the privileges and all the responsibilities that devolve upon that state. Most other Australians don't even know they exist, and of course one wonders how long they will exist in their present state.

Civilisation will take over, and responsibility, and material ambitions, taxes and plastic flowers and shoes on the feet and respectable alliances and temperate behaviour. The drum in All Souls' will be silent, the Department of Native Affairs a memory, and the new Royal will hold cabaret with due decorum and a four-piece orchestra.

I am glad I have tasted Thursday Island while the taste is still rank and wild. It will turn bland soon enough.

The Outer Limits

He told us, the manager of this cultured-pearl outfit, that the workboat left Engineers' Wharf at a quarter to seven, and we could go if we liked. We asked about food, but he said not to bother; he would contact Muroi, whoever Muroi was, and Muroi would give us lunch. So we only took some mangoes and a bottle of wine and our swimming things and presented ourselves, fairly clueless but as instructed, on the wharf at the proper time.

The workboat was already shuddering impatiently beyond a moored lugger where a beautiful serene old man in a purple lava-lava lounged, idling through a comic book. We had to drop from the pier where the women were already fishing to the lugger and then jump from the lugger to the workboat. Nobody offered to help us and not one of the natives on the workboat smiled, which shocked us momentarily. June said in a puzzled voice that they might be Badu natives, a more dour type. They were certainly in a hurry: we had scarcely skidded clumsily onto the deck before they had pushed off. Nothing indolent about this work gang: we sensed a stern authority operating from the island we were headed for, and were, I think, slightly and deliciously thrilled.

We had reached it by half-past seven, after threading the channels through the closer islands—ardent blue race of current and a black prince from a Roman triumph standing haughty in green board shorts and spindrift speckling him silver. But he was as anxious to get to work as the others. They all piled off the workboat into a launch, and he piled too, and scrambled out on a floating landing stage where pine-log rafts, supported on empty petrol drums, were moored. A pine and bamboo catwalk, jiggling perilously on the lively sea, led right out into the jewelled channel to other rafts. There was a green sun-awning, a couple of sheds, piles of tarred wire baskets, a generating plant, a tractor, and a churned sand path that led up the steep dunes to a long prefabricated steel hut with a row of doors painted cerise and yellow. The work gang scattered urgently, to machine shed, pitch barrel or, with the pretty balance of tightrope walkers, along the floating catwalk.

We were ignored, and something irresolute, but thought that we ought to find somebody to present ourselves to. Eventually Muroi found us, squatting disconsolately on the beach and staring back to Thursday Island—still visible but not, alas, accessible.

He was a big Japanese, broad in the shoulders and broad in the face, and his hands were the most powerful looking I have ever seen. He wore white shorts and a fine loose white lawn shirt and he didn't smile either, and I think he had been watching us for some minutes before we saw him. But he gestured us to follow him up to the hut and led us into what was obviously his private office, and called the native cook in the adjacent kitchen to bring us coffee, and when he had given us the coffee and a big round green Granny Smith apple each, he bowed politely, indicated the awning at the landing stage, and left us to uneasy speculation. There were shelves filled with tattered Japanese books, piles of gramophone records, an old console radio, a blackboard with the cryptic chalked message 'Nucleii gloves', a set of golf clubs, a desk piled with papers, an abacus—everything neat enough, but old and worn and used. The room of a lonely man on a lonely outpost. We would have liked to have had an inquisitive riffle, but didn't quite dare.

When we went back down to the landing stage activity was intense. There were natives bent like black interrogation marks on the further raft raising and lowering baskets of shell. On the stage there were tanks of sea water with baskets of shell immersed in them. One native was selecting single shells according to some obscure law of preference and wedging each open with a wooden chock. Another, gloved, scraped each shell free of barnacles and growth and scrubbed it furiously.

Muroi himself was intent at a small table on which there was a foam rubber pad, containers of various chemicals, two jars of plastic beads of different sizes, and a row of surgical instruments. There was a wedged-open shell in a clamp at eye level, and inside the living flesh of this shell Muroi was performing an operation with those huge muscular hands of his, inserting a plastic bead deep into an incision and grafting live tissue over it again. The shell, unclamped, winced shut. I said, stupidly: 'Do they ever die?' Muroi, clamping the next victim, said with convincing brevity: 'Yes.'

But he didn't seem to mind how long or how closely we watched him, and he answered all our ignorant questions with unsmiling politeness. And his hands never stopped— probe, scalpel, surgical scissors, tweezers—so fast and so delicate and so rhythmic that if we had watched for years we would have been no closer to knowing how he did it. Once I asked him if there were any Australian technicians yet who could perform this operation, and for the first time his impassivity flickered with something like amusement. 'They try,' he said.

But however interesting all this was, we were superfluous there, and knew it—idle ignorant women interrupting urgent work with silly questions. Piqued and humbled, we took ourselves off to the furthest tip of the island to swim and explore. Sandhills and she-oaks and native figs, bunches of fat green pods bursting with black seeds, vegetation so weird and primeval that it was scarcely vegetation at all. We lost ourselves in burning sand gullies, ginger-footed on spiky dry carpets of oak needles, gathering seeds—for what?—such seeds as these would never germinate in civilised gardens. They would only burst darkly in the climate of a mangrove creek wading with witch claws, and a dead turtle putrid on the sand. We were far then from the blur of the Cape's tip just visible on the horizon between Horn and Prince of Wales, far from semi-civilisation as represented by the distant small clutter of habitations on Thursday Island, far even from the mysterious complexities of pearl-culture and the mysterious complexities of alien Muroi performing unnatural operations to the end that throats and ears and fingers might be decked with sea-lustre.

We were on the outer limits of all our civilised continuities. We lived in weird green mansions, we bathed in virgin sea, and let the warm blue current take us, unresisting, and beach us on white sand. We were beyond the outer limits of everything, apparently, except the range of Muroi's binoculars, because in the middle of the day a launch came chugging up inside the line of pearl rafts, with instructions to collect us for lunch. But even waist-deep in water we couldn't pull ourselves up to the deck, and had to walk back, soaked, sandy and discomfited.

'You rike bath?' Muroi asked so blandly that June and I dissolved into schoolgirl giggles, and marvellously Muroi became scrutable. We pantomimed our efforts to get into the launch, we clowned for him to keep him laughing, and back in the office he served us raw tuna steeped in green ginger, fluffy rice, sardines delicious in batter, raw cabbage, soy sauce, with a fried egg each and a piece of steak in case our tastes were rigidly Australian. He was hostly with the wine we had brought, and fathomable, a lonely man enjoying rare company. His wife and family were in Tokyo; he went back there every year. Yes, he was lonely. Five of his compatriots were on leave in Japan, and four others were working on other pearl farms in the Strait. He went in to Thursday Island every Saturday, but through the week he stayed here. He read, he listened to Japan on the radio, he played music, he putted on the sandhills. Our feminine egos reasserted. We discussed pearls as if we were ladies who habitually wore such adornments. We poured buckets of charm over him. And then the native cook cleared away and Muroi stubbed out his cigarette and enquired shatteringly if we took nappings.

We turned timid as snails. Dismay overtook us. Married ladies and mothers-of-three—what etiquette applied on the outer limits? We took nappings, each in a neat little cell with a bed and a hammock and touching personal things, postcards, and photographs of slant-eyed children, and the wind in the she-oaks sent us off like babies. And afterwards we swam below the hut, wading through the dugong grass, and knocked oysters off rocks, and found Muroi again late in the afternoon, supervising the beaching of a barge with quiet, persistent authority. It was so ancient, and so ritualistic, the black bodies straining on the ropes, glistening with sweat and the late sun, the chanted work-cries. Is this really Australia? And are we really here, June and I, soaked and saturated in this strangest of days, sun-addled, sitting with our feet scruffing through discarded pearls? Blister pearls that didn't grow properly. The shells that did not survive the operation.

The workboat left late. The barge had to be beached first, and beached to Muroi's satisfaction. He apologised for this, and held each of our hands warmly on parting. Work was over. He could smile again. In the end there is no communication between people. As our boat raced down the channel we watched him climb the path to the hut, a lonely white figure scuffing sand. At the top he turned and held one hand in salute. We wished we could shout him some words, some message, but there was none, and anyway he was out of earshot.

The black prince from the Roman triumph burst a dazzling smile on us, like a bonus, and our boat leapt against the current and raced for home.

The Hippy Warriors

In the evening of a most satisfactory day we are sitting, as has become our habit, in old cane basket chairs on a verandah, just around the corner where we can still see the front steps— and who comes in and goes out—but also keep the lounge under observation, and, through the lounge and across the passage, the bar, where we are not allowed, this being technically North Queensland and we being technically ladies.

The verandah is wide and wooden and there are plants growing in kerosene tins, including a weird white lily which has just plopped open, releasing a gust of indecently sweet scent that quite overpowers the more delicate smell of the dusty frangipani blossoms that are being blown in on us from a gnarled tree that grows beside the front palms—lashing and crashing about as usual, fragmenting a lurid sunset. We have just been told that there will be no plane into Thursday Island for several days, the pilots having flown their sixty-five hours already, so we are marooned irrevocably enough to relax about it.

Inside the lounge, which has been modernised to the extent of moulded plastic tables and chairs, black and orange and white, vinyl flooring to match, and paint, in a discreet riot of pastel shades, on the very old weatherboard walls, the jukebox is playing something about San Francisco and flowers in your hair, which doesn't seem all that inappropriate considering the number of hippies who are gathering for the evening Happening. Hippies in families and groups, happy hippies by the charcoal ton. What would be the yardage of flowered cotton required to so modestly encase mountainous Nelly?—Nelly laughing into beer froth with a hibiscus stuck in her woolly hair, a baby stuck on her apocalyptic bosom, clinging for dear life, as well it might. We might get a nurse of it later if we're lucky.

Big Florence, in a neat blue overall, is setting out more flowers in the lounge, but plastic ones, and reserved notices on the tables. The members of the band are setting out themselves and their instruments in the dining room at the end, which has been cleared, and the orange curtain (plastic again but pretending to be bamboo) drawn back. Satin shirts. Electric guitars. Microphone. An elaborate and expensive set of drums emblazoned with the legend 'Y-Bens'. Florence is jiggling a bit with anticipation—how their bodies move, these girls, joyfully and instinctively, as though their muscles still remember something that has atrophied in our starched lot, or been squeezed out of us by centuries of rectitude and foundation garments.

The Y-Bens have called themselves after the original name of Thursday Island, Waiben, which means dry. What the original names of Sunday, Monday, Tuesday, Wednesday and Friday islands were before dogged Bligh doggedly ticked them off day by day on his epic journey through the Strait to Timor, I don't know.

But names are interesting here. There are ordinary European ones, acquired secondhand, I suppose, from admired or feared or powerful white men, but the more suitable surname of Sailor is current. And so is Warrior. Sailors and warriors these people were before Bligh, and before Cook, before Torres's journals were ever discovered, and before Torres himself passed through the Strait in his search for the Great South Land. And missed it entirely.

This morning after breakfast we spent hours in the stony cemetery over the hill on the back road to Tamoi Town, deciphering old legends on old headstones guarded by crumbling angels. Younga David from Yam Island, Spear Sambo from Murray, Richard Fred Abednego, Poey Akiba, Sosefo, Assea Fonomoa from Rotumah Island, Aliasa Warrior, Dadu, Rosie Rau, Kuap Tiati, who was a government teacher and Island councillor, Gagie Mosby from York, David Sebasio from Darnley. And Wigness. Just Wigness. Nothing else at all. And all these graves were eloquent in the dusty baking morning of a long proud tradition of sea people, warrior people, missionised, perhaps, but never quite tamed. (I thought of that savage drum beating in All Souls' Cathedral—onward, Christian soldiers, indeed.)

Many of the graves had cups and saucers and plates laid out on them, in which offerings of food and drink had dried. There were some enclosed by ropes from which paper streamers fluttered. Some had their headstones swathed in wrappings, waiting, I suppose, for some Grave Festival. And poking up among the Spear Sambos and Wignesses the austere stone fingers of the Japanese headstones, uniform shafts cabbalistically charactered, excepting for one, which read in English 'Ritsu Taguchi, Hiroshima, 1898'. Better perhaps for the blue salt sea to flood your lungs with death than the poison flood that lay in store for Ritsu Taguchi's home town.

But all that was far from then forethought of, the year of 1899 when William Vigers of Scone, NSW died on his way to India with horses. Did John Thomas Bebrouth, Master Mariner of Limehouse, 1853, leave any descendants? Love a girl as dark and gay as Florence, jiggling joyfully to the first tentative twanglings of the Y-Bens warming up? Who dictated the poignant words under the name of André Boitelle?—'*mes memoires eternelle*'. In that harsh, sunbaked, stone-strewn resting place one would not have been surprised to find, among all the half-obliterated names, one that said, simply, 'Lord Jim'.

Although it is more likely that Lord Jim is in the bar across the passage, talking pearls, customs duties, tides and shipping. Or taking his place at one of the plastic tables decked with plastic flowers and ordering a long cold drink for his partner, who is pretty and knows it. The European colony is out in force tonight, the men in crisp creased shorts and shirts, the women in shifts that are short and fashionable, and hairstyles that reflect ingenuity, since there are no hairdressers here. It is, for all the plastic flowers and the Y-Bens' marvellous percussion and the determined twisting of officialdom being gay, a curiously old-fashioned scene. Australian colonialism passing before Australia ever really knew about it, shadow and echo of British colonialism, not fake exactly, but not quite credible either, like an amateur theatrical company in costume, acting their heads off before the curtain comes down. Real professionalism is represented by a huge man in rumpled shorts and split sandshoes at ease in a basket chair, a British ex-governor of an African state who came in on an untidy yacht today and is being patronising in a hearty British way to a couple of imitation beachcombers. The curtain has come down already for him, but the professionalism stays, like a hallmark.

Here on the verandah the hippy warriors and sailors are loosening up. The beer jugs are emptying, the beer jugs are refilled. Couples essay the lounge and the waltz, which they perform with wonderful dignity and sometimes in shoes. Laughter rises, and voices take on a beautiful singsong lilting intonation, using English words to the melody of native dialects. Four big men begin a chant in opposition to the Y-Bens, growling and stamping, and the women laugh until they shake all over, telling the men not to be such fools. The tin cans tacked on the verandah posts are overflowing with bottles, and the flower people are bringing more from the bar, for time is passing, and licensing hours, and supplies will be needed to continue the party on the beach later. And now the young girls, singly or in pairs, take over the lounge and the last of the twist. They twist with every muscle. They twist until you cannot believe such twisting is possible. They twist with such laughter that everybody else must be laughing too at such fantastic parody. They twist the band out of music, and me out of breath, and the weekly cabaret out of further possibilities. Nothing can happen now but for the party to end. Which it does.

And we sit for hours on the empty verandah, blown over with frangipani flowers, thinking that San Francisco has a lot to learn, and laughing until we have laughed ourselves into gravity again and peace and wonder. Who, oh who, was Spear Sambo?

The Great South Land

How very far south it seems after being so very north. Even with all those relays of aeroplanes to snatch you and your bright new torch of discovery and hop you down the long long coast in great dizzying leaps, every aeroplane bigger and glossier than the one before.

The last great impersonal jet, pressurised, deodorised, plasticised, whispering lofty over the tamed southern coast to piped music and the flicked-on smiles of young ladies who might quite credibly be made of plastic too, does not seem to be of the same order of transport as yesterday's old Fokker, with a handful of disparate individuals as passengers, all known to each other by sight, or rumour at least, and the rest of the seats filled with netted and roped bundles of freight, punching holes in the storm clouds over the desolate Gulf and the Cape. (And our turtle meat in the luggage rack seeping nastily through its wrappings.)

Neither does the Great South Land seem to be the same country as the Great North Land. Even if our north is uncompromisingly south on a globe, under the world's belly as it were, it is still so far north that when a northerner speaks of going south he means to Cairns, which is still so very far north in our terms that the weather reports predict for the Coral Sea, and one finds oneself listening, absorbed, to a long radio discussion on the eradication of the dingo. I had never really considered the dingo before, or expected to encounter one on the road switchbacking down from the Atherton Tableland (only a couple of hours after we saw the cassowary stalking haughtily out of the rainforest), much less to have one tied up on the front porch making the most desolate noises for its beautiful young Samoan owner who, occasionally, and with the prettiest giggles, goes out and pretends to be stern with it with the heel of her sandal: she has been taking it to obedience classes in Cairns, at the most properly pedigreed school, and is only concerned that it will not sit, not for a second, with its back to the nice Dalmatians and Poodles and Pomeranians and Basset hounds.

People seem more like real people in the northland. Perhaps because there are so very few of them, and each one of the few has so much space to move in that everybody is quite distinct, individual, a figure in a landscape. It is not that the people are really larger than life, or even, I think, unduly eccentric. It is more the feeling that nobody in the north is anonymous. Perhaps there is something in this sense of being wholly and identifiably oneself and nobody else at all that lures so many pressurised southerners north, and keeps them there, not only the painters and the potters and the writers, who are all mad anyway and live where they choose, but respectable citizens like pilots and teachers and doctors and cooks and dressmakers and mechanics, and quite unlikely fringe-type people who have escaped the south and anonymity by growing orchids or setting up restaurants or going prospecting or fishing or crocodile shooting or carving coconut husks into soup bowls or salt cellars or stringing berries and shells into fancy jewellery for the tourist trade.

I have met so many southerners who have repudiated the south entirely that it teases me to try to understand why. Because the glamour of the tropics is, in a way, the great deception. Townsville may have a most healthful climate, but nobody could call it beautiful, not before the rains anyway, when a passing acquaintanceship reveals only, and disappointingly, provincialism parched brown and wilting, even if it is wilting quaintly on stilts and decorated with tulip trees, and waiting cautiously for the advent of 10 000 army personnel and army families who will occupy the new (and beautifully designed) Lavarack Barracks and spend, it is predicted, $9 million a year. On what, I don't know. Certainly not dining out or whooping it up or nightclubbing if ever so genteelly.

Further north the coast is actually majestic, mountains and brilliant tropical sea and the precise geometry of canefields pricked with the tenderest green or flaring dramatically in ordered rows, so many pillars of smoke by day, so many pillars of fire by night. But in Cairns the Fun in the Sun Festival fizzles, in spite of window-dressing competitions, beauty queens, a tired roundabout, variety nights, yacht races, an art exhibition, and whipped-up enthusiasm by perspiring dignitaries in leis of artificial flowers. It is too hot; when the tide is out the city waterfront stinks, and the beaches that look so inviting from the air are muddily churned and discoloured at the edges and abound in dangers like sharks and stingers and sea-wasps. Green Island, reached by ancient and dangerously overcrowded ferry, abounds in day-trippers, luncheon vouchers, souvenirs, postcards, and stern itineraries that include glass-bottomed boats, an underwater observatory, a marineland complete with stuffed and dusty crocodiles, and a film theatre in which you can see the wonders of the coral reefs without the exertion of actually going outside to look for yourself. Glory be. The crown of thorns starfish was provident indeed to eat up so much of 'the loveliest island that is anchored in any ocean' before it is cemented over altogether. Which will be more convenient, of course, for the day-trippers, and provide more space for more Attractions.

But the southerners who go north, and stay north, are not there for the shoddy awkward come-ons of the great Australian tourist industry, although some of them find it expedient to live on the tourists. There is more to it than that, more to it than climate, or health, or informality, or friendliness, or any of the other reasons that have been advanced to me as valid for declaring for the north permanently. There is a curious time-lag somewhere, as though the crowded, pullulating, anxious, busy, desperately with-it south is still thirty years away from really influencing the north, whatever the politicians say at election time. The south, and the problems of the south, which are the problems of the rest of the world, are so far away that the weather for the Coral Sea and the eradication of the dingo are more immediately important. The year of 1967 has no real meaning: it hasn't even dawned here.

As for populating the north, or defending the north, the mind, for want of a better word, boggles. There is so incredibly much of it. If you look at the map there are a lot of place names, but if you go to the places they are little more than postage stamps of colonisation stuck on, quite insecurely, to such an enormity of blankness that any label or address would be a joke.

If I cry my beloved country, what country is it, and how shall I cry it? How could anyone try to encompass it? For weeks and weeks the thousands of empty miles have spread out under my hired wings, awesome miles, so vastly indifferent, to wings, or me, or threats or promises or predictions as to how and to whom they should be apportioned, how maintained, how defended, how raked for profit. After such austerity and loneliness the southeast corner of the Great South Land is such a maggoty little patch that it almost seems as though one could break it off and not even miss it, crawling and swarming as it is. And start again. There is so very much to start with.

On Coming Home

My suntan has just about peeled off now, and people, I think—although I might be oversensitive on this point—are beginning to look ever so slightly pained or forbearing at any mention from me of the word 'north'.

Also I am grieved to learn that apparently I missed out on so many really interesting things, failed to see so many really interesting places, and to meet so many really interesting people, that I might just as well have stayed at home.

'What?' they say in disbelief. 'You mean you went all that way and didn't go to (Croydon, Einasleigh, Cooktown, Aurukun Mission, Laura, Coen, Mornington Island, Dunk, Burketown, or any other of a hundred pinpoints on the map)?

'Oh, you met him, did you? Yes, he's quite an interesting sort of person, I suppose, but if only you'd been able to meet (somebody legendary and deceased—or made up?—anyway, certainly not available for meeting).'

And, 'What a pity you had to fly,' they say. 'The only way to get the real feeling of the country is to drive.' (If I had driven I suspect they would have regretted that I had not been enterprising enough to travel by camel.)

I understand also that I went in quite the wrong season and at least several decades too late to taste the authentic flavour of the north, and from all this I realise that I am not to be above myself just because I've been on a bit of a caper, which anybody else at all would have contrived more expertly, knowledgeably, and rewardingly. I am above myself all the same, and rich in so many rewards that are touching, intriguing, illuminating, that I won't be able to sort them out for years.

One of the best rewards for going away, of course, is coming home again, and I don't mean that entirely sentimentally, although it is reassuring to slip back into a familiar pattern, and the familiar recurrence of familiar events, even of familiar worries like the yearly cramp of apprehension about examination results, the yearly resolution of prudence and moderation in all plans for Christmas. And not sending cards. Familiar irritations, also, like people welching on the washing-up, and not picking up their own litter, and swiping one's comb and pen and the last of the shampoo and forgetting to turn out the hall light and switch off the record player. This is the sort of family correspondence the very ordinariness of which gives one a secure perch to land on if one has been flying a bit high and solitary.

But coming home is more than coming back to one's own familiar people going about their familiar affairs, and more than the path that still hasn't been fixed and the porch that still hasn't been tiled and the now familiar wince of shame at the scraggy desert of front garden, the planting and ordering of which we have postponed from season to season out of completely defeated imaginations: there must be something to do about it, but what? It is such a comfort to know that at this time of the year any decision about planting must be put off until autumn, and I can walk through to the back of the house and admire last autumn's plantings there, all recognisably young trees now, and grown visibly since I have been away (I don't know why that should surprise me so much, as if, perhaps, everything should have stayed quite static until I got back to it).

This is a nice neighbourhood for back yards, if you like back yards, and I do. I mean these are lived-in back yards,

family back yards, used for children's play and drying
washing and hair and burning off the rubbish in home-made
incinerators and stowing the empties until the next collection
and open-air workshops for home handymen. And there are
many trees, and old rooftops of pleasing shapes, and for a
high-density area there is a great quantity of sky.

I was thinking that it is exactly a year now since we moved
into this neighbourhood, like a nomadic tribe to a strange
new encampment, and had to learn the territory, and the
particular territorial customs and territorial taboos, because
such things vary subtly from place to place, and the language
of milk and paper deliveries, garbage collection, postal times,
bus services, wastepaper pick-ups, is quite particular to the
area. Almost a dialect.

Now the dialect is so natural that one gets to the postbox
exactly as the postman raises his whistle, and to the bus-stop
precisely in time to raise one's hand, and on the bus there is
bound to be somebody one knows, or even if there isn't there
is bound to be somebody one will know by the time the bus
has reached the shopping centre, because this is an area for
easy conversations as well as old inhabitants of fixed and
settled habits and places of abode.

After so much high-keyed experience, so much that has
been novel and exotic and strange and absorbing, so much to
comprehend and sift and compare, I am charmed by such
ordinary things as bus conversations about weather and
families and illnesses and shopping lists, and childishly
pleased, with my own list in hand, to be greeted by name in
the shops that were all strange to me a year ago.

But what is fresh and new and exhilarating about coming
home is that for the first time I know that I actually belong
here, not just in this familiar house, and not just in this

familiar territory that includes other people's houses and other people's back yards, and trees and streets where one's footsteps instinctively avoid bumps and awkward kerbing, and shops where one is greeted by name and saved special delicacies, but I belong in this city too, which is only a further extension of my territory, and I belong in this country. Three years ago it was as strange to me as a foreign land, and it seems to have taken three years to graduate from migrant status—probationary, questioning—to that of a real Australian. I mean as real as the real prawn-fishers on the Gulf of Carpentaria, or the real pearl-divers on Thursday Island, or the real bush-pilots flying the lonely cattle-runs, or the real cattlemen too, if it comes to that, and their real women who live on familiar and easy terms with solitude, just as my real bus-stop acquaintances have lived in this suburb for twenty years or thirty or more and wouldn't dream of living anywhere else in Australia.

So that even if I did go north in the wrong season and the wrong decade and missed so much that is essential to real understanding I feel that I have reaped much that is rewarding. And among my souvenirs (the most precious of these is a handful of human beings) is also a root of *cusibghere*—I don't know how it is spelt but that's what it sounds like—which was gathered in the dawn on the top of a mountain, and this root I intend to plant in a pot, and if its properties are only a hundredth part as mysterious and powerful as alleged by my Thursday Island friends it might turn out to be a very interesting pot indeed to keep in anybody's kitchen, and then it will be my turn for one-upmanship and an excuse to begin many conversations with the words: 'When I was in the north ... '

On England, My England

Well, Australia Day is coming up, and Coral Sea Week is going down, and Britain has declared herself to be a tiny island only, and perversely I, who have always been anti-Empire, feel a twinge. There must be something in the blood after all.

My father was English, my paternal grandparents were English, my great-grandfather served in the Indian Army, and all his ten sons, excepting for my grandfather Will, served in the army too. All ten were over six feet tall, and every one was in a different regiment, and just once they all had leave together and marched into the village church, each in his different uniform, and it must have been a fine sight. Grandfather Will was bitten on the head by a sacred monkey when he was a baby, which seems to have exempted him, or perhaps my grandmother Emma, a frail blonde creature of implacable will, caught him while he was still a youth only teetering on the brink of enlistment, as it were, and firmly dragged him back to the safety of a nice commercial office, where she could keep her eye on him.

One grows up on this sort of family thing, stories and legends, and what is true and what is false I haven't the faintest idea. Did my great-grandfather, dying in cold England, really set his beard alight to keep his chest warm? Among his plunder from the Zulu Wars was there really King Pempe's stool? My grandfather Will used to tell such things, and he was a truthful man, but then he was old too, and memory is a tricky thing, forever discarding, rejecting, or embroidering what is retained, making transformations, building up the small and ordinary into the grand and exceptional. Anyway, certain it was in the matter of Empire, that my grandmother Emma was absolutely pro and my father absolutely anti, and they fought it out every Saturday afternoon on the verandah under the staghorns and the maidenhair where my grandfather, upon his arrival in Australia on his retirement from his nice commercial office, had hung his bowler hat upside down on chains and grown a fern in it as a symbol of his new freedom. My grandmother Emma spoke of England as 'home', quoted Kipling on Empire, and furiously drowned out my father with her huge contralto turned on full-belt in 'Land of Hope and Glory'. My father spoke of 'that dismal little island' and quoted Norman Douglas as saying that 'living in England was like living in the heart of a lettuce'. My grandfather Will played 'The Boys of the Old Brigade' on the wind-up gramophone and held his peace.

I concluded that my father was a Roundhead and my grandparents were Cavaliers. A renegade also, my father. But how that renegade feverishly paced the house through the Battle of Britain and the debacle of Dunkirk, and how he trotted out all his martial ancestors and the family stories of their exploits on the outposts of Empire as irrefutable proof that the English could not be beaten.

I first saw England in the early months of 1951, with late winter still gripping it harsh and the aftermath of war still glumly apparent. We queued for everything, even welfare state cod-liver oil and orange juice for the children, and people looked dank and shabby and terribly meek, and I wondered how it was that these same meek people, meekly queueing, could have been capable of such heroism so very recently. I had an inkling of what it was about twice, once when I was trapped in a lift in Selfridges, and once when I drove to Stratford in a blizzard. On each occasion the reticent English sharing the moment of drama became positively exhilarated. In the lift they made jokes, were solicitous of old ladies and small children, and actually seemed to enjoy the experience. On the icy road to Stratford, with the cars waltzing behind a snowplough or caught in drifts by the side of the road, they waved and laughed and stopped to help each other and me too, and I have never met such courtesy on the roads before or since. That was the year of the Festival of Britain too, and there was a lot of pageantry one way and another, and England was going to be great again.

And then when summer came we explored the English countryside, and came to know the pleasures of drifting in a punt among the swans at Bray on a Sunday afternoon, and watching a village cricket match, walking in Burnham Beeches, picnicking in apple orchards and castle keeps, discovering pubs that forever would be 'our' pubs, and it might have been like living in the heart of a lettuce, but I understood my grandmother's deep love of it, just as I understood my father's deep anger with the social system he had fled a world away from, and my grandfather's unquenchable delight in the bravery of uniform and drum. I wished very much that they were not all dead, all three of them, so that I might have written to tell them so.

All the same, after a driving holiday in Europe, I felt a bit uneasy about England. If the aftermath of war was evident there it was so much more terribly so in France and anguished Germany, with the crosses in the fields to remind you all the time, and so many mutilated young men still wearing army greatcoats, but in Germany the fields were ploughed right up to the very edge of the roads, and you were conscious of the intensity of the effort towards reconstruction. As one of my friends said later, talking of the doughty Lion of Empire: 'You're not tryin', lion.'

But then we had the death of a king and the coronation of a queen, and there was lots and lots of splendid pageantry, and many people said that the new Elizabethan age had come and England was going to be great again. I enjoyed all the pageantry, being Cavalier enough to respond with as much delight as my grandfather to all the bravery of uniforms and drums and flags, but the Empire seemed to be dwindling away, and I didn't see how England was going to be great again unless she got on with it at a faster clip. The welfare state was in full swing and everybody took it for granted now, and there was no more rationing of anything, and the countryside would make you weep for beauty sometimes, and people didn't look meek any more, only fretful, and they seemed to complain a lot.

We left England at the end of 1954 and didn't go back until the winter of 1960–61, and in the meantime the Angry Young Men had lisped out their anger and been absorbed into the Establishment, and London was beginning to be really swinging and the shops were filled with every wonderful thing in the world, and in the country village where we were living the wives of gentlemen farmers served champagne cocktails and the gentlemen farmers lived handsomely somehow on their losses and kept their shooting woods well stocked, and National Health had become, I thought, shockingly unwieldy and expensive. I didn't want to live in England any more.

I've never been back since that winter, nor wanted to much, particularly now, what with the Thames rising and London sinking and foot-and-mouth raging, although I think it would be interesting to see the flower people sleeping in Trafalgar Square in the summer, and the girls marching about in jackboots, and nobody meek at all any more, but apparently declining and falling with some panache and a derisive thumb to the nose.

Still, Germany is doing well. And so is Japan, which might be able to take over the east-of-Suez role and even produce a Japanese Kipling, which is an interesting thought, or some lines like these:

'And what good came of it at last?'
Quoth little Peterkin.
'Why that I cannot tell', said he,
'But 'twas a famous victory.'

The Voices of Greece

I have hesitated about writing anything on the Greek situation, mostly because I felt I didn't entirely understand it, and I have been afraid to write to friends there for elucidation since I might very well compromise them by doing so.

The voice of Melina Mercouri, stripped of property and citizenship, rings clear as a morning bell. 'I was born Greek, I will die Greek; Patakos was born Fascist, he will die Fascist.' One would not expect less than that from her. 'When I am 'appy,' she said once, 'I explose. And when I am angry, I explose.' One imagines her to be very angry indeed, and that she will go on explosing. Melina's is the authentic Greek voice of resistance, the voice of Marathon and Salamis, of the pass at Thermopylae, of the Byzantine Constantine Palaeologus, of the klephts harrying the Turks from their mountain lairs through all the hundreds of years of Turkish overlordship, of the heroes of the War of Independence, of Metaxas' famous 'No!' to the Italians, of the underground fighters who waged unremitting war on their German masters. This is the voice of people of the Dodecanese Islands who, during their occupation by the Italians, painted their houses blue and white, the colours of the Greek flag.

Melina is, of course, a wealthy and famous woman, living in America, and it is perhaps easier to hurl defiance if you are not going to be seized for it and beaten up and hurled yourself into some terrible prison camp. All the same I do believe the note would be just as clear and just as authentic if she were inside Greece, as the note of conservative Eleni Vlachos was clear and authentic in refusing, in spite of all persuasion and all threats, to publish her newspapers under censorship. What the composer Mikis Theodorakis said in defiance we don't know, because he was nabbed pretty early and we haven't heard anything of him for a long time, excepting that when he was due for trial he did not appear and it was said he was in a coma, having most curiously developed diabetes a couple of days before. I would guess he was in a coma, all right, but for very different reasons. One of the letters smuggled out of the prison island of Yioura to London last year states that prisoners were arriving in such terrible condition from security headquarters that the military doctor said: 'But for God's sake! Were they beaten up by cannibals?'

But torture has never broken Greek spirit before. For 3000 years they have been starved, beaten, burnt, roasted on spits, they've had their tongues cut out and their ears cut off, they've been blinded, enslaved, and for 3000 years they have cried, 'Freedom or death!'

And this is what I can't understand about the present situation. How can it be that they are so completely intimidated, or appear to be so intimidated, as to accept this monstrous regime that has wiped out every constitutional liberty, and imprisoned every liberal, every humanist, every intellectual of even moderate persuasion, every trade union leader, professors and poets and lawyers and the mayors of municipalities, the aged and the sick, pregnant women and the mothers of large families, under the most appalling circumstances and with no right of appeal? Even an ordinary Greek gaol is nothing short of frightful. (I know a European woman who spent three months in gaol in Athens and she said sometimes she thought she was playing Moll Flanders. She had a lot more grey in her hair when she came out. Although, on the other hand, she came out speaking fluent Greek: she always did learn everything the hard way.) The prison islands are notorious.

It is bewildering enough that the United States and Britain, as avowed enemies of fascism, should accept the Junta with no more than a 'tut! tut!' of disapproval, more bewildering that Australia appears to approve of it so heartily that we deny a visa to anyone who is likely to speak out against it. But it is most bewildering that the Greeks in Greece seem to have taken it so tamely. I say 'seem to have' because the resistance could be underground, as it has been so many times before, and if it is it could erupt violently and bloodily. I've known a lot of those resistance fighters of the German occupation, including a few who were caught—one girl had her baby kicked out of her by the Germans, another was under sentence of death after being forced to watch her mother executed—and the one thing they had in common was an insatiable appetite for heroism. I wonder very much what they are doing at this minute. I've gone through the names in the smuggled Yioura letters, but of course they aren't complete lists, and although many names among them are names I know well—like the poet Yannis Ritsos, the Biennale prizewinner Vaso Katraki, the actor Karousos, the marvellous liberal journalist Papadimitriou—I haven't found the names of any personal friends, so I hope desperately that security hasn't caught up with them yet, or they've gone to ground. I can't imagine them keeping their mouths meekly shut under tyranny of any sort.

In fact I can't imagine any Greek keeping his mouth meekly shut. Every man is a politician and an orator. The most impassioned speeches I ever heard on the Cyprus issue came from Tzimmy the pedlar. And once, before an election, I watched two labourers unloading asbestos from a caique. They were engaged in political argument, and put their sacks down on the quay while they got on with it. A crowd gathered, and each protagonist appealed to the bystanders, until at last they turned their backs on each other completely, the better to harangue the audience. As they were both very resonant orators each began moving away in opposite directions so as not to be drowned out by the other, until finally one, with attendant audience, was at one end of the waterfront, and the other, with his audience, was at the other end of the waterfront, and the neglected sacks of asbestos lay in the middle. I have also seen an electioneering politician thrown into the sea, and another hurled back into the steamer from which he was trying to land. How can spirit like that turn tame overnight?

It has been suggested to me that resistance is easy, indeed inevitable, when you have nothing left to lose. But in the last ten years or so there has been emerging in Greece a definite middle class, who for the first time have a great deal to lose. Jobs, prestige, property, possessions, children's education, investments—things which might weight the scales against conviction. I watched through ten years just one island's development out of absolute poverty into relative prosperity and the change in manners and attitudes that the change in economics brought about. It wouldn't be simple for those people to risk their very new security. The voice of caution might suggest that it would be prudent to wait and see how things turn out and keep mum in the meantime. It is exactly the sort of prudence on the part of decent middle class people that allowed the Nazis to take over Germany.

Well, as I said at the beginning, there is much about the situation that I don't understand, but oh Lord!, I know where my emotions lie. With Melina the Greek, and all the Greeks like Melina, outside Greece or inside Greece, and whether I can hear their voices or not. They'll all ring out loud and clear one day soon. After all, they always have.

What Are You Doing It For?

One day last week, by reason of a bit of bad timing, I was forced to come home from the city in peak hour, which is a pretty hideous ordeal if you're not used to it. Although, at that, it might be an even more hideous ordeal if you are used to it. Actually, does anybody ever get used to it?

So I sat in my taxi, caught in the nose to bumper stream, with lane beyond lane beyond lane also packed nose to bumper, like a series of monstrous metal caterpillars sluggishly crawling, and I looked at the querulous and fretful and angry and impatient faces, and I thought of all the thousands and thousands of people who had to go through that every afternoon and every morning too, and of the further thousands and thousands hanging on straps in trains and buses, jostled and pushed by irritable strangers, irritable and harassed themselves, suffering discomfort, indignity, and downright rudeness in order to get to or get away from jobs in which most of them would have no passionate interest or sense of dedication or burning belief, and I thought that they would spend five days of every week like that, for fifty weeks of every year, and I wanted to ask them:

'But what are you doing it *for*?'

And I know that although ambition comes into this, and status, and the acquisition of more possessions, and 'getting on', the basic answer is survival. Survival, of course, on the best possible terms, and with the maximum of immediate comforts.

I shouldn't think that many people have a distinct purpose in life beyond that—always excepting the dedicated few, the visionaries and the dreamers—unless a further purpose is to give their children a better education and greater opportunities than they had themselves (and then upbraid them for not being grateful enough, or for having it too easy).

But beyond the immediate goal of education we are not much inclined to labour for our children, or even plan for them in the sense that older races plan for descendants yet unborn, planting the trees and the vineyards, acquiring the property, arranging the alliances that will be most beneficial to those who come after.

I have been told that the salt mines in western China are actually subterranean reservoirs of brine, which is pumped up through bamboo drills to the surface where the brine is evaporated into salt. There was a time when a Chinese man would spend his whole life putting down a new drill, and his son would do the same thing after him, to the end that the original miner's grandchild would benefit. What happens under Chairman Mao I don't know, but I do know that most of us are incapable of even the concept of two generations working entirely for the third. Or even one generation working entirely for the next, as happens still in peasant economies, where survival could be dependent upon such a fixed pattern of past proof.

There was a family I knew well in Greece, two brothers and their wives and assorted children, who had pulled themselves up from the illiterate peasantry to become small-time grocers. They never employed anybody, the wives worked as hard as the husbands, they denied themselves every comfort that cost money, they were frugal to the point of stinginess, but they sent their children to school, and they brought their nephews and nieces over from the mainland tomato patch and sent them to school too, or provided the girls with dowries and arranged marriages for them, and so, in one generation, raised the social level of the whole family to solid bourgeois. Their grandchildren will no doubt speak four languages and aspire to art and letters and despise their grandparents' uncouth ways, and whether this is a good thing or a bad thing I don't know, but it was impressive to watch such utter determination in action.

I think the same thing still happens with some migrant families here in Australia. They will work all day and all night too, or take two jobs or three, and work weekends and never take a holiday, sleep a whole family to a room and live off scraps, so that their children will inherit the Promised Land on terms of equality with—if not superiority to—the indigenous inhabitants, who are inclined to wonder whatever happened.

On the other hand, talking of Europeans, a Czech art dealer, himself very successful, told me that Middle Europeans, persecuted for so long, work only for food and wine. The very best food and wine. His theory is that they have suffered so much and lost so much in the way of possessions and material things, they have started again from scratch so many times, that they have lost faith in the efficacy of possessions as a means to security and have come to believe that the good things of life are the only things worth having, things that can be consumed and enjoyed here and now. Thus they don't own houses. They rent them. And they would rather, he said (I thought rather gloomily), buy good delicatessen than a good painting. He is himself, naturally, a gourmet.

And while we are on the subject of paintings, there is a quaint notion still current that painters and poets and sculptors and novelists and folk of that kidney do have a higher and loftier purpose than survival and immediate comfort. They are working—shhh! please—for posterity.

I admit that most of them work under an imperative—nobody would be such a fool as to engage himself in such arduous labour for so little reward otherwise—but I think the posterity bit is poppycock.

The real drive and purpose of Shakespeare's life appears to have been to establish himself as a landed gentleman in Stratford, with his very own coat of arms. And this he achieved by dint of a lot of writing and a lot of sycophancy to the great and influential, and one imagines that he was very happy about ambition fulfilled. But of course his line died out and there was nobody left to inherit the coat of arms, and posterity, in any case, judged him quite differently.

Balzac too, who wrote like a tormented fury, wrote only when the clamour of his creditors, to whom we should all be eternally grateful, drove him back to his desk and his pen. His stated ambition was to marry a very rich woman and be kept in luxury. He was a dreadful social climber at heart. And Dostoyevsky wrote for the gambling tables, which were his great obsession.

It is the most pretentious nonsense to believe that the work you do will live after you. It might, but then again it might not, and history will be the judge of that, not you. What most of us leave to posterity are only a few memories of ourselves, really, and possibly a few enemies. A whole human life of struggle, bravery, defeat, triumph, hope, despair, might be remembered, finally, for one drunken escapade.

So what are you doing it for? If you are doing it for fame, that is a transient business. If you are doing it for posterity, she's a fickle jade. If you are doing it for money, you can't take it with you, and it will be little consolation to have engraved on your tombstone—like the Connecticut conmen of the last century—'He Amassed Wealth'.

My greatest admiration and respect goes to the few who do it—whatever it is—for the betterment of other human beings, now and in the future, but few of us are capable of that sort of dedication or even have the talent for it. So I suppose survival and immediate comfort will continue to motivate us in our labours, and self-interest will prevail.

You are perfectly entitled now to ask me what I am doing it for, and I promise to answer you honestly. I am doing it to please myself.

Long Live Democracy!

'A democracy,' wrote Aristotle, 'is a state where the freemen and the poor, being in the majority, are invested with the power of the state ...

'For if liberty and equality, as some persons suppose, are chiefly to be found in a democracy, it must be so by every department of government being alike open to all; but as the people are the majority, and what they vote is law, it follows that such a state must be a democracy.'

I was bound to be nosing around after definitions (and I found this one in volume 7 of the *Encyclopaedia Brittanica*, Daisy-Educational) because a couple of Sundays ago I could have been discovered, rather surprisingly, on the stage of a scungy suburban cinema shouting 'Long Live Democracy!' to some hundreds of people, with absolute fervour, and what's more in Greek. Greek is a much more suitable language than English for fervour.

Now this is not the sort of thing I normally do, but it was a rather emotional evening one way and another, and a lot of other people were letting off steam too. One Australian poet recited Cavafy's 'Waiting for the Barbarians' in English, another Australian poet said 'Aghia Sophia' in Greek, a Greek group sang Australian bush ballads, another group danced Zorba, a very well-known folk singer belted out 'Freedom', another belted out Cuban folk, the lights dazzled, the mike went on the blink, a slide of Melina Mercouri flashed on the screen brought cheers, and one of King Constantine hisses and some cries of 'Pig!' There was bouzouki music (amplified to torture pitch), and sweetly harmonised songs sung cantata-style and unaccompanied. There were also speeches.

It was a grand evening and we all enjoyed ourselves hugely and made a bit of money for the funds of the Committee for the Restoration of Democracy in Greece, although whether our efforts will really contribute anything to restoring democracy in that unhappy country is something else entirely.

There are some who believe that only the outside pressure of world opinion can oust from their seats of power Europe's first military dictators since the war. And certainly the Scandinavian and Benelux countries have already protested vigorously against the supposedly temporary tolerance extended to the colonels by America and Britain. But cynically one feels that the tolerance is more long-term than temporary, and what disapproval has been expressed was never more than token anyway.

Last Saturday was the first anniversary of the colonels' putsch. The tanks rolled in and constitutional government rolled out and no democrat could raise a finger or a voice to stop it. To many Australian Greeks it was a day of mourning, falling as it did on their Easter Saturday, with Christ not yet risen and feasting not yet in order. It was a sad day. Fascism had been tolerated for a whole year, and many felt that the longer it was tolerated the more tolerable it would become to the western world. Even token disapproval would very likely diminish with time, and it would even be possible that the colonels could be transformed into respected ornaments of the 'free world'. Such things have happened before.

To simple-minded people like me it seems that such things ought not to happen. Nations which declare themselves pledged to safeguard the principles of democracy, individual liberty and the rule of the law should, in my view, honour their pledges. Or declare openly for fascism if that's what they intend to support anyway. They might even have some arguments in favour of fascism that would be worth considering. Like Hitler built good *autobahns*, and Mussolini drained the Pontine Marshes. And the colonels have cleared up the festering corruption of Greek bureaucracy.

But is that enough? And is it even true? Why should one believe that the representatives of the new regime are somehow more resistant to bribery than those of the old? And did nepotism really die with democracy? Some reports coming out (I am presently reading one from Gordian Troeller and Claude Deffarge, two reporters from *Der Stern*, the mass-circulation West German weekly) suggest that the promised economic revival is a figment of propaganda. Many factories, they say, have in fact had to shut down night and holiday shifts, and there has been a big jump in unemployment. Also, prices have gone up.

Other reports, it is true, would have us believe that it is all for the best in the long run. I can't accept that any regime whose power rests on soldiers, police, stool pigeons, informers, intimidation and torture is for the best. Anywhere.

Troeller and Deffarge report that at the beginning of the last school term 6000 children were rejected from enrolling at their schools because their parents had left-wing pasts. Civil servants don't get jobs without signing loyalty oaths, or keep them if their relatives are politically active. Pressure is applied to anyone who visits a 'left-wing' doctor for treatment or consults a suspected lawyer. Those who hold the Greek flag in too much honour to display it compulsorily on holy days and colonels' days end up in gaol.

To me all this reeks with an old, familiar, and extremely nasty smell. And I think it is too high a price for a proud people to pay for a bureaucratic clean-up. If the clean-up has, in fact, taken place. Even too high a price for the west to pay for a conservative, client state. At least I think that prolonged toleration of fascism is too high a price to pay, but then, as I said, I am rather simple-minded.

In a new book by Stephen Rousseas and others, *The Death of a Democracy: Greece and the American Conscience*, Rousseas quotes six Italian economists who say, in part: 'How is it possible for any army which is part of NATO to suppress that very freedom it is supposed to defend, without as much as losing its good standing within the structure of NATO? We have always believed that NATO was designed to defend us from tyranny, but episodes such as this cannot fail to erode our trust in NATO and the United States.' Ah well. Perhaps the six Italian economists are simple-minded too.

I think, though, about condoning fascism, or condoning intimidation, or condoning torture, or condoning any infringement of the civil liberties of people capable of governing themselves constitutionally, for whatever the reason the toleration is extended, that it is rather like the story of Saint Denis, who walked three leagues with his head under his arm. A great lady, puzzled by this feat, asked her priest how it was possible for the saint, headless, to walk so far. And the priest said: 'Madame, it is, after all, only the first step that counts.'

And the German people, once, walked all the way to the gas ovens.

And I say, 'Long Live Democracy!' in any damn language I can get my tongue round.

The Borrowers

When my children were much younger they had an enchanting series of books by Mary Norton about some little people called the Borrowers.

Like all the best children's books these chronicles of the Borrowers were really much too good for children and I came to believe unquestioningly in the existence of Arrietty and Homily and Pod and Hendreary and the other wee people who inhabit nooks and crannies in very old houses and furnish their apartments with such serviceable items as they can borrow—thimbles and cotton reels and snuffboxes and matchboxes too, and paper fasteners and thumbtacks and hairpins, and all those other small homely articles that are constantly disappearing in any establishment.

Wherever I have lived there have always been Borrowers living too, otherwise there is no accounting for the quantity of little useful things that vanish.

I have never minded for a moment (or not for more than a moment, anyway) about these little acquisitive people. But there is another race of Borrowers, of normal adult size, disarmingly friendly in appearance, quite winning in their ways, apparently trustworthy, and these are the sort that bother me. Because they get off with books and records, and the books and records never come back. At least the same books and records don't come back, although sometimes one is landed with quite different ones, borrowed, I suppose, from somebody else entirely, while one's own precious possessions are being lent out further along the line.

I do not want two copies of Elizabeth Jane Howard's *The Sea Change* or an extra volume of Pausanius, but I do want my own *Will Durant* and my nice edition of *Madame Bovary*, and the Edith Piaf record and the Nana Mouskouri special and the only copy of the American edition of my own novel and my cookbooks and George Johnston says he wants, and rather desperately, the only copy he has left of *Journey Through Tomorrow*, which is long out of print and the only record he has of his Asian journeyings. Oh, and I want the Tom Lehrer record too.

I know that the simple solution to the problem of the Borrowers is never to lend. I can't understand why it is so difficult to stick to such a simple resolution, but all the incorrigible lenders I know are weak-minded about it. One could say, of course, that one wants to share one's pleasures and enjoyments, but I suspect that the process is actually more complicated than that. And just as there has to be a Susannah for the elders, and a murderee for every murderer, so there have to be lenders for borrowers. A fatal attraction exists.

I admit to having done a fair bit of borrowing myself in my time. I have borrowed money, and clothes, and cups of sugar and flour and half-pints of milk and just a couple of spoons of tea, and books and records too, and sewing patterns, and once, shamefully, I borrowed a saucepan from a little peasant lady who had a large family and presumably needed all her saucepans, and I kept that saucepan for ten months instead of simply buying one for myself. I was so guilty that I flinched every time I passed the lady's house, and I took to avoiding her in the marketplace, but I hung on to her battered old saucepan as if my life depended on it: for some reason it was the most desirable utensil in the world and I doubt if I could have cooked two boiled eggs in anything else.

The lady must have been a born lender herself because she seemed terribly surprised when I finally gave her saucepan back, and oddly enough, once I had given it back and bought a new one I never missed the old and to this day have no idea what exactly was the fatal fascination of such an undistinguished piece of kitchen equipment.

I am only telling this story to show that I am anything but a Simon Pure in the borrowing business, and could even show little Arrietty a couple of points on the borrowing of useful articles for housekeeping.

But books are different, especially when they are out of print, and records are different too, especially when they are rare, and I think both borrowers and lenders should adopt a more scrupulous attitude, or make a new set of rules.

The trouble is that when you live in a sizeable family in which every single individual member is a lender by nature, it is very difficult to keep track of all the books on all the shelves and all the records in all the sleeves. Did one only lend it out upstairs, or did one of that lot upstairs lend it out of the house? It is missing, but who has it? And when did it go?

Now when I was a little girl every single book on our bookshelves had its appointed place on the shelves, every single record stayed in its album. My parents did not lend. Neither did they borrow, not even the odd cup of sugar or a few fish-hooks or a screwdriver or a half loaf of bread until the baker called.

So I do not know from where I inherited this reckless instinct or compulsion to press on the merest acquaintances possessions which are actually precious to me, nor why I should pass it on to my own children in an even more reckless form. Maybe I had some ancestor who was glad-handed to the point of sheer dottiness. In fact there are tales about my great-grandfather, who was said to have given away all the furniture, even to the grand piano, and to have lent all his money out on no security whatever, and to have died in a bare house by setting his beard alight to keep his chest warm.

I have no intention of going as far as that, although indeed I have lent out furniture more than once, mostly because I had no place to put it, and rugs if they didn't happen to suit my colour scheme, and paintings I wanted to have a rest from, and money when I had it, and clothes if somebody else really needed them or wanted them. (Money's different too: I think actually you have to give that never expecting to get it back—or lend it to people you don't like so that you'll be rid of them for good and all.)

But please, please, whoever has those records and those books, will you return them, even to confirmed lenders like us who probably deserve to be stripped of every valuable or sentimental volume and disc we own? Or did own.

I swear for the hundredth time that I am going to buy a big exercise book and rule it out in columns and label it 'The Borrowers' and be meticulous from now on about entering names and dates and titles.

And whoever brought back *The Dove of Ishtar* can take it back to whatever other crazy lender lent it. We would like *Journey Through Tomorrow* instead.

A Matter of Conscience

The case of conscientious objector Simon Townsend, brought to public attention while indignation still seethes in at least some democratic breasts over the attempt to turn ordinary citizens into pimps, is making a great many people sit down (or sit up) and have a good old think about this matter of conscience.

Conscience, as I understand it, is the moral faculty of recognising one's own thoughts and actions as right or wrong, and far from making cowards of us all the possession of this faculty seems to make some people very brave indeed. At least I think it is brave for one single individual to defy the whole panoply and majesty and authority of the law, provided he is defying it out of deeply held conviction, I mean, and not from exhibitionism or ratbaggery.

I have been acquainted personally with quite a number of young men of draft age, and have listened in on a great many conversations of which the theme was 'To Register or Not to Register'. I say 'listened in' deliberately, because their case was not my case, and I did serve in the Australian army myself for exactly 1110 days and look back on that period as one of the best times of my life, and in any case I didn't think then (and don't now) that any adult not liable for call-up was (or is) competent to advise or instruct prospective draftees. Quite literally it is their lives that are at stake.

Anyway, of the young men I have listened in on, some favoured dodging, some favoured public defiance, some were of the 'Oh what the hell, they'll get you anyway' school, and as the time approached for them to decide upon their actions I was very sad and worried for them, such kids as they seemed then to be facing such a harsh moral test. Because although they were all eligible for student deferment I thought that one or two of the more earnest of them might feel themselves to be morally obliged to make their protest anyway, and I didn't want to see them in trouble.

No, I'm not pimping, because what actually happened was that every one of them finally registered, some sheepishly, some shamefacedly, some angrily, and I believe that every one of them got their deferments, and I for one was glad it had worked out like that. Legally, I mean, and without drama or complications.

But it was about that time, or soon after, that an American friend sent me an article torn out of an *Esquire* magazine, and on the article he had pinned a little scrawled note that said: 'This thing hit me so hard that I pulled back in fear of going over-emotional. But for these aged, tired spirits it was a welcome tonic-relief from the waves of the unwashed.'

The article was about a young man called Tommy Rodd, who had just been locked up in the federal reformatory in Petersburg, Virginia, for a term of four years. He was a pacifist like other young pacifists, a demonstrator like other young demonstrators, he refused to register for the draft, he was convicted and paroled, he violated his parole by demonstrating again, and so he was put away for four long years of his very young life. He was nineteen years old and he said his conduct was decided by the law of God and his conscience.

Now the friend who sent me this story is a highly sophisticated and civilised gent of middle age, urbane and somewhat cynical. What he calls 'the waves of the unwashed' do not impress him, so it seemed quite odd for him to be getting emotional about a young demonstrator.

Only when I had read the article did I begin to see that aristocratic young Tommy Rodd, born to the very best upper middle class advantages of the Great American Society, handsome, educated, a little spoilt even, might be one of those rare shining people with the so deceptively gentle strength that is required to follow the path of conscience without a single deviation to easier paths or an uneasy pause for reflection and reconsideration about where the path is obviously leading, and to do this quietly, calmly, firmly, politely, and without a trace of bravado or shrill defiance.

What Tommy Rodd said, in effect, was that although he knew the government had made some provision for people like him who could not conscientiously learn how to kill, in that it was prepared to classify them as conscientious objectors and send them to serve for two years in various types of constructive civilian work, he could not accept this. He said that if he registered for the draft he was giving the government the right to determine whether he should learn to kill or not. He thought that the government did not have that right, and that by registering and applying to be a conscientious objector he was applying for a permit not to murder. No one, he said, should need a permit to love.

Tommy Rodd is, evidently, a complete conscientious objector. That is, he does not object only to the Vietnam war but to all wars. His conscience dictates to him not 'Thou shalt not kill Vietnamese', but simply 'Thou shalt not kill'. With devastating sincerity, in a world exploding with violence, he demands for himself the right of non-violence. In a world suppurating with hatred, he demands to be allowed to love.

He has been called crackpot, nut, yellowbelly, Vietnik, exhibitionist, and all the other choice epithets reserved by the outraged many for those stubborn few who will go so far as to force society to do violence to them rather than disobey their own fundamental beliefs in non-violence.

He calls himself a 'civil disobedient', a term coined by Henry David Thoreau, and says it means that a person so respects the institution of the law, and the laws of his country, that he openly, willingly, submits himself to prosecution while that law exists. 'For no law,' he says, 'can be proved unconstitutional until a person breaks it.'

Anyway, I was thinking of Tommy Rodd again while I was watching, on the television screen, young Simon Townsend being manhandled into a paddy-wagon en route to a cell at Ingleburn, the place where I did my rookie training.

'Spectator sports' somebody said grimly, and I thought, yes, there are some pretty devastating sports on that screen these days for us spectators whose consciences rest easy because we are not required to be on the playing field.

Let me say here, now, that I am not personally a conscientious objector. And if I have to face it I don't think I am really a pacifist either. But oh Lord, how they haunt me, these people of true conscience. How dare they be so brave, in this world, to preach non-violence? And love of all things. Love! Young Tommy Rodd and young Simon Townsend, tracking firmly in the footsteps of Gandhi, and Martin Luther King. And I do believe, quite a long time ago, that Jesus Christ had something to say on the subject too.

The Habitual Way

I thought I would write about habits this week because all of mine seem to have been somehow smashed up overnight, and if this is fate at least it is my own fate and I must learn to sit down and live with it.

I like habits, bad ones particularly, because habits make days into rituals, and it is easier to live a day by ritual than to play each one off the cuff. In theory I love the unexpected and the unprecedented, but in practice I think I would rather put the kettle on at the usual time.

Anyway, when you get to my time of life you get to a state of what is called 'set in your ways', and to have your ways unset suddenly is odd and unnerving. I mean, if you have always got up at six-thirty and squeezed the orange juice and stirred the porridge it is fairly scary to find you can stay in bed if you want to. In fact you don't want to. You would rather stir the porridge. Only because that is your habit. And you feel secure in it. I do think I understand about people who retire with an illuminated address and a cuckoo clock and promptly drop dead. Because being lazy or self-indulgent is not their habit, and their poor constitutions just can't stand it.

I began writing this because my husband is incarcerated in a hospital, my eldest child has left home to pig it alone (I must add quickly with my cheers and blessings), my second has just come back from the local church all dewy with wedding plans and the bells of St Paul's (recorded) and choristers at ten cents a head and whatever extra extras are offering, including floodlighting, I do believe, and I am left with my youngest and the pair of us rattling around like the last two peas in the pod and all my habits smashed.

Now some very curious things happen once you start smashing up habits. It has been one of my habits, for instance, to deplore opera and make mock of it, and of all operas to be deplored Wagner has always been to me the most deplorable. I grew up on Rhine maidens shrieking and Valkyries whooping and Siegfried hoop-laa-ing about his wretched sword until at the age of ten I swore that I would never again in all my life listen to such beastly noises. (I must confess that I did listen to Anna Russell and fell about and howled with laughter, but then she was making mock too, so it seemed nicely conspiratorial.)

Anyway, such is the smashing of habit that I might have been discovered (actually I was, by people who expressed some surprise) twice in one week at the opera, and one of the operas was Wagner. Beastly Wagner whom I repudiated at the age of ten. Shriek, whoop and hoop-laa and all. And what was awful was that I enjoyed it. Enjoyed it so much in fact that I could be very critical.

Tannhäuser is discovered in the lap of Venus (as I was discovered shamefully at the opera watching Tannhäuser being discovered in the lap of Venus), and Venus was very gilded and deep-bosomed. I don't know why I think that is wrong. Habit again, probably. I have got into the habit of Botticelli and Cranach, and my Venuses are little and light and not very gilt, and of course I did once know a small girl actually named Aphrodite, and she was little and light and black as pitch and she had straight jetty hair all tangled and eyes like ripe olives and an unpleasant habit of stoning newborn kittens to death and of course she will be grown up now with a smile like heaven and she is my idea of Venus. Not gilt. Not gilt at all.

But in spite of Venus I revelled in all that beastly music. I rewrote the plot, naturally, and got rid of Elizabeth, who does muck it up rather, I think. I would prefer more rousing choruses, and pilgrims tottering, and musical contests. But I'm not grizzling, really. Having smashed my habit of hating Wagner I'm getting out to buy me a nice LP so I can have pleasant breakfast sessions with the gentleman and sort of make up for all the years that I mocked and reviled him.

Or maybe I will make it lunchtime sessions with Wagner, because I need another lunchtime habit to replace the smashed one of sitting around with my husband every midday and lapping up beer. That has been going on for more years than I can count, and I don't say that it was a good habit exactly, but it was a fun habit, and a habit of talk and ideas, and I do miss it most dreadfully, especially as I find that I don't like beer at all, awful bloating stuff, and it does seem very odd to be liking Wagner instead. Oh dear.

The habits I can't smash, I find, are my worst ones. And indeed I often wonder why vice is so much more interesting than virtue. I am sure that if someone could find a way of making virtue as interesting as vice we would all turn good overnight. If the good Lord had intended me for a saint why is it my revolting habit to reach for a cigarette first thing in the morning instead of a tomato juice? I mean, I like tomato juice too, but after the cigarette.

Why do I prevaricate, procrastinate, habitually promise myself remarkable deeds of self-improvement which I know I am quite incapable of performing? Or perhaps I am? Once you start smashing habits anything can happen. I might make a habit of frivolity, for instance, instead of endurance, I might make a habit of good works, or long walks, or collecting stamps, or just lolling around with a hibiscus behind my ear listening to Mr Wagner, or birdwatching, or having roast beef for breakfast and porridge for supper, changing the sheets on Mondays instead of Wednesdays, keeping a diary of my Secret Thoughts (because of course I don't tell everything in these columns), eating oysters for lunch every day (with champagne, which I've always hated but which I might get to love, like Wagner, who has rather rocked me about habits). Anyway, the possibilities of new habits are endless.

The nicest habit that I ever knew anybody to have was one of my grandfather's, who, having been poor and careful all his life, found on his retirement that there was enough to live on fairly comfortably, so he kept his trouser pockets filled with small coins which he had a habit of jingling: I expect they made the sweetest music to him. And whenever he saw a small child in the street he had a habit of inviting the small child to have an ice-cream, always with a cherry or a strawberry on top, according to the season. My father always said that he had never known as a boy what a very nice father he had. And I think it was the changing of habits that did it.

So perhaps there is some hope of me becoming a nice old lady. But oh dear, I do wish my kids were all at home and I was drinking beastly bloating beer with my husband every midday and I still hated Wagner the way I used to and was forced to squeeze the orange juice and stir the porridge at six-thirty every morning, but then, as I said, the possibilities of new habits are endless, and I might dream up some really wild ones. If I do they will go into my diary of Secret Thoughts, and not, I promise you, into this column. Although you might, of course, dream up some new ones of your own and let me know. We could even swap. And make, I do believe, a new social scene in this lovely land of Oz.

On Being a Culture Vulture

The other day I was interviewed for television on that old chestnut of why Australians go away. Actually, I thought it was why, having gone, Australians should bother to come back. And I thought too that every possible thing must have been said on this subject, but apparently not, so here we go again.

Why does it so still rankle and niggle? Why does a man choose to live in the country rather than the city? Or the city rather than the country? Why does somebody say: 'The Mediterranean is my spiritual home' and somebody else say 'Wagga Wagga'? And somebody else say 'the Barrier Reef', or 'Upper Kurdistan' or 'the Maldive Islands'? Indeed, why not? I had a letter from a gentleman who finds the Canaries much to his liking, and again I thought, why not?

There is a lovely poem by John Donne, a gentleman who somewhat takes my fancy (being dead doesn't count in this, as I am sure you all know). Anyway, he wrote this:

> Is the Pacific Sea my home? Or are
> The Eastern riches? Is Jerusalem?

Well, I felt that he felt that it didn't matter, 'whether where Japhet dwelt' he wrote, 'or Cham, or Shem'.

I think you dwell where you dwell and build firmly with the bricks to hand. And if it happens to be Australia it is Australian earth and mud and bricks and the lot, nor do I think it peculiar that some people decide to leave it and go play with some other mud. When we were little kids we all stood against the kitchen door and had a book put on our heads and our parents measured out our height to see if we had grown half an inch or one or two, and if we had caught up to our brothers and sisters, and if you want to go measure yourself against Europe I see nothing wrong with that at all. You might be even taller than you thought.

What I find peculiar is the attitude of some people when you come back, having measured yourself (and maybe found yourself a bit short on the European kitchen door), who say, like patriot vigilantes: 'You were a traitor for leaving. But you are a coward for returning.'

Personally I never know whether they are blaming me for failing, or blaming me for trying. Nobody ought to be blamed for trying.

Culture, as I understand it, comes from the Latin *cultura*, meaning a cultivating, meaning agriculture, rearing of plants and animals, production of articles of commerce which are due to animal or vegetable activities or functions. We can talk, for instance, about the culture of rice, or the culture of cotton, or pineapples, or cabbages, or even babies under the cabbages, or rose bushes if they happen to be girls.

The culture of human beings might be something different. It might be the result of mental training. It might mean the refinement of taste, the keenness and balance of intellect and judgement. It might mean a quality and elegance of manners.

When we speak of a country's culture, or the culture of a civilisation, we usually mean its art and letters, its architecture, its handicrafts.

We talk of folk culture and we talk of mass culture. So that culture could be, in fact, the way of life of a community. (As a matter of fact that's what I think it is.) So Australian culture might well be venetian blinds, plastic flowers, feature walls, roller door garages, television personalities, pop groups, rotary clothes hoists, pubs and horse-racing and surfboards and supermarts and commercial palaces. Also the clubs, which are our version of temples. (As a matter of fact I was taken into the stock exchange a little while ago and I thought that was the closest thing to a heathen temple I'd ever come across: outside real ones, I mean.)

And this, of course, is the image we project. Our very own identity. Because whether you will or no, what survives of a civilisation is its buildings, its art, and its literature. We read with some titillation of the Greens and the Blues (or was it the Reds?) careering around the stadium of Byzantium, but what we actually go to see is Agia Sophia.

What do we know of the trade in currants or oranges of ancient Greece? Indeed, what do we care? We have the Parthenon, and the Temple of Aphaea on Aegina, and Poseidon in bronze (and he must be the most beautiful male man ever sculpted in the world) and the Charioteer of Delphi (he might be the second most beautiful but a bit camp for my tastes), and we have the theatres of Dionysus, and Epidaurus, and Herodes Atticus, and that is enough. And if it is not enough we have Pericles' funeral oration as well: 'Future ages will wonder at us. . . .' And, golly, wasn't he bang-on right!

What do we care about the oil trade of Renaissance Italy? Nothing, and less than nothing. We care about Michelangelo, about Bernini, about da Vinci. We care about Dante, as we care about Chaucer, who, most extraordinarily, popped up at about the same time. (And, indeed, I sometimes wonder what divine breath blew over Europe just about then, when you consider the Romance poetry of France, I mean, and all at the same time.)

So what do we care about the Japanese car trade? Or nickel? (Yes, I do understand that in that heathen temple they are all going potty.) But shouldn't we be caring about Russell Drysdale and Patrick White and Peter Sculthorpe? Shouldn't we be going down on our filthy bended knees and thanking the dear Lord for the ones who actually came back to us?

The gentlemen referred to above are all successful and therefore eminently respectable. Even though they went away and came back. That's just our luck. They might have preferred Barbados or California or the Black Forest. They might have been sick to death of struggling and being called arty types. I don't think it matters much. Because they would have been what they would have been wherever and whatever. I'm not sure that locale is all that important.

Alexander the Great was offered three hundred elephants by an Indian king for one philosopher. There is no record of the eventual deal. But when I read my daily news-sheets I do think we might offer three hundred kangaroos for one Bertrand Russell just to come and say a few commonsensical things to us.

Like: 'Go away by all means and find the taproots. Find the Parthenon, find St Peter's, find St Paul's, find Poseidon and Mary Magdalene and Ghiberti's gates to paradise, find architecture that is simple and harmonious, rock cubes growing out of rocks, find flowers and sun and wine and dancing and laughter, find love if you will.

'But don't feel you are an awful failure if you should just so happen to want to bring it back.'

A New Generation of Protestants

Everybody has said everything there is to say about Mr Askin's little blunder already, so I don't need to say any more, but now there is Mr Willis banning a play he hasn't even bothered to see and talking about 'hippies' and the 'lunatic fringe' and I think he is blundering too, and I am being very thoughtful just now about authoritarianism. Australian brand, I mean. Paternalistic brand, I mean.

Father knows best.

But does father know best really? Complacent father, smug father, slippers-and-pipe father, well-fed father, I-know-best father, you-follow-in-my-footsteps-son-and-everything-will-be-all-right father?

Maybe son doesn't want to follow in your footsteps, father. Maybe, just maybe, son wants to think for himself. And maybe also—I've got news for you, father—daughter does too.

And it's just too easy, father, to say 'Ride over the bastards', or to label anybody who disagrees with you 'hippy' or 'lunatic fringe' or 'pseudo-intellectual' or 'quasi-intellectual'. You are being arrogant, dear papa, without any justification whatever. You are being dismissive, dear papa, without any real thought about what you are dismissing. And that's not really wise, papa, because there are forces stirring in this world—oh, surly if you will, but intelligent forces, angry forces, frustrated forces, and oh so powerful forces, papa, that might rock you out of your complacency. And quite soon too.

Never underestimate the power of the intellectual, papa. Quasi or pseudo or lunatic fringe. The only exciting things that have ever been done in this world have been done by people who think. I know that's disturbing, but it happens to be true.

Why do you think that a large majority of the Christian peoples of this world are called Protestants? Because, papa, they protested. There was a man called Martin Luther, once, a long time ago, and he protested. There was a man called Martin Luther King, once, a short time ago, and he protested. There was a group of English colonists in a country called America, once, who protested and, by protesting, made the mightiest nation in the world, to which you genuflect these days, papa, with some sickening sycophancy. There was a group of frustrated and angry and hungry French, once, who protested and, by protesting, changed the whole pattern of European civilisation: and it wasn't banners they were carrying, dear papa, it was heads on pikes. There was a group of Russians once—raging dreamers, they were—who protested and, by protesting, made the other mightiest nation on earth.

There were coal miners who protested, and pit workers who protested, and railway workers who protested, and carders and spinners and weavers who protested, and there were women too (please remember, papa, that you have daughters as well as sons) and they chained themselves to railings and kicked policemen and were force-fed in gaols because they were protesting.

And where do you think we would be—what sort of society do you think we would live in—if there weren't people brave enough to protest? Not the 'lunatic fringe' or the 'pseudo-intellectuals' or the 'quasi-intellectuals', but people who think and get fed up and exercise their democratic right to protest. If nobody had protested in the past, there wouldn't be any democratic rights. If nobody had protested, our little kids would be down in the mines and the pits and in the factories for ten or twelve hours every day, our men would still be working an eighty hour week or more, and no woman would have a vote. We would still be living in feudalism and slavery. That we are not is only because people protested.

As far as I know, no injustice has ever been overcome, no wrong ever righted, by putting up with it, or by meekly accepting the dictum that father knows best. I may be wrong—some outraged people tell me I am sometimes—but if there is anything to distinguish man from the brutes, to lay the foundation for his singular dignity, it is his very singular faith in absolute and eternal values, in justice, in his own rights as a dignified human being—not as a child to be soothed and patted and scolded, papa—and against this nothing has ever been set, nothing has ever held any weight, not his own freedom nor even, at times, his own life.

Oh, 'lunatic fringe' if you will. When you are counting the heads, papa, count mine. Brown it is, and rather turbulent. I think the lunatics of the world have rather a regal air, and a style I admire. (I do admire style intensely, and hope I have a certain style of my own.)

You may think there is nothing regal in students lying down in the middle of a city street. But at least it has more style than somebody saying 'Ride over the bastards.' The students, at least, were brave. I like bravery. It makes my heart sing. And they were within their democratic rights to protest, if they felt like so doing, as their ancestors have protested through generation after generation. And I repeat and repeat and repeat that nothing has ever been accomplished without protest.

I would suggest, papa (papas?)—Australian variety, I mean—that you have a bit of a thumb through history and philosophy, and even current affairs in Europe (about which you seem to be singularly ignorant, or singularly insulated) before you construct your no doubt admirable theories about 'pseudo-intellectuals' and 'quasi-intellectuals' and 'hippies' and the 'lunatic fringe'.

I think, after the manner of artists, you should make some preliminary studies. I think you should consider a little more gravely the world in which you live. I think you should not rely so absolutely upon the safe phrase and the safe cliché and sit smug and complacent (those are terribly overworked words, I know, but I'm overworked too and can't for the life of me think of better ones) saying: 'Father knows best.'

Among the cunning bargainers, hucksters and investors, the astute and slippery profiteers of the markets and the bazaars (we read about them in our papers every day, caught out— sprung, if you will—and that is apparently their only sin: to have been sprung, I mean), the protestants to me have a positively princely gait and carry their heads high.

Lunatic fringe? Oh, but lunatics with their colours nailed to the mast. Brave colours.

Perhaps it might all be foolishness. But, as I said, the foolishness has a style and a manner and a creed, and nothing has ever been done without it.

Dear papa, will you not consort, even in imagination, with plotters and revolutionaries, with angry souls in small back rooms? Will you not consort, even in imagination, with buffoons, with mountebanks, charlatans, sadists, pimps and procurers, as well as with priests and professors and solicitors and councillors and members of the RSL? You might learn something. How about consorting with a few hippies and pseudo-intellectuals and quasi-intellectuals? You might learn a little bit more.

You might, even—perhaps this is too much to hope—never use a thoughtless cliché again.

Betrothing a Daughter

I realise that there are all sorts of very important and meaningful things going on in the wide world at the moment, but the most important and meaningful thing that is going on in my more constricted one is that my daughter, as a prelude to marriage, is being formally betrothed.

'Engaged' they call it now, but I like 'betrothed' better, and if there's some formal plighting to be done let us by all means have it of troth, and with proper ceremony.

It's all right. I promise I'm not going to be sentimental—although I've no doubt I'll weep buckets on the night—but I find myself walking around her warily and looking at her sideways and blinking suddenly to try to surprise the image of this young woman who is my only daughter. And sometimes she looks about fourteen and sometimes she looks about ten and I find myself thinking wildly that this contract is quite impossible—child-brides are out in this family—but then I realise I am getting her mixed up with that incorrigible little barefooted mahogany-brown island kid who sat on the rafters in slaughterhouses, chased funerals, jumped from the masts of sponge boats, played five-stones, disappeared down trapdoors, I think, whenever she knew there was a possibility of being carpeted for misdemeanours.

And when I blink back into focus again she looks so adult that I feel like asking her for advice on some of my own problems, and wonder why on earth somebody didn't nab her years ago. Then of course I remember that various somebodies did try just that and what my reactions were—ranging from consternation and dismay to absolute outrage.

It's a very mysterious business. I've never had a daughter betrothed before—at least not with parental consent: what contracts she contracted privately herself, on sunburnt rocks overlooking the jewelled Aegean, in damp misty-green English villages, or on the moonlit decks of various liners, I wouldn't know; I've never dreamed of asking. Girls have to practise a bit for the real thing. I know I did.

And then again I've never been betrothed myself but for once, and that was in wartime, and not formal in any way at all and no parents involved, and the restaurant was sleazy and he fumbled the ring. In any case the betrothal proved to have been an error, although I did like flashing that half-hoop of family diamonds around the barracks for a while, and was quite reluctant, really, to have to give it back.

No, when I finally married it was only as formal as nipping around the corner to the registry office and signing up for life. I sat on a beach in the morning and darned the seat of my husband elect's pants (he having but one pair) and then we waited for a man getting a dog licence.

Asking around among the friends of my generation I find that most of them did much the same thing, and I am wondering now, with all this formality facing me, whether this generation of our children are not perhaps rebelling against their nonconformist parents as their parents rebelled against their own conformist ones.

I even know a couple of mixed brace of students who did everything that was wild and outrageous and designed to shock and turn their mothers grey and wear their fathers out of weary patience. And then, quite suddenly, they walked with perfect composure up conventional aisles in conventional mists of tulle and flowers and conventional dinner jackets to the conventional manner born, not only forsaking all others but apparently their former wild ways.

I don't mean I disapprove of all this at all. But it puzzles me. Perhaps the wheel has turned full circle and the conventional has now become the unconventional. The need for ritual and ceremony might be manifesting itself. Or maybe girls just love to wear all that white gear, like the bride-dolls they played with when they were little.

Anyway, being involved willy-nilly in this betrothal, I begin to realise what I spared my own mother by just nipping around that corner to that registry office.

It's not that I haven't turned on parties before. Indeed I have. I love giving parties when the mood and the time and the people are in harmonious conjunction and I know I can sit on the floor before the night's over. But I am entirely unpractised and unlettered in even the ABC of formal ones. Australian style, that is. I think I could mock up a fair imitation of a Greek one fairly well, having danced the soles off my shoes at so many village betrothals, but then I lack the requisites, such as the gallery of the bedshelf for the old people and the very young children who are there as spectators, and the wicker flasks of retsina, and the musicians—with violin, bouzouki and tsabuna to play and play and play the whole night through. And, alas, I lack the innumerable black-garbed ladies of close or distant kin who bog in and do the actual serving and cooking and the cleaning up after.

I even turned to the encyclopaedia for guidance, and found there many betrothal customs that kept me interested for hours.

In ancient times I could have had all this over and done with when she was between the ages of seven and twelve.

That made me thoughtful. The party would have been jelly and custard and hundreds and thousands, and I think that would have been simpler.

'If you lived in rural France,' I said, 'all I would have to do would be break a coin and give you a piece each in front of witnesses. And your betrothal gift would be a crooked sixpence.'

And she said—quite sternly, I thought: 'Come on, Mum. Smoko's over. Back on your head!'

So here I am back on my head (that's the tag-line to a rather ribald joke that my children enjoy) surrounded by lists, and I am quite certain I am doing everything quite wrongly and it might have been more practical to look up a book of etiquette instead of a fascinating encyclopaedia.

'Wouldn't a crooked sixpence do?' I wheedled. And she said warningly: 'Mum . . . '

'But look,' I said, 'if you've turned all conventional why do you have to bulldoze me into being conventional too? Why should I turn into a conventional mum now when I've spent all my life sheering and dodging and even bolting upon occasion?'

She said: 'Catering equipment for hire in the pink pages.'

I suppose every other mother in Australia is conversant with what one can hire when one's daughter is being formally betrothed, but to me it was a revelation. I lost myself in it as I had done a little earlier in the encyclopaedia. I lost myself in urns and pot plants and marquees and portable dance floors and festoon lighting and folding tables and trestle tables and tablecloths and red carpets, and even slippery dips (that would be fun, I thought). I grew ambitious. In imagination I transformed my house into a sort of glittering gala nightclub.

'Smoko's over,' she said again.

And I thought, still reeling with revelations but coming out of it fast, there's the wedding after this. Oh Lord.

'Look,' I said, 'why don't you two elope? It's terribly romantic. Your brothers will hold the foot of the ladder so he won't fall off getting up to your window, and I promise I'll pack your suitcase beautifully and hold the curtains back so you don't get hitched up.'

I think I might give the crazy little biddy a crooked sixpence anyway. As well, I mean. One day she'll know what I meant.

A Portrait of My Mother

My mother creeps into my writings quite often, as she should indeed, with one small swollen blotched ragged-nail over her mouth. It was a gesture that was characteristic of her, but whether it was because her teeth were in shocking condition, or in case we should interpret correctly the wickedness in that loving tobacco-stained smile, I don't know. I suspect the latter. And the honey-coloured eyes all melting with mischief and delight at our misdoings. She had misdone them all.

Somebody said, the other night, looking at old photographs, that I should write a portrait of my mother. As if I needed to, she being so indelibly etched upon my heart and my memory that sometimes I don't know where she leaves off and I begin.

I don't know when she was born, because she was the most endearing liar about her age, but I think it was in the middle or late 1880s, at Inverell in New South Wales, of a Scottish father with a dash of French in his blood, and a mother who was a beautiful Irish Jewess. She won waltzing competitions, my mother said, with eggshells on her heels and a glass of water on her head, and her hand was so small she could put it inside a lamp chimney. She had six children, of whom my mother was the only girl (what a pity, they said, she'll never be as pretty as her mother), and died of the sixth of them, not putting aside until the last moment of agony the lace she was making to trim my mother's petticoat for market day. Her name was Sara.

When Sara died my mother, with all the others, was farmed out on various relations, and it was my mother's misfortune to be allotted to her Jewish grandparents, who kept a store. They immediately took my mother from school, sacked the maid and put my mother to work. This grieved and angered a young girl mad about learning but she bided her time, read books at night by a candle, and saved every penny she could. (The first photograph was taken at the beginning of this period: looking at it I always think of Beth in *Little Women*.)

Four years after this, or it could have been five (as I said, you could never pin her down on precise dates or years), she judged she had enough money to get to Sydney and have two pounds over. And after hasty and secretive conversation with her favourite brother one night she let a sheet down from her window in approved fashion and slid right into the buggy which her brother had standing there, and in a mad midnight dash across the countryside held up the train for Sydney at a siding and set out for adventure. Besides her two pounds she had, I think, the most terribly innocent faith in her own future. She believed in a personal star. She had, as it were, exchanged a wink of conspiracy with God. She skivvied again in a boarding house in Kings Cross, graduated to selling lingerie, and all the time worked at night at shorthand and typing until she was accomplished enough to apply for a job. She became a Gallery Girl, she went to concerts and theatres, she wrote romantic verse in secret notebooks and locked them up in her tin trunk. She must have blossomed in those years. Anyway, they must have affected her deeply because she never made a visit to Sydney without making a pilgrimage to the old boarding house. Until, one day, it was gone.

The second photograph was taken on her wedding day, maybe ten years after. I don't know about the time, but she was married sensibly in a coat and skirt and chiffon blouse to a young English engineer she had landed in the boarding house at Kings Cross, where he, just being down from the Newnes Valley, was staying while he decided what to do next. My mother, against the competition of the daughters of the house—blondes all, and fine figures of women—won my father by pretending to let him teach her chess (she spending her savings on private lessons from a chess-master), and my father said he had never met a more intelligent pupil in his life. Oh Lord, she was immoral! I can never remember her playing a single game of chess in all the time I knew her. Certainly not, she said, it was the most boring game on earth.

They moved romantically from the city to the coastal town where they lived until my father's death, and for years it must have been a golden idyll. My father had a fine set of machines to tinker with at his place of employment, and there was a great sweep of ocean at their doorstep for swimming and fishing, and the lovely hills for strolling and Saturday shooting, and my father bought for her pleasure as well as his own a secondhand schooner which they refurbished at the weekends. And she planted vines and shrubs to hide the little cottage, which was only temporary, of course. Next year, if they could sell the schooner for a decent profit, they would have a good scout around for something roomier, where she could display her pretty linen and lace and china, and scrap the old deal furniture they had only bought to Make Do.

I wonder how long it took her to realise that she was stuck. She didn't have children for six years, and in the meantime life was pleasant enough, although she couldn't go on fishing expeditions any more, and found herself spending her weekends entertaining the wives of my father's fishermen friends. And then my father heard of a better schooner and sailed his up to Port Jackson to get it, and was in such a hurry to get home to show it off that he forgot to insure it, and they were caught in a terrible storm and the schooner sank. And now there was no money any more for houses. I wonder whether she upbraided him, or threatened to leave him with storms of indignant tears, or was she just so thankful that he had made it to shore safely that she held back—at least until another day?

I only remember her really from the time of the last photograph, although I have little glimmerings before and beautiful sharp little pictures of picnics on the beach. That last photograph has been retouched, but it doesn't matter, to anyone excepting me, and I remember that her face was crumpled and sagging with neglect, seamed with worry lines, and her fine silver hair floated in wild wisps, like a hobgoblin, which indeed she was.

By this time she had transferred all her dreams and ambitions to her children, and spent most of her time, while scurrying out to the clothesline, wrestling with the copper-stick, weeding the back vegetable rows (to save on the greengrocer), or treadling away at the old sewing machine, or elaborating our glorious futures. We understood quite clearly that we would never have to shin down sheets to make a getaway. If we didn't go we'd be pushed.

But when she was watching the sea her face was different, calm and ardent, and sometimes at night, very late, I could hear her scribbling away with a scratching pen, writing more poetry to be crumpled up and shoved into the fire, and once I saw her (having heard a commotion in the kitchen and poked my head around the door) stamping on a dress she had been making until three in the morning and kicking it around and around the kitchen.

I wonder, all in all, if she had a happy life. Whether the Yang and the Yin balanced out finally. She was a little bit of a selfconscious martyr sometimes, but never in an accusing way. Oblique, rather, and flurried and flustered, as if she really didn't want us to worry about it.

But she was never less than ardent (which is such a good word for her), and loving and kind. And I think these three photographs merge into one eventually. She was the same person all the time.

On Not Answering Letters

On the subject of letters I've had a couple of very plaintive little ones within these last two weeks. Gently reproachful. Puzzled, even. They go something like this:

'I wrote to you on such and such a date about such and such a matter, but since I have not had a reply must suppose that the letter went astray.'

There is no need to suppose anything of the sort. I'll take a bet it is on my desk now, somewhere in one of three stacks, each equally mountainous and weighed down respectively by a set of goats' bells, a river pebble, and a rusty bolt from the buggy of the Kelly family.

On the corner of every letter in the first stack is scrawled firmly: 'Answer'. On the corner of every letter in the second stack is scrawled—less firmly—'Try to Answer'. And on the corner of every letter in the third stack is scrawled absolutely nothing. Even my optimism won't carry me that far. Because if, as is being borne in on me quite inexorably, I haven't got Buckley's of even reducing the first stack (more being added to it each day), let alone rolling up my sleeves and whaling into the second stack (which is actually the most interesting stack because not one of the letters is begging specific questions or asking for information or advice or issuing invitations to speak at this luncheon or that or to open festivals and fêtes or to address meetings, but just extremely interesting letters from extremely interesting people whom I would love to answer: I can't get near that lot), then what on earth am I to do about the third stack?

Burn it? I can't. If all those people took the trouble to write to me a letter of commendation or praise—or censure, if it comes to that—they deserve the courtesy of a reply. Theoretically, that is. But the credibility gap widens daily. I am like a politician making promises to myself with my tongue in my own cheek. Tomorrow, I say. Tomorrow. Phooey. Tomorrow there'll be more.

Why do I not employ a secretary? Because, upon my word of honour, I cannot afford one. Besides, there are very few of my letters that could be answered by a secretary. The invitations, perhaps, but what could a secretary write to the enchanting old lady who is saving a crooked sixpence for my daughter's wedding, or to the whimsically contentious young one who has thrown down a gage to me on prior possession of John Donne? She says he wrote 'Busy Old Fool' for her, and I say he wrote 'Busy Old Fool' for me. Or to the lady who also owns a cat called Jeoffrey, named from the very same very obscure poem by Christopher Smart. Or to the letters filled with personal and family reminiscence, valuable human and historical stuff, worth exploring further. Or to the senders of manuscripts and poems asking for comment and advice (I feel terribly guilty about those: I try, but reading manuscripts takes time and extreme concentration).

The point being that I *love* my letters. I can't get out to the mailbox fast enough in the mornings to see what the day's bag is. The only way a writer can judge the depth or degree of his communication is by the response it evokes. It's like an exciting conversation. I say this. You say, yes but. And ideally we should be off, thrust and parry, poste and riposte. But not even D'Artagnan could thrust and parry with quite so many people at once. The very thought is exhausting.

I even like *writing* letters. At least I used to. I used to fancy myself rather as an eighteenth century lady of wit and charm and negligible domestic duties seated at a silk-polished escritoire with lots and lots of cunning pigeonholes and secret drawers and sticks of sealing wax and intricate seals and a finely wrought sandbox and a jar of quill pens and a single rose in a fine glass vase, and my taffeta sleeves rustling secretively as I scribbled scribbled scribbled delicious confidences and spicy observations to the wittiest and wickedest people (taking great care, of course, to make a fair copy of each letter in my own journal in case my *bons mots* should be lost to posterity).

Oh, but that is a far cry to the set of goats' bells and the river pebble and Kelly's bolt.

I am trying to remember how long it is since I wrote a letter to one of my friends abroad. A year? Eighteen months? Something like that. Through lack of communication they have been metamorphosised (is that a word?) into Other Worlders. When I try to imagine them I find I am making them up, piece by piece, quite laboriously. Actually, they don't exist at all.

I am not being flippant, or grizzling about all this, but in fact any freelance writer has quite a considerable amount of secretarial work to do on his own account. I have a filing cabinet which I am forced to keep in order every day or I would never know to what I am committed or who paid me for what or what might be deductible when the tax man cometh. I have a receipt file and I have a bill file and a bank file and a contract file and two dozen other files as well, and I have a diary for deadlines and a Teledex that has to be kept scrupulously up to date. I have a filing system for carbon copies and another for tear sheets. All this takes more than five minutes out of every day, and is boring to boot.

Come to think of it, most of my writer friends are, and have been, men. And they always have devoted and efficient wives who look after all that bit for them and put fresh flowers on their desks as well and call them for meals. I do think that if the wife of a writer is a writer herself she should be allowed a wife too. Just a little one. No, I'm not becoming a perverted and nasty old lady. I would just like to be free to get on with my business. Which is writing.

Because I am a housewife like any other. I do have a cleaning lady twice a week but that is the extent of my domestic help. And houses, as any woman knows, don't run themselves. If there are to be meals the meals must be planned for, shopped for, prepared, cooked, and cleaned up after. If there are to be clean clothes in the closets the clothes must be washed and ironed. If the bed linen is to be changed somebody has to change it. Also, one cannot have a family and pretend they don't exist. They do, imperiously and demandingly, each with his own problems and his own particular claims for attention. And I cannot sell them short for a heap of mail, no matter how fascinating the mail is. That's for career ladies, of whom I am not one.

If I could take one whole day off every week I could clear it all up and keep it clear. But I cannot afford one whole day a week. Nor even half a day a week. And if I had a whole day free each week there are so many things I would like to do, like taking a ferry ride, or going to the zoo, or sitting on the beach with a book, or browsing through bookshops and boutiques, or stripping down my sitting room chairs, or covering cushions, or planting more trees, or just visiting a friend.

However, writing this I have made one resolution. Today I will go through those piles and fish out all the invitations and at least have them off my conscience.

But the next time any of you are puzzling, pen poised, about how to fill up the requisite two pages of duty letter to parents or grandparents or godparents or aged aunts, will you think of this poor Sisyphus, eternally rolling her paper ball uphill?

Only, I would hate it if you stopped writing to me.

Bewildered on the Bourse

'Bourse', says my dictionary, is a 'name given to the place, in foreign countries, corresponding to our (Stock) Exchange, where merchants and financiers meet to transact business'. It also says something of the low Latin root of the word, meaning 'hide (stripped off and tanned)'.

There now. I'd always imagined that the Bourse was one single particular street somewhere, cobbled, with solemn old buildings of rosy brick and curved white plaster mouldings, and all lit with the calm light that old prints have.

I'd never thought exactly where this street might be. My sense of geography at the best is shaky and at the worst utterly baffling to my family and friends, who cannot understand why I persist in locating Spain on top of France, or get so terribly confused about ports of call on sea voyages. So I had never been so bold as to assign my Bourse a particular city or even a particular country, unlike the Rialto, of which I have an actual photograph with myself under a striped umbrella drinking something out of a long glass and looking pensive, possibly because I had just been through a very tiresome hour persuading a banking gentleman that an Australian travellers' cheque was valid money. The Rialto had let me down. 'You'd do better on the Bourse,' I was probably saying to myself.

I have been moved to pinpoint the Bourse more exactly by the current world crisis in finance. What with trembling francs and tottering pounds and stubborn marks and dithering financiers and incomprehensible economists, it is disappointing to me to have my solid and dignified Bourse, so satisfying to the imagination, reduced to hide stripped off and tanned, or just any old foreign stock exchange. Because I've been to one of those (stock exchanges, I mean) and came away convinced that everybody inside was mad. I'd had some sort of crazy notion that if it were only *explained* to me I would be able to sort bulls from bears as well as the next one and even come to some sort of simple understanding of the real nature of money, which is quite as mysterious to me as geography, in spite of the fact that I need money more than I need geography and have found that the heedless use of the one has more far-reaching consequences than the insouciant use of the other.

I still don't know what money is, apart from being the root of all evil, as some pious folks would have us believe, or not being everything, as others say more moderately. Secrecy and shame and guilt hang around it, and furtiveness, either through not having enough of it, or through not wanting to reveal what an amount of it one's got.

'Money,' wrote the economist Ralph G. Hawtrey, 'is one of those concepts which, like a teaspoon or an umbrella, but unlike an earthquake or a buttercup, are definable primarily by the use or purpose which they serve.' Further, the *Encyclopaedia Brittanica* states firmly that 'money is anything'.

Well, if that's the closest the experts can get, it's no wonder that currencies reel and tremble and shake and flounder about, let alone poor bemused people like me, who still can't grasp the principles of the gold standard or Fort Knox or why all those ingots have to be shuttled around from vault to vault. How do we know the ingots are gold, anyway? They might be bars of salt or peanut toffee or sawn-up railway sleepers for all anybody is going to tell us. Stranger things have been used as money before this, sheep and oxen and elephants and skulls, pigs and palm nuts, feathers, cowrie shells, handfuls of nails, gunpowder, slaves, serfs, or those colossal millstones that were used by the islanders of Yap as negotiable lolly. (I am very proud of knowing that Yap is in the South Pacific, although I have never met a Yappese, and do not know if millstones are fluctuating these days or devalued or holding steady or out of circulation altogether.)

Anyway, millstones don't seem to be any sillier than those bundles and bundles of dirty crumpled paper that used to pass as a foreign concept of money. How gingerly and unconfidently one handled it, representing as it did thousands and tens of thousands and hundreds of thousands of monetary units—in other words, two cups of coffee, a tip for the waiter, a museum catalogue, and half a dozen coloured postcards. And which traveller has not eventually been stuck with pockets or purses full of leftover lire, gulden, drachmas, dinars, escudos, roubles, shekels, taels, yen, or even a stray zloty or two? (I bought some leftover drachmas once from a traveller in London, only to find when I tried to use the stuff in Greece that all the noughts had been dropped from all the currency in the meantime.)

The one thing I know about money is that it sticks to some and not to others, by what principle of monstrous inequality I don't know. Contrary to Scott Fitzgerald's profound conviction, I've never found the rich to be noticeably different from the rest of us. A Rothschild I knew, who might justifiably have indulged in a bit of swank, actually lived in a Thames-side pad (sparsely furnished at that) at Whitechapel, and often seemed hard-up for spending lolly. Millionaires, at least the ones I've met, have turned out on acquaintance to be about as amiable or dim as lesser beings, although perhaps they went in for wives rather more extensively than most men can afford to do, and were either meaner or more ostentatious about tipping (whichever way was bound to be wrong, as one of them rather sadly pointed out to me: he was very sensitive about it).

And yet they must be different, because they have the stuff and I don't. Also, they keep the stuff and I can't. The knack must lie in knowing how many rupees go to the krone from day to day or hour to hour, or bolivars to the rial, and where the ingots are stacked this week and what is happening on the Bourse. It seems a terribly risky game to play, particularly at the moment when you can't put your trust in any sort of money because it's likely to turn into something else entirely by tomorrow.

I suspect they are wisest (if not presently richest) who put their faith neither in paper nor banks but gold pieces in their socks stowed under the floorboards, or well-set skulls piled in the loft, or pigs or elephants or bundles of feathers or jawbones or herds of yak or bricks and mortar or diamonds or olive groves or palm nuts or anything else evidently tangible and negotiable. Millstones, even, if you happen to be Yappese and millstones are steady.

Then you needn't fret yourself about the precise location of the Bourse nor whatever madness is happening there with francs and marks and dollars and levs. You'll have a little something with which to barter when all that paper stuff collapses. Even something with which to ornament yourself. We're bound to get back to barter and ornament sooner or later. Sooner, I hope. I will feel much safer.

Death by Misadventure

Criminal abortion is indeed a grave and terrible subject, and all responsible adults must be glad that, in the press and on television, it is again under discussion. Discussion is good. Indignation is good. Anger is good. Nothing yet was ever accomplished by resignation, no set of circumstances ever bettered by the willingness to submit to it or put up with it.

The Victorian police surgeon, Dr John Birrell, has estimated the annual total of criminal abortions in Australia at 90 000 and has stated his belief that one conception in every five is terminated in this way. It is therefore a practice so general and widespread that it must be regarded as just one of the risks implicit in woman's situation.

It is a criminal act. But who is the criminal? The woman who seeks deliverance from the callous demands of nature, the doctor who helps her from compassion, or uses her dilemma for gain, or the law which makes a relatively simple operation clandestine and therefore open to abuse?

Enforced maternity brings into the world wretched, unwanted infants. All the world now accepts the necessity for contraception in some form. The fact that all the world does not accept the necessity for abortion rests on a dubious moral point, and if such a morality condemns women to shame, degradation, secrecy, sterility, and sometimes death, what is one to think of it?

Human life is sacred, says morality, and fortified by this argument, proceeds to sacrifice the life of the mother to the life of the unwanted foetus.

Abortion must be necessary if for no other reason than that so many women undergo it in such appalling circumstances.

That the circumstances are so appalling is the fault of the law. In countries where abortion is legal, it is under control, and standards of medical skill, hygiene and after-care can be maintained to safeguard the health of the unfortunate woman who has surely suffered enough in making her terrible decision. For I do not believe that women make this decision lightly or callously. It is for most a traumatic experience, and that mental anguish should be heightened by shame and humiliation as well as physical anguish turns what is already an ordeal into a punishment.

A punishment for what?

It is interesting to note that the majority of abortions are performed, not on young girls 'in trouble', but on married women who are already mothers, who love their children, and wish to restrict their families for the family's benefit, in accordance with accepted modern social teaching which urges parents to plan their families and sets up birth control clinics to the end that unwanted children should *not* be born. Even with advanced forms of contraception complete safety is still uncertain and accidents—as the town gossips used to say with such pleasurable smirks—happen in the best-regulated families. So the wife and mother, the pillar of her home and the respected member of the community, becomes a potential criminal because she has been 'caught'.

If she is in a good social and financial position she will find it relatively easy, crime or no crime, to find expert assistance. Of course at a price. And a price which has nothing to do with the actual expense of the operation, but might be regarded more as 'risk-money' on the doctor's part (at the best), or as extortion by the patient (at the worst). Fortune favours the privileged as always. But even at her most privileged a woman seeking an abortion is a suppliant, and under the best possible conditions the operation is still performed secretly, furtively, in complicity, and as a moral and legal transgression.

If her financial position is not good she will find it more difficult, she will need to beg and cringe more abjectly, she will have to turn to people of more dubious qualifications, be denied the boon of anaesthetic, suffer excruciating pain, risk internal injuries, and be bundled out into the street immediately afterwards as something not only undesirable but positively dangerous. If she has the support of her husband she will find even this severe torture more bearable than having an unwanted child.

Then how much more pitiable is the plight of the unmarried girl who, having made a 'mistake', must at all costs conceal it from her employer, family, friends, teachers, or become an object of pity or scorn. Unmarried mothers are still, to our abiding shame, the subjects of lewd jokes and smoke-room sniggering.

If she has a lover he might marry her. More often than not he urges her to 'get rid of it'. The relationship may have been casual and ended before she was aware of her pregnancy. In these days of sexual licence she may not even know who the father is.

She might, if she is lucky, be taken under the protection of the lover who will find out an address and pay for the operation. She might have an experienced girlfriend who knows where to go. More often than not, even now, she is most dreadfully alone, and in her terror and ignorance lets weeks and even months go by or resorts to quack pills, making the abortion finally more dangerous and painful than it need have been and increasing the risk of serious illness, sterility, and even death. And girls still commit suicide rather than become unmarried mothers.

One thing is certain. No repressive legislation will prevent women terminating pregnancies they do not want. Surely it is in the best and truest interests of society to accept this, as it has been accepted in so many other countries already, where abortion is no longer considered a crime but a social safeguard, carried out under strict controls, safely, and without stigma, when circumstances warrant it.

This is not to belittle the value of human life, but to dignify it.

For surely it is a little ironic for the law to be so nice about the rights of an unwanted embryo and at the same time put the lives of twenty-year-olds into a lottery barrel?

A Pride of Lions?

I was asked to write something about Australian men. But nobody has specified precisely what sort of Australian men I am to write about. And they do come these days in all sorts of shapes and sizes and degrees of confidence and sophistication and weights of chins and bellies and rumps.

Actually I do think Australian men are getting a bit rumpy in this generation. That's not really a criticism, only an observation. I don't object to solid hindquarters on either men or women. Or horses if it comes to that. Sculptural, in a way. Those great white rippling Percherons ploughing through the poppies in fragrant French fields.

Well then, since I am Australian born (and bred, I suppose, if you can call my rather zany upbringing breeding: although my father did say we all had fine wrists and ankles and therefore might class ourselves as thoroughbreds; he did loathe women who were, as he said, 'beef to the heels like bull-calves') obviously I did my first practising on Australian men. There was nothing else to practise on in a small Australian country town.

And they were young quarry workers and farm labourers and a few taxi-drivers cruising down the coast for Sunday larks (our town had the reputation for the prettiest girls on the Illawarra coast) and a stray commercial traveller or two. Or even three, if I am to be honest. And very worldly the commercials seemed too, at the time.

In fact, I suppose, I practised on anything handy in pants. From the moment I could distinguish. And I think I distinguished quite early.

But of course I had no standards of comparison then, apart from literary ones (Byron and Marvell and Lovelace and Keats and Shelley and that lot, and the gloomier and more thrilling Russians: Raskolnikov sent me quite wild), and current film stars of whom, perversely, I romantically preferred Conrad Veidt ('there's a lighthouse shines across the bay'), and Peter Lorre and Claude Rains, when all the other girls were swooning for Robert Taylor. I didn't tell the other girls, naturally.

But my very first romantic attachment was to twins who were called—I know that I will never be believed—Honk and Donk. They used to bring me sticky sweets when I was eight and endeavour to lure me down into the aloe cubby we had on the beach. And after Honk and Donk came the Bawny Crab (I swear the name is true) who died, poor boy, of the lockjaw, contracted while pinching the obligatory number of little brown eggs for me through the rusted wire of his mother's hen coop. And then there was Tom Fly (whose sister was called Flossie Dog), and Geik and Splonge and Googles. And Dai, who was of Welsh parentage and nicked lots and lots of chocolates and tinned peaches from his father's grocery shop. And Eric, who had been to America and showered me with a fortune in cent pieces and all his scout badges.

And writing this I wonder what sort of Australian men they grew up to be (excepting the Bawny Crab, who didn't get to be grown up). They were country boys of working class parentage and mixed ancestry—their fathers were Yorkshiremen and Derbyshiremen and Welshmen and Cornishmen and men from Ireland and Scotland—but my father was a Derbyshire man too, so it didn't seem strange. They were loutish lumpish boys, I suppose, with big soft ears and great mottled hands, clumsy and slow, and they had bad teeth and no education and inarticulate yearnings towards grace and beauty and stifled ambitions towards they didn't know what and no prospects whatever excepting the quarries or the farms or the steel mills or, if they were clever enough, a place in a bank or behind a grocery counter or on a butcher's cart or in the post office, and a war which they couldn't have predicted but which liberated so many of them into travel and romance and adventure and more intoxicating thought-patterns than they could have dreamed of then. Even in the aloe cubby. I have an idea that wars—and I am against them—hold some sort of clue to Australian men.

They will all be middle-aged now, and the fathers of families, and good members in standing of the Leagues Club or the RSL. They will be Sunday fishermen and weekend gardeners, members of the shire council, and their names will have been reverted from the wild and whimsical nomenclature of childhood—Honk and Donk and Geik and Splonge—to the staider names of baptism. Contracted, naturally, in the Australian way. Keith and Alan and Bruce and Harry and Vince and Cec and Dave and Christy, and they will have been married comfortably and complacently for twenty years or more to the girls called Molly and Valda and Isobel and Joycey and Sylvia and Thelly and Audrey and Gwen, and they will all have modest cars and modest bank accounts and modest houses jam-packed with plastic and modest dreams for their children, so much better educated than they were. Or maybe they have raging dreams for their children, who are bound to let them down.

Now, I may be quite wrong about this, but I don't think there was a Sir Lancelot in the whole bunch. Or even a potential Sir Lancelot. Tirra lirra never sounded, however muffled, by the rank and reedy creek that flowed sluggishly beneath my splintered window, although I listened for it desperately enough and performed prodigies of imagination in trying to transform coarse country adolescents into parfait gentil knights.

I know it is not wise to generalise—it may even be impertinent—but I don't think Australian men are good at the Sir Lancelot bit. A girl needs a phoney Hungarian count for that, or a Jewish poet with eyes like ripe olives, or practically any cosmopolitan conman with a bit of the real flair for the game.

It is a flair, after all. Because what Australian men, however worthy, seem to lack is any real sense of the romantic or the erotic. As a game, I mean. As that delicious knowledge of a preordained conspiracy between the sexes that European men are born with. And I don't mean bottom-pinching either, but something much more subtle—the whatever something that enables a short, bald, tubby French boulevardier to turn on one sweet slow heavy glance in passing and make the dowdiest middle-aged English spinster walk like a young queen, nonchalantly tossing her hair.

It is a very vibrant and very sensuous quality, a very melting quality, and I like it rather much myself. Because above all it is completely confident.

I think I might be beginning to generalise after all, and that is presumptuous on my part, but if I could just be allowed to sneak in one generalisation I do believe that Australian men are terribly unconfident about their own masculinity. The Lord knows why. But they seem to be so sensitive of their virility that they must constantly prove it. Not to their women, however, but to their drinking and surfing and sailing mates, their weekend mates with whom they engage in constant competition—of physical strength, mighty oaths, beer-swilling capacity, and Arabian Nights tales of erotic conquest. They protest too much.

Just on observation I would believe that their mistresses are mechanical ones—boats and cars and lawnmowers and handymen's toolkits—on which they can lavish (and do) passions that their wives never knew existed. To watch them tinkering with mechanical innards on a blithe Sunday morning is to avert one's eyes hastily.

I was just thinking in passing that if you can have collectives like a cry of players and a gaggle of geese and a flock of martlets and a flush of roses and a pride of lions and a school of barramundi and a boil of prawns, what collective could you apply to Australian men? A boast of Australian men? A swagger of them?

Now, my great and glorious period of Australian men was in wartime, when it was fairly simple to transform them into romantics. Lancelots abounded, vowing vows and throwing down gages and begging for hair ribbons to wear over their hearts. Australian men were still lean and slouchy and brown in those days (poor damn Depression kids that they were) and under the emotional stress of partings came up with the occasional poetry of inarticulate men, poignant beyond telling. Tirra lirra rang like a tocsin through those years, and even such a glutton as I was glutted with eternal vows and perfect red roses and locks of sandy hair and regimental numbers and sets of airforce wings and champagne corks and the Song of Songs. And silver chains for my thoroughbred ankles.

Well if they were capable of that sort of abandonment then, they must be capable of it now. Perhaps it is the women who are at fault. I don't like to suggest that, having feminist leanings myself.

And of course I know nothing, or next to nothing, about the new generation of Australian men. They may be Lancelots all. I've been married to one of the old breed, lean and slouchy and brown, for more years than I need to confess, and we have three nice children and are paying off a nice house and I don't think I would know quite how to react if you put me back on the boulevardes again, or into the aloe cubby with Honk or Donk, or sighing out of my splintered window for tirra lirra by the rank and weedy creek.

Actually I think men are gorgeous. I adore them, and couldn't bear to be deprived of one around. My mother used to say, wickedly I thought, that they were only forked radishes anyway, but I will settle for that, as long as they sing tirra lirra occasionally. Whatever nationality they are.

And when I am a little old lady in lavender lace I will say with absolute certitude and Dorothy Parker: 'There was never more fun than a man.'

I Shall Not Want

Well, now we're over that again and can tune down our oscillating metabolisms, say from full panic to only normal panic, at least until next week anyway.

I do hope that the celebration was worth the preliminary panic after all, and all the thought and organisation and planning and headaches and hangovers, and that the cleaning up isn't too formidable, and that all the people who said they weren't going to bother this year changed their minds at the last minute and bothered as frenetically as anybody else. They usually do.

And now that we've had the candles and carols and gifts and feasting and family reunions, and we've been surprised all over again to find ourselves gushing goodwill in spite of everything we said beforehand, and will no doubt say again, we should all be feeling—if not actually in a state of grace—at least a little more benevolently disposed towards the mad sad erratic human race to which we so surprisingly belong. There might be something to it after all. A lot of quite extraordinary people have thought so, including Jesus Christ.

Admittedly we did not choose our human condition, but since we are landed with it we might as well be loyal to it, just in case there is more value to this peculiar experiment in existence than often appears.

But being loyal to human existence means being loyal to all of it, and of course it is difficult for us who exist in a more or less privileged mode to recognise or accept the value of human existence that is so degraded and demoralised as to scarcely seem human at all. The Biafrans, for instance, could be rejects in the experiment, as could most of the peoples of Asia, of India, of Latin America, or any other of the two-thirds of the human company that look like being discards for want of sustenance. No peace or goodwill for them, or turkey-and-pud either.

Even if some of them can summon the incredible will that must be necessary to want to cling to life under such appalling conditions they are unlikely ever to realise their human potential of creativeness, humour, laughter, love, generosity—those best parts of our human dole that somehow make up for the rest and even, if only occasionally and unexpectedly, give us an intimation that we might yet be capable of being nicer creatures than we had supposed.

Most of us felt something of this yesterday, and today we're still trailing a few wisps of our better and more generous natures. Or if we're not we ought to be.

Traditionally this is the day of collection boxes, when we are supposed to distribute gratuities to the people who have served us obligingly through the year—the postman and milkman and the garbage collectors and those other collectors who are dignified now, I think, by the title of sanitary workers and perhaps don't leave a Christmas poem the way they used to do. But if indeed these people have been obliging through the year (and there are many who would quarrel with that) we've probably distributed our gratuities already: besides, they're all off duty today, maybe polishing up their smart new cars or lolling on the patio.

Still, tradition is tradition, and before there ever was a Boxing Day, or a postman either, alms-giving was an obligation. In medieval England every house had its alms-scuttle for donations to the needy, every traveller of degree carried an alms-coffer as part of his luggage, every religious institution had its almshouse attached, and wealthy households employed a full-time almoner to supervise the distribution of its considerable charity.

Perhaps they had more faith in the possibilities of the human condition and the value of it than we do now. Certainly they were more religious, and considered charity as part of their Christian duty. There was no condescension or patronage in the giving, and no shame in the taking. The proper spirit was humility on both sides, and if a bit of graft crept in, or penitential bargaining with the Lord (as with King John, who used to compound for breaking rules of abstinence and fasting by feeding hundreds of the poor at a time), Christian duty was still Christian duty, and it was the duty of everyone to contribute whatever he could towards the feeding of the hungry and the clothing of the naked and the relief of the distressed. Your fellow man was your fellow man and nobody questioned it.

Oh dear. But the scale of human misery was probably so much easier to comprehend then than it is now, when what most of us feel in the face of our unfortunate fellow men is only utter helplessness.

It would be simple if we could take the broken meats from our Christmas tables as they did then, or empty the refrigerators bursting with leftovers that are going to be a bore to the most ingenious housewife before she's through serving them up again and again some different way, and distribute them personally, or through an almoner, to the hungry of the world. I am sure every decent person would do so gladly.

There are still some rare ones who have managed to retain this sense of personal involvement with the needy and the hungry and the oppressed, but usually they've done it by giving their whole lives to it, and that's beyond most of us. We might wish to be as good as that but we know very well we're not, and we've got our own lives to live anyway. Besides, our stomachs turn up so easily, even at newspaper photographs of the diseased and the deformed and the mutilated: we could never endure a confrontation with the real thing.

So what we've got left is only money, impersonal and unsatisfactory, but necessary to our contemporary almoners—the relief organisations—if they are to get on with their dedicated work of feeding the hungry and clothing the naked and relieving the distressed. I know that everybody has spent too much already, but I believe that most of us could tip up the alms-scuttle and still find something there to put in an envelope and send to the Freedom from Hunger Campaign or the Save the Children Fund to help those splendid almoners to get on with it.

And not penitentially, or to compound for self-indulgence and gluttony, or even in the name of charity, which is a beautiful word sadly debased, but in common justice.

If we believe in human existence, that is. We have to be loyal to all of it and have faith in the experiment, which might, after all, have more value than is presently evident.

The Rule of the Olds

I am an Old. I didn't know about it until quite recently and I find it quite distressing. I mean, I've never been an Old before, nor, if I had thought about it, which I didn't, would I have considered it conceivable that I should be so labelled. I've never known such a place for pinning labels on people. You're not a Young, lady, so you must be an Old. Go buy yourself a fancy hat and a pair of winkle-pickers (so becoming to the Old legs) and make up a bridge four and join a women's club of an educational nature, take up a charity, put on a white nanny's uniform and play bowls.

I don't think I will mind so much being really old. Old age carries authority and can be terrifically stylish. Colette could paint the sun and the moon on her raddled old face and get away with it, that Gothic belle Sitwell went in for fancy dress and many jewels and firmly ordered martinis for elevenses, and I have always admired the other Gothic lady, the Baroness Blixen, who got to look like a heathen idol in her old age, and subsisted entirely on oysters, fresh asparagus, wild strawberries, and the finest Moselle wines. Why not? For myself I fancy a red wig and a parrot and a silver-topped cane and a fund of risqué stories with which to regale my grandchildren, who are bound to adore me.

But what really distresses me most about being an Old here, now, in Australia, is that I just might, quite inadvertently, be identified with the bigots, the moralists, the reactionaries, the disapprovers of the Youngs. The Olds who rule, who instruct, who admonish, who warn, who exhort and preach and censor.

The Olds who must envy the Youngs with a bitter corrosive envy to go to such lengths of prurience and authoritarianism.

Unfortunately there seem to be so many of them in this country, and so much more firmly entrenched and inflexible than anywhere else I can think of. They are parents and often teachers, they fill the pubs and the clubs and the shire councils, they hold high public offices, they wield the big stick of authority. And they know best. Because they're Olds.

I sometimes think they are rather like the dinosaurs, surely the most stable society the earth has ever known, a society so resistant or impervious to change that they refused absolutely to go even one little mutation towards adapting to it, and died out, sluggishly and torpidly, in the creeping cold they had been too inflexible to acknowledge, saying, no doubt, in outrage and disbelief and dinosaur language: 'Whoever would have thought it?' Or maybe nature was just sick of them.

Not that there is much fun in being an Old. It's one of nature's nastiest practical jokes. (I wonder if it was any fun being a dinosaur?) Olds have coronaries and ulcers and dyspepsia and rheumatism and hernias and haemorrhoids and hysterectomies. And bad-tempered livers. Olds (it's one of the signs of becoming one) begin listening fearfully and compulsively to the working of those interior organs that control their very thoughts, absorbing, secreting, expanding, contracting, quivering and pumping and sucking and blowing ... the whole sluggish, viscous, wave-like motion of life on which they (and I too, of course) are floated inexorably towards the ropy hands, the hairless freckled skull, the abdominal itch, the stringy blotched wattles, the skinny shanks, the grinning set of clackers, and the dull and plodding reasoning that passes as Olds' wisdom.

Cyril Connolly once said that inside every fat man there was a thin one screaming to be let out. Perhaps inside every Old there is a Young, screaming too. For a second chance at it. Alas, there never was but one. That's the joke.

In the whirlwind climate of change we live in I sometimes think that Olds are really migrants in the Youngs' territory, the Youngs having been born in it and not knowing any other. It is a territory where the only valid passport for the migrant Old is tolerance and an attempt, however groping, however muddled, towards understanding the queer tribal customs of the natives. And of course no communication is possible without at least a smattering of the colloquial language. 'Flog 'em!' and 'Run over the bastards!' belong to an outdated phrase-book, and do nothing to establish goodwill. In fact, such nineteenth-century phrases are more likely to bring about active hostility.

Not that I think those little punks are always right. Sometimes, mercifully, they are terribly, devastatingly, wrong. Sometimes they are irritating beyond endurance. Sometimes, like any other migrant in a foreign country, an Old can become so bewildered he can despair of ever reaching even the glimmer of understanding.

But what the Youngs have is time on their side—if the virtuous Olds don't exterminate them first, and everybody else too. Time to adjust their balances and their values, time to learn, time to experiment, even time to devise a new set of rules to replace the old rules, the Olds' rules, the rules that don't apply any more in this explosive, exploding world of shattered morality and fractured faith and all too bitterly plausible cynicism. Any game to be played has to have rules, but the Marquess of Queensberry is anachronistic on these sidelines.

The Youngs, I do believe, even have time—if the Olds allow it them—to discover razors and toothbrushes and soap and the pleasures of hot water.

And they have all that energy, energy to burn, energy to spare, energy to squander, energy to create. Create what? Good or evil? One has to make a blind act of faith here, they are so strange and barbarous and beyond comprehension at times, this McLuhan generation.

I don't believe for a minute that it is possible for a migrant Old to become thoroughly acclimatised to the Youngs' culture patterns. The gap is too great. And there is something infinitely pathetic about an Old trying to pass as a native Young, like those desperate women who spend two days a week at the beauty parlour and put sticky tape between their brows at night to keep the fear-frown at bay and resolutely wear minis in spite of their knees and their knobbly shinbones, and the hearty males who risk rupture and worse by strenuous exercise, and the lonely terrified ones who expend all their energies going faster and faster to keep up with the trendy movements and the trendy jokes and the trendy gear until they fall down dizzy and defeated, like those old predators who tiredly litter the fashionable rocks of the Mediterranean, sans everything but their pale-blue Mediterranean gear and their laboriously acquired suntans. Poor old wrinkled pachyderms, come to their elephants' graveyard at last.

But those, of course, aren't the Olds that rule. The Olds that rule don't try to pass as Youngs. They have grown thick defensive skins over the Youngs they actually were once, the more easily, I suspect, to idealise themselves.

'When I was young,' they say. 'When I was young'... When they were young decency prevailed, and chastity, and obedience, and king and country, and short-back-and-sides, and children honoured their parents and were dutiful to their elders and accepted advice and sixpence a week odd-job money and braved the University of Hard Knocks to get where they are today, established pillars of society, powerful, secure, rigidly rooted in outmoded and inapplicable concepts, stern guardians of public taste and public morals. Knowing best. And like the English of another generation, refusing absolutely to learn a word of the native tongue. It is the business of the dirty foreigner to learn ours.

'Dirty' is one of their favourite censures. Dirty, immoral, beat, Vietnik, peacenik, quasi and pseudo, irresponsible lunatic fringe, ratbag, hippy, druggy, junky, disruptive minority, tool in the hands of outside influences, feckless, rootless, heedless, improvident.

To be dismissed with a spiteful quip as not quite human. Or to be punished severely for the crime of being young in the most frightening time ever to be young in. 'Flog 'em!' 'Run over the bastards!' Spy on them, pimp on them, club them, fine them, gaol them, conscript them. How dare they not accept what the Olds, knowing best, have decided is good for them? How dare they ask questions? Think for themselves? How dare they be disrespectful of authority?

How dare they be young in the time of their own youth, which just happens to coincide with complete social upheaval?

No, I don't like rape packs either. Or gang bangs. Or hoodlums or thugs or vandals. The casualties, the social cripples, lacking the will and the wit to keep up with the terrifying acceleration of knowledge and skills and ideas. The bewildered dullards who see only the permissiveness and not the challenge. The human dropouts pitiably divested of any identity and lacking adequate mental equipment to keep up the required fierce pace for successful survival, informed by nothing but the mass media of sensationalism where sin and sex are rewarded if they're fashionable enough and, if they're not, at least are newsworthy and more exciting than anything that happens at the milk bar. They're resentful all right, but I suspect they don't really know of what. Being casualties, perhaps. Being wounded. Being failures.

All casualties are nasty and messy and offensive. Once upon a time every small town had at least one village idiot.

I am an Old. I find it quite distressing, but must accept it with what grace I can muster. I must accept that I shall never again walk to the manner born in the territory of the Youngs. But since I don't want to subdue it, or conquer it, or devise repressive legislation against it, or rule it, I hope I will be allowed to walk freely as an interested foreign observer, though maybe a bewildered one sometimes. I might even be allowed to trade and barter. Experience for new ideas and a glimmer of understanding.

I have an idea that the ruling Olds are so frightened of the Youngs because the Youngs are the future, and the Olds know that they're not going to be there, knowing best. As a future it is at the moment dicey. The spiteful hidebound we-know-best Olds have seen to that. They may even yet blow the future into smithereens rather than miss out on it. I wouldn't put it past them.

I am an Old, true enough. But with a long exciting run for my money's worth, or my imagination's worth, or my talent's worth, and no desire to rule. Perhaps it is a symptom of being an Old that I think it is infinitely harder, in the present inclement climate of greed and repressiveness on the one hand and woeful human deprivation on the other, to be a Young, inheriting it.

On Being Alone with Oneself

Like anybody else who for twenty-four hours of every day is surrounded by—embroiled in, part of—an interdependent society like a family, I have sometimes muttered to myself, in exasperation or frustration or sheer weariness: 'Oh, how I wish they'd all go away and leave me alone.'

And so they did. Not, I hasten to add, in pique, or to teach me a lesson, but quite fortuitously and separately they all went away. And for the first time in exactly half my life I was quite quite alone, as I had so often longed to be, really alone for a whole week that was mine to do with as I chose.

My plans were not dependent upon the plans of anybody else, my meals were not dependent upon other people's appetites, preferences, appointments or comings and goings, and my moods were not dependent upon other people's uncertain temperaments. There was no involvement, no demand, no interruption, no whirlwind of movement, eddy of activity, chatter of voices, slamming of doors, blaring of radio, calling of queries, rattle of coffee cups, flaring of anger, no snatch of careless song, and no laughter.

They went away and silence rushed into the vacuum of their absence and filled my tall house to brimming.

At first I dabbled in it quite cautiously and tentatively, not being certain of my ability to maintain equilibrium in such a quantity of the stuff, for silence, whatever it is, is not buoyant: one sinks in it rather than rises. Some sort of spiritual water-wings seem to be necessary. My heartbeats were audible and even my thoughts too loud. I felt guilty and furtive and slightly out of control. Nefarious even. As though I had no right to ... to what? ... to be alone in my own house? Or just to be alone? I felt apprehensive, in imminent danger of discovery, but by whom or what I couldn't have said.

There was the telephone, of course. And friends dropping in. And going out to a party or dinner. And some necessary marketing. I was not in any way cut off from human contact. But the normal and familiar human contacts seemed in some peculiar way to have changed subtly—almost to have become artificial—and in them I had the most curious sense of exposure, as though I was play-acting at being myself and not doing it very well. And always, after the voices and the laughter and the last goodnights, I would close the door and the silence would stealthily expand again to fill in the echoing pockets, and I would be alone in it, listening, waiting, and filled with an indefinable excitement.

I thought, I am myself alone at last, and I can do anything I please. What pleased me was evidently quite childish. Like making my breakfast on hock and iced peaches, served to myself quite ceremoniously with flowers and Beethoven quartets and nobody except Jeoffrey the cat to see, and he wouldn't tell. And lying in the bath for an hour, trickling in fresh supplies of hot water and extravagant quantities of cologne, and then going back to my great brass bed in the middle of the morning (the brass bed spread with the best lace-trimmed sheets) with a novel and a plate of fruit too beautifully arranged to be eaten, just as the novel was not actually to be read, because I was too intent discovering the scene to myself in the mirror. With satisfaction.

But of course these childish indulgences palled. It is probably not my nature to loll in bed in the middle of the morning, desirable though such a practice has often appeared in the past. What was more to my taste was spending the middle hours of the night, the really nefarious hours that are always potent with limitless possibility, in my study, going through old manuscripts and notebooks and letters and photographs, or just sitting in the dramatic shadow outside the exciting circle of the work lamp, listening to my own thoughts with astonishment and sometimes dismay: it didn't seem to be myself thinking at all, but somebody else entirely. You just wait, I thought, until *she* hears what you've been up to. You'll cop it. And heard myself giggling defiantly.

Or in those hours I prowled from room to room very quietly, surprising things that had moved themselves from the places in which I had put them—an ashtray, a book, a jug, a shell. The house breathed and creaked and settled itself more comfortably on its foundations, not furtively, as it had done at first, but quite openly and confidently. Somewhere upstairs a door unlatched itself with a discreet click, a window chattered momentarily and was silent again. The refrigerator shuddered and hummed and there was a tune in it somewhere, and words, as there is in train wheels. The bathroom tap dripped with a sharp bright ping. The chimney shook down a little puff of soot and a card toppled slowly and significantly from the mantelpiece. I locked the doors and lit all the candles and felt mysterious and reckless and expectant, like a lady in a Gothic tale—the one who walked around in only her skeleton and all the family jewels.

I forgot to eat for twenty-four hours, and heard myself addressing Jeoffrey the cat at length and with excessive courtesy. Some mad story I told him, I don't know what exactly, but he seemed to appreciate it. I sat in front of the looking glass for an hour, staring at myself. I woke from a dream with tears on my face and there was no one to tell.

By the middle of the week the telephone tempted me almost unbearably—it wouldn't be giving in, would it, just to ring up somebody? Anybody. Or to turn the knob of the radio. Or even, because after all nobody would know, to switch on the television. Just for an hour? But I didn't. I had made no conscious pact with myself about the renunciation of these ordinary little props to the lonely, but I knew quite definitely that they were not allowed. Not this time, anyway. Not if I was to discover whatever it was. I stared at the telephone, begging it to ring. It lay stubbornly mute. It became a contest. Any other day, I thought wildly, the damn thing never stops. And finally, weakly, with sweat in my palms, I snatched it and gave in.

The house turned against me after that. Even while I was having that nice companionable chat on the telephone I'd known that it would. The high stool I was balancing on to reach the reserve tins of food in the top cupboard slipped from under me and I crashed most painfully. The sharpest knife cut my finger viciously. The big Portuguese basket deliberately spiked my leg. And I began turning all the lights on at night because I was scared. It wasn't at all nice to be alone any more.

They're all back again now, of course. Clattering and chattering and demanding and interrupting and involving me, and sometimes I wish they'd all go away and leave me alone. Because, next time ... Why do I feel so strangely that there was some mysterious marvellous opportunity in all that silence? That I missed.

Last of the Old?

I didn't write anything about Australia Day this year because it always seems such a damp squib of an occasion that it is better perhaps to let it fizzle out without notice or comment. More polite, anyway, to just pretend it isn't happening.

So it was interesting to find that, for the first time, Australia Day made quite a respectable bang this anniversary. Interesting and surprising. Because it was not, after all, the stately set piece of the First Fleeters and other Heritage Worshippers that attracted attention, but the rather acrid fumes that hung about over a whole series of sharp explosions of query. Who are we? What have we done? Where are we going? And why? The questions crackled with a new urgency which I, for one, found stimulating after all the years of soggy self-congratulation, pious platitudes and official smugness that used to be considered not only suitable, but necessary, for public utterance on Australia Day. Advance Australia Fair, and all that.

It seems to be a good time to ask questions. This is the last year of the most violent and disruptive decade the world has ever known—the seditious sixties, the suspenseful sixties, the subversive sixties, and finally the sordid sixties—and the last year before we Australians set out into the third century of possibility for a nation and a people, unique, distinct from every other people and nation on earth.

True we are still attached by an umbilical cord of habit and sentiment to old Mum England, but there is no real need to cut it since it is, in fact, withering away of itself. And that makes me remember that it is seventeen years ago today that the drums and tuckets sounded for a new young Queen and the dawn of a new Elizabethan age. And look what happened to that. Oh well, there was no foretelling then. The sixties were unimaginable. Just as well, perhaps. We might all have slashed our wrists. Or taken an overdose. Opted out. Got off.

I wonder if there is any foretelling now. About the looming seventies, I mean. A lot of the old breed will die off. Digger breed. Alf next door. Mum in winkle-pickers who never did have much of an education and waited all those years for her 7th Divvy bloke to come home. A fundamentally decent and kindly breed, unimaginative maybe and sometimes even dull, but with nothing perverse about them. And another breed will take over, a new breed who will not be able to remember back beyond the sixties. Come to think of it, who can now without an effort?

That damned decade of human confrontation over the gaps of our own silly human devising. Black against White. Haves against Have-nots. Ins against Outs. Humanists against Materialists. Hawks against Doves. Students against Authority. Authority against Dissent. Respectables against Irreverents. Olds against Youngs. Intellectuals against everything. Very angry it's been, very violent, very self-righteous, with everyone being holier than everyone else and getting themselves arrested to prove it or beating up someone or being beaten up or defiling telephone booths and railway carriages or killing savagely and without provocation or freaking out in despair. And getting around the moon where the world, they say, looks small, and all of a piece.

And through all this we Australians have gone on regurgitating: we are young yet; we have the most marvellous climate in the world; it's a great place to grow up in; we have a glorious heritage; we have a glorious future (like just around the corner).

I don't know that we're so young any more. Youngish perhaps, but old enough to stop making youth an excuse for our dreadful irresponsibility towards ourselves and our inheritors. Old enough to stop indulging ourselves in one long lazy hedonistic weekend that is not a reward for any real achievement but only an endless public holiday, self-decreed and honouring nothing—excepting our marvellous climate, perhaps, which is actually not marvellous at all, but brutal, savage, fickle and conducive of much skin cancer. Old enough to start doing things for ourselves, inventing things for ourselves, making things for ourselves, our own sort of things, I mean, and not bad copies of other people's things.

I don't know why one should be embarrassed at expressing some hint of idealism. Maybe because cynicism is easier, and of course more fashionable. But I don't see why it is not possible, now, to stop the sweet rot of hedonism and get back to breathing that high thin air of endeavour that is more bracing, really, and I believe would suit our constitutions better. It used to, anyway.

I don't see why we can't look after our aged and sick ungrudgingly, generously, and without that iniquitous and totally unnecessary means test. I don't see why we should accept poverty in this country at all. We ought to be outraged and ashamed that it exists. I don't see why we shouldn't have an education system that would be a model to the world and a guarantee for our own future instead of the shoddy, shabby, patched-up, creaking, clumsy structure that we put up with. I don't see why we can't call a halt to the vandalising of nature and begin conserving, intelligently, lovingly, and with a long-term plan. I don't see why we shouldn't be a proud people, and a creative people, and an original people, and an adventurous people, and a resourceful people. It's all at hand to do, and I am still idealistic enough to believe that we could do it, and be much the happier for the doing.

Only, of course, we'd have to call off the long weekend. And we'd all have to work harder. And think harder. And maybe share out more generously. Even do without some of the luxuries we are beginning to take for granted, be more frugal, tougher, self-reliant.

I've never thought self-esteem to be a bad thing, providing it is for self-achievement. It's better than being demoralised, which we might be in danger of becoming in the future as we are outpaced and outdistanced and outthought by more vital and less self-indulgent peoples.

That's why it was good to read those editorials and comments on this Australia Day. Maybe, just maybe, it might have been a really important Australia Day after all.

On Flying the Coop

This subject has come under discussion so many times lately with so many different people that it might be worth exploring a bit.

Are you a parent with children of an age to fly the coop? Do you want them to fly the coop? Or, even if you don't really want them to, do you think it desirable that they should for their own sakes? Or do you deliberately pad the coop with such comforts and enticements as to keep them safe in it, dependent, and where you can keep your eye on them?

Most of my friends and acquaintances who are approximately in my age group and also parents are either coming up to this situation, or disturbingly in the middle of it, or irrevocably through to the other side of it and thinking, either sadly or adventurously, of looking for a smaller house or a unit (with one spare bedroom, of course, in case one of the chicks needs a temporary roost some time).

It's a queer business, coop-flying. You know that it is coming up one day, but the day is always unexpected, and shattering somehow. For nineteen or twenty years the pattern of your life has been dictated by the needs and desires and whims and temperaments and triumphs and tragedies of these creatures you so recklessly brought into the world. Laboriously, creatively, with hope and love and pain and sacrifice and much joy and some bitter disappointment, you have spent nineteen or twenty or twenty-one years building a complicated edifice called Family. Not perhaps an entirely satisfactory edifice, not perhaps entirely as perfect as planned, a rather surprising edifice really, but your own, and therefore the most interesting edifice in the world. And just when you might sit back and contemplate it and enjoy it with just and happy pride, its very cornerstones casually remove themselves and the whole crazy structure lurches and topples and falls about your ears. It was, after all, never more than temporary.

Some parents feel a kind of outrage at this point. But look, they say, we would never have mortgaged ourselves to this great place if we'd known you were going to leave it so soon. Why, it was only last year that we went to the expense of all those built-in cupboards for you (or bookshelves, or stereo, or desk, or whatever). And it's not as though you can't have your friends when you like, they say. Or come and go as you please, they say.

I sympathise with this attitude, mortgaged as I am up to the ears, and with all those expensive built-ins gracing those empty rooms upstairs. But I have found that this first flying of the coop is likely to be experimental in nature and more or less brief in duration. I mean, it is not yet time to start looking for a smaller place to live. Those big empty rooms will have lots of use yet.

Off the young go, certainly, taking with them everything they can scrounge in the way of old cooking and eating utensils, worn sheets, faded blankets, tatty towels, knobbly pillows, tinned food, rolls of toilet paper, cakes of soap, jars of sugar, anything they can prize off their own walls and make portable, and a choice selection of their parents' books slyly reefed from their parents' shelves. Dear God, you think, how are they going to manage? What are the cooking facilities like? Is there a laundry? An iron? A juice-squeezer? An alarm clock? A refrigerator? A bath, even?

None of these luxuries will matter in the least at first. They will set up camp in some decrepit old terrace house with others of their kind, pool the loot they brought from their parental homes, and sleep as soundly on lumpy kapok as ever they did on inner springs. They will cook nothing but cups of coffee, so the cooking facilities won't be important: they will nourish themselves adequately and happily on hamburgers, Chinese takeaway food, flagons of red wine, and nights of smoke-wreathed conversation. They will not need chairs, because they will sit on the floor. They will not need built-ins, for they will hang all their clothes on the floor too, and pile their parents' precious books on old planks propped up with bricks. The state or colour of their walls won't matter, because they will paper them interestingly enough with blown-up posters, revolutionary slogans, political pamphlets and such like. As for baths and laundry, these are minor matters, because they can always come home for a visit when their best friends begin telling them, or when they get so whiffy it is evident even to themselves, whichever is the sooner. They will be delirious with freedom but probably, in this first period, will 'keep in touch' quite prudently, if only for the occasional orgies of hot water, mum-style washing and ironing, and a real baked dinner with three veg and lots of gravy.

Also they are not likely to go really far from the home coop, for the same reason. One young woman I know rather better than any other young woman, on her first flight out, moved only as far as the end of the street, and nipped back home practically every day to change her clothes, wash her smalls, shampoo her hair, pick up her mail, use the telephone, and write out recipes. The flat at the end of the street where she cooked weird meals and entertained weird friends in fabulous confusion was, in this case, nothing more or less than a cubbyhouse, and she and her girlfriend were playing cubbies as assiduously as they ever had at five years old. When they were tired of playing cubbies—it took two months or so—they both came home.

Usually it takes more like six months before the discomfort and inconvenience begin to tell. Not to mention the expense. For it is really instructive for them to learn that toilet rolls do not actually grow on lavatory walls nor coffee jars replace themselves without a money transaction. Even bread and cheese costs. And electricity, and gas, and those simple things that have always been there. Like light bulbs. When the bills start coming in they, in their turn, are startled and outraged, and probably reduced to candles as everything is cut off. But candles cost, too. You, the parents, may expect them home soon now.

And of course you are wildly happy. Because you've been really concerned lately how scruffy they've been looking on their rare appearances, and pale, and underfed, and nervous, and you've been certain they've not been eating enough or sleeping enough and suppose the flu epidemic does hit, they won't have any resistance at all. Et cetera. How joyfully you shop and cook again, buying up all the little delicacies they've been missing, like peanut butter and Oxford marmalade, and making big, balanced and really nourishing meals. How willingly you rush backwards and forwards from the dry-cleaners with the revolting garments they've returned in (quite unrecognisable as the ones they departed in), and sing in the laundry, soaking all their washables in enzymes, bleach, detergent, or even disinfectant, preparatory to a wash that will take a week. How happy you are. Or are you?

Because in the last six months you've become accustomed to lighter domestic duties and lots more time to yourself.

You've become accustomed to tidiness and quiet. You'd forgotten that litter always did exasperate you, and lights left burning all night, and soggy towels on the bathroom floor, and electronic music full blast, and doors banging, and the forgotten toaster burnt out, and dirty coffee cups on the rug, and spillings and droppings and crud and crumminess everywhere, and lids left off jars for the ants to get in, and nothing ever picked up or put away, and ...

Never mind. Get as much happiness out of it as you can. Because after a certain recuperative period they'll be off again. Spasmodically. But for longer periods as they gain confidence in coping for themselves. And you should be glad really, because it will lessen the blow of that final day, the one yet in abeyance, when they find their mates at last, and begin to build themselves.

That sad genius Edward Lear put it prettily: 'Calico Jam/ the little Fish swam,/ over the syllabub sea' ... Do you remember the ending? You'd better. 'But he never came back,/ he never came back,/ he never came back to me!'

On Tick and Tock

I have a clock, very small, round, of chased gold (for gold read gilt) with beautiful numerals backed with black. It is not in any way valuable but it is a pretty thing and I like it very much and it makes me cross that my family disparage my clock only because it doesn't tell the time accurately.

I know it doesn't. Sometimes it is five minutes fast and sometimes it is fourteen minutes slow and very occasionally it is almost right and what I say is that it's close enough for my purposes. My purposes don't particularly depend upon seconds and if they did depend upon seconds I think I would abandon my purposes as not being worth it. Somewhere between galaxies and electrons there is an eloquence that begins with tick and ends with tock and that's the sort of time that suits me just fine. In fact I think that's the only sort of time I could possibly cope with.

Although, now I am considering the subject, what I might like even more than my little gold (gilt) clock is a sundial. I have one actually which I will get around to setting up and levelling in the garden one day when I feel like that. It's a very handsome sundial too, hand-made, of brass, and on it is written: 'Some tell of storms and showers: I tell of sunny hours.' How very sensible that is. You might not be able to tell the time at all in dirty weather but maybe you'd be better off in bed anyway.

Some of those old sundial inscriptions are most instructive and conducive to deliberation. Like: 'I shall return: thou never.' Or: 'Hours are Time's shafts and one comes winged with death.' Or, so prettily and negligently: 'I count only the hours that are serene.'

And wouldn't that be nice? To count only the hours that are serene and to the devil with the rest of them. Let somebody else have that lot. Ah, but who? Dorian Gray managed it by way of a portrait, and then there was that Shangri-la lady of Hilton's, but time caught up with them too in the end, probably because their creators were so enmeshed in the time-trap themselves that their imaginations finally couldn't extend to a conception of timelessness.

Timelessness is unimaginable. But then time is too, apart from the tick-tock sort, I mean. And of course the older you get the more enigmatic it becomes and if you get out of the tick-tock area you are likely to get bushed.

Creatures of time we all are, but what sort of time, and time for what? Ecclesiastes maintained that there was a time for every purpose under heaven, Marvell saw deserts of vast eternity, and the computer operators at the Parkes radio telescope concern themselves with a million messages, or a billion messages, bounced back from heavenly happenings that took place thousands of millions of years ago.

When I was young and my heart beat faster and I lived at a furious rate, there seemed to be immense quantities of time to play with and use and burn up and the days were long and the nights were long too and the right place most often coincided with the right time and even the right state of mind and body for whatever physical or intellectual need I was grasping. And I think it is very peculiar that as you grow older and your blood flows more slowly and you live more slowly, the days get shorter and shorter and the years whizz past and time, as they say, flies. Something has obviously happened to your inner clock and the spring of it is unwinding.

It has always fascinated me that among men of genius there have always been those who knew in some mysterious way how much or how little time they had at their disposal. Those like Mozart, for instance, who developed his talent early and worked and lived in a frenzy and died young. Or those like Titian, who can afford to be more leisurely and save their best work for the long slow years, as if they know they have lots of time to spare. Or is it that the early starters die young just because of that early frenzy? It seems as though the hotter the faster is the general rule about life spans.

But that's genius and genius is extraordinary anyway. We ordinary mortals can probably expect an ordinary life span, a very ordinary amount of time to do our very ordinary business. And commonsense tells us that our ordinary business is real only when it is happening now, at the present moment. Reality is served up to us in thin slices of now. 'Unborn tomorrow, and dead yesterday, why fret about them if today be sweet?' One does fret, of course, against one's commonsense, which is so wedded to 'now' that if somebody says they have had a glimpse of the future, or looked back into the past, one's commonsense will denounce that somebody immediately as a charlatan. While still fretting. What happens between tick and tock anyway?

Between tick and tock time passes. But passes what? Has it passed us? Or do we flow along with it, and if it is flowing and we with it then surely it must have stationary banks, like past, present, and future, which would mean that everything is fixed and determined. And if everything is fixed and determined, then of what use is our vaunted free will? Or do we have any free will?

How can we use 'now' to throw a beam onto the future, or to illuminate the past? If our consciousness is only a torchlight moving along a back alley, what is the use of it? Did we invent time to explain change and succession, the irreversibility of events, the ageing process, the 'moving finger writes and, having writ, moves on' bit, or does it really exist as people like Priestley and that hard-headed military engineering type J.W. Dunne have believed, as another dimension, a fourth dimension in which we exist as irrevocably as we do in the other three?

And how about those 'deserts of vast eternity'? If they are there do we really want them? People get bored so easily in this life it continually surprises me that they should so passionately insist on another. Lasting forever. People are always 'filling in time' or 'passing time' or yawning between tick and tock. What are they going to do with eternity? Even, who are they going to be in eternity? Young selves, middle-aged selves, old selves? Will they even recognise themselves? Or their loved ones with whom they are reunited?

Funny business. I have never worn a watch in my life, because that has always seemed to me like wearing your death on your wrist. But I like my little gold clock, which is quite eccentric and has its own ideas about time past and passing and to come. Tick, it says. And tock, it says. And anything could happen in between.

Like I could finish this article. It's about time.

The Loftiest Form of Springtime

The poet George Seferis said that the Easter Passion Week—Greek Easter, that is—was the loftiest form of springtime he knew.

We used to think so too, those years we lived in Greece, where the seasons declare themselves more definitely, and more significantly, I think, than they do here, and each season has its appointed ritual, so old and so potent with earth-lore that you can understand it in an atavistic way without recourse to Frazer's *Golden Bough*, Graves' *Greek Myths*, or the liturgy of the Greek Orthodox Church.

May wreath and Midsummer Eve fire, the autumn vintage with its ceremonial tosspotting, the blessing of the waters at Epiphany when shivering young men dive into the winter sea to retrieve a gold cross, the weeks of hectic carnival that precede Lent, Soul Saturdays for the propitiation of spirits, Clean Monday for purification, each has its proper time and purpose, each ceremony is always true to itself, yet mysterious, pulsating with life, and whether it is Demeter or Saint Demetrios, St John or Poseidon the Earth-Shaker, Helios the Sun God or Elijah the Prophet, what does it matter?

Christ and Dionysus merge in torn flesh and flowers, and life is resurrected from the dead earth. The pagan world is always there, lingering on, dark and impenitent.

And every year it did indeed seem miraculous that those austere crags and stony fields could spring again, so suddenly it happened. Overnight rough mountain tracks were starred with clumps of camomile daisies, as though for a bridal way or a triumph, and the slopes were stupefying with wild thyme and spotted with crimson anemones, crinkle-petalled and fine as silk. Red as blood. You could wade in the ragged asphodel. There were little hooded green lilies sprung up between the stones, trails of wild caper blossom drooping fringes and tassels from every crevice, tiny pale violets, narcissus, pink hyacinth, strange delicate trumpets and spikes whose names I never knew, brown bells on acid yellow stalks almost as fine as hair, and flowers so minute in size and simple in form that we called them 'dolls' flowers'.

The irregular ploughed patches high above the white town were washed with a green so tender as to be almost transparent, in paved courtyards the hard sticks of pruned vines nubbed with little swellings of bud, ancient figs put out new leaves like tiny green hopeful hands, and the broad spiny plates of prickly pear bloomed with soft-fringed magenta flowers.

Even in the long vacuum of Lent you were stirred by this vernal festival preparing itself in leaf and bud and shoot: there was a heady sense of imminence. We whitewashed our houses, inside and outside, with brushes tied to long poles and long hair tied up in kerchiefs. We whitewashed courtyard walls and cisterns and well-heads. Pious ladies already faint and exhausted with fasting scrubbed doorsteps and cobblestones and outlined paving flags with new paint. Their men submitted without complaint to the meagre Lenten dishes they were served at their own tables, and then nicked off down to the waterfront taverns to fill up on something more nourishing. Form had been observed, but working men must eat.

I sometimes think that the observance of form is the key to the strength of the Greek family structure. There are so many rituals and ceremonies through the year that family tensions can be sublimated in the involved preparations necessary to carry off the occasion with the proper flair. Everybody, from grandparents down, knows his or her exclusive duties on these ceremonial occasions; even the very little children wait and watch expectantly for their cues from the adults so they, too, can participate.

In the second last week of Lent, just before the Day of Lazarus, the mountain shepherds came down into the town, wearing their wide flat hats tied with leather thongs beneath their chins and high soft goatskin knee boots. They herded before them the paschal lambs. All that week the waterfront was blobbed and clotted with little lambs, delicate crinkled creatures still awkward on thin legs and with their fleeces dyed rose pink and crimson and yellow and blue, whether to distinguish separate flocks or just to please the children I don't know. Because the lambs were the children's responsibility, and as each householder selected the family lamb with weighty deliberation and much haggling, the children would take it and tend it up on the slopes all dizzying with herbs and flowers and weave garlands for its throat and deck it with woven leading ropes of brightly coloured wool and the intricate woollen pompoms they had been making for weeks. Children and garlanded lambs and flowers. It was very pastoral and ancient and beautiful, and perhaps the more so in the knowledge that it was a prelude to death.

In the meantime the men made home-made fireworks in preparation for the resurrection, and sometimes blew themselves up. There was often torn flesh before the due date.

The Day of Lazarus, eight days before Easter, was children's day too. Bands of them went from door to door singing the Lazarus songs and receiving eggs or freshly baked Lazarus bread, which was made in sweet little loaves exquisitely stylised into a formalised body in a winding sheet of intricate folds, with crossed hands and stiff thick legs with crudely indicated toes. The bread tasted delicious but it was also so aesthetically pleasing that we were inclined to prop our own children's loot of loaves on the shelf above the oven hood, just to look at. Foreigners, no matter how willing, or even eager, apparently can't pass over into the old ritualistic world quite as easily as all that: sophistication gets in the way.

And then it was Palm Sunday, with its crosses of woven palm fronds and laurel, and a great foretelling of the future. And after that it was really Holy Week, Passion Week, and the emotion began to build with an aching intensity. The women were frantic with final scrubbing and polishing, the making of new clothes, the dyeing of red eggs, and the baking of small sweet pastries twisted into the shapes of flowers, and baskets, and serpents, or pastry cradles with a red egg for the baby's head, and the huge cartwheel loaves of sesame-scented Easter bread brushed with beaten egg and stamped with the Easter symbols. And every day in Holy Week every bell of every campanile rang for service after service. There was not a church on the island that was not packed with emaciated women, fanatical in this final week of fasting, and almost beside themselves with a mounting sense of tension and excitement. Imminent liberation too, I should think. You couldn't help admiring their fervour and their fortitude, for while they starved the whole island was heavy with the smell of food cooking.

On the night of Maundy Thursday religious ecstasy took over absolutely. Christ was seized and Christ was crucified, to candles and Byzantine chanting and grievous sobbing as the crude cardboard effigy, with a silk cloth about its loins and a wreath of mountain thorns on its head, was brought out on the cross and taken in sad, solemn procession around the church before being placed upright in the centre of the nave. It was accomplished. The women threw themselves to the floor in their grief, wringing their hands and clutching their hair. Children wailed and men covered their eyes. Christ was dying on the cross, now, as Christ would die on the cross this night, and now, forever. You felt very close to the beginnings. It has always been the women who have wept, the women who have mourned, and the women who have sewn the winding sheet. This night they spent shivering on the cold marble of church floors, mourning the King.

But even the men fasted on Good Friday. The haggard women in the churches had been busy since dawn, preparing the funeral biers. Every church had its own, very elaborate and mostly very beautiful. They were roofed with little domes of silver or blue enamel, hung with glittering gauze and white satin, with wreaths of mountain flowers and tinsel bows. One was covered all over with hand-made flowers of white organdy, thousands of them. Another had gauze curtains worked entirely with silver beads. There were candles at each corner, and a carpet before each bier, flanked by tubs of mint and sweet basil and flowers, and flowers wreathed too about the cross, bare now, for the King was to be taken to his tomb.

At nine o'clock in the evening you could hear the chanting. The dark waterfront began to flicker with hundreds of points of candle flame and the bobbing orange glow of lanterns, and within five minutes all the processions from every church had poured down the lanes and mountainsides in lurching streams of fire, with the white biers swaying above like nuptial howdahs borne by invisible elephants. It was mysterious and magnificent and awesome. They moved to the throb of drums and the solemn chant of voices, the deep tones of the men, the strained shrill voices of the women, the high piping of the children. Candlelight flickered on taut, pale, exhausted faces suddenly illuminated out of the dark massing and grouping. Gold blazed high in the darkness above the swaying biers, where tall swinging lanterns burned on tasselled shields and raised crosses. Faces swam out of the crowd, closed eyes, straining throats, mouths stretched wide in agony or ecstasy. And very high, high on the dark shape of the mountain against the stars, a ridge of dancing points of flame. The nuns always brought out their candles to the great rock that overhung the town.

Emotion still held the town on Saturday morning. In every lane and doorway the little coloured lambs that the children had loved and tended on the slopes were being ritually slaughtered. Men's work. Crosses were being smeared above every doorway with the running blood from their throats. That was too much. I could never bring myself to move outside, not until the butchery was over and the streets clean again. But by midday the lambs were on their way to the bakehouses, curled—poor little things—in Easter pots of red earthenware patterned with curious white symbols, and stuffed with rice and liver and cinnamon. The air was thick with the smell of blood and spices and cooking. And imminent joy in the miracle about to happen.

At ten o'clock the night was wild with bells, Agios Christos, Nicholas, the urgent clamour of I-Papandi, the throaty clangour of Stephanos, each of three hundred and sixty-five churches outpealing each other, and the whole population dressed in their gladdest best, and carrying tall white candles decorated with tulle and flowers. Pockets bulging with red eggs and those lethal home-made fireworks.

Outside every church a wooden platform had been set up, decorated with palm leaves. The courtyards were strewn with mountain herbs, trampled into such a smell as would bowl you over. There was scarcely standing room. And after the singing and the chanting, just before midnight, the chandeliers were doused, and all the tall candles. Apart from the little oil lamp that burns perpetually before every high altar, it was the darkness of the tomb. We all sighed, a long sigh of near-hysteria.

This was it. The officiating priest suddenly appeared, holding up a lighted candle and crying, 'Come ye and take light from the eternal light!'

There was the wildest surge forward in the darkness, a tumult of gasping, pressing bodies, a sea of upraised hands holding candles. One by one the candles took flame from each other and spread and multiplied, running and jumping up flights of stairs and along cool arched cloisters, while on the palm-wreathed platform the symbolic stone was rolled away, and at exactly midnight an angel cried: 'He is not here! He is risen!'

Great explosions like cannonfire shook the night and everyone, laughing quite wildly, was caught in a great bombardment of red eggs and those terrible fireworks. Children went completely out of control and whacked each other with red eggs and hurled fireworks like the very little fiends of hell.

'Christ is risen!'

'He is risen indeed!'

The parties went on all night, all the next day, and for many days after. People feasted themselves into a stupor. Life could go on, with marriages and betrothals, with christenings and quarrellings and feuds and nagging and worrying about dowries and crops and where the next meal was coming from. And soon the sun burned the flowers away and the mountains reverted to parched rocks, and spikes and thorns.

But something had been accomplished. It was reassurance. And triumph. Everything would come, this year, and every year, in its appointed season.

Even we, ignorant foreigners that we were, had the strangest feeling that we had helped the year along.

Hallelujah for a Good Pick-Up!

They came in from the letterbox with a printed notice and whooping for joy. 'Hallelujah!' they cried. 'There's going to be a pick-up.'

It was not, of course, the Resurrection with a pick-up of seemly souls bound for everlasting bliss, but only what our municipality nicely refers to as 'Household Waste'. Meaning garbage.

We live in quite a benevolent and resident-mindful municipality, and earlier on there used to be a pick-up at least every two months of all the junk and crud that people accumulate and all the leftovers that just won't fit into the regulation-sized garbage bin no matter how many of you take turns in treading it down like a wine press. (We do it by numbers and to various treading-down songs. 'Step Inside Love' we find most encouraging.)

But for some reason or another that is known only to our benevolent municipal fathers, their benevolence has not extended to pick-ups for at least six months. Seven, maybe. And I won't tell you how I date that particular pick-up. But no doubt our municipal fathers had other things on their minds, like rates and high-rise development and stray dogs and tree-lopping and street-sweeping and their Image and whatever other little matters councillors squabble about in council and worry over in their beds at night.

What we'd been worrying about in our beds at night was whether benevolence in regard to household waste had ended altogether, and if it had ended how on earth were we going to dispose of our accumulation of the sordid evidence of two student parties, one welcome home, three birthdays, one Christmas, one New Year, one Easter, and general hospitality dispensed in a six (or was it seven?) month span resulting in waste considerably in excess of anything that Hannibal's elephants—all of them, I mean, and before they got to the Alps—could have trampled down. Step Inside Love. I wonder if elephants do.

Let's face it. All those empties render gross, if not vile, a smart back deck that was designed for gracious living. How can one live graciously surrounded by cardboard cartons bulging and sagging with such squalid evidence of completely ungracious hijinks? Some would say 'boozing', but of course I don't, knowing the circumstances and how many guests pass through this house and my own hospitable instincts and the regulation size of the garbage bin. There are others, more sophisticated, or better equipped perhaps, who have what one young friend of mine calls 'a set of wheels', and they can load up and whizz off and dump it all on a municipal tip somewhere (like some shady leafy glen wild with flannel flowers: how do our municipal fathers choose where it is proper to dump garbage?) and pretend it never happened.

We don't have a set of wheels, excepting two very small ones belonging to a motor scooter, and that's not much good for loading up and dumping purposes. Although stylish enough in its own right and useful for other purposes. But that's another story.

We got everything out onto the pavement before Hallelujah Day. In work gangs, hauling away two by two, and singing or whistling loudly to cover up a natural embarrassment at such public exposure of our domestic detritus. And since we had about a ton of old newspapers—there hadn't been a

374 / Charmian Clift

collection of paper for six months either—we arranged these artfully, in bundles, on top of the cartons to disguise their contents. And a more conspicuous bit of camouflage I have never seen in my life.

You believe that you don't care what your neighbours think but when it comes to the public exposure bit you find that you squirm with just such a degree of abashment that would be more proper to Aunt Julie or Maude, tucking the brandy bottle (for medicinal purposes only, dear) behind the sheets in the linen press.

Well, it is such a respectable street, after all. Nice. Lined with camphor laurels and desirable residences of the gentlemanly kind. My wicked wicked children, in a spirit of bravado that I could not muster, arranged to have themselves photographed sitting on top of that most formidable heap, under the camphor laurel tree and on the only unmown strip of grass in the whole street. With beer cans in their hands. Grinning.

'Oh, don't be such a square,' they said. 'Just wait till you see what the neighbours bring out.'

And what didn't the neighbours bring out! Boggles this mind at what orgies must have been going on—carrying on, rather—behind those discreet gentlemanly-residence-type doors and polished knockers. Funny, one was never aware. Although, come to think of it, there has been music—sort of on-and-off—and shrieks of girlish laughter and tootings of car horns and maybe it wasn't a dream after all that one night (waking?) I observed from my bedroom window a young man running up the street quite starko except for a net curtain and a German helmet. Dear me.

Anyway, emboldened by all this evidence of a suburban depravity that far exceeded our excesses, I added to our disgusting pile of household waste all the old clothes that had been shoved into the backs of closets and under the stairs on the chance that they would 'come in useful'. In the meantime the moths and the silverfish had found them more useful, and the mildew had claimed them, and, quite frankly, they stank.

But the neighbours added yet more. Old cane chairs and wicker whatnots, lengths of plumbers' piping, mouldy boots, garden taps, old-fashioned pink stays (the lace-up Scarlett O'Hara kind), busted bedroom lamps, astrolabes, chamber pots, umbrella stands, tired mattresses, feather boas, computer parts, cracked soup tureens, ceramic marvels, and such odds and ends and intriguing bits and pieces that kept us housekeeping ladies off the buses for days. We all walked up to the shops, prodding and examining as we went, and with such acquisitive instincts as would make me ashamed, excepting I know that all the ladies felt the same overwhelming urge to do a little picking-up for themselves.

It rained before the official pick-up. Torrents. The cardboard cartons sogged up and drifted apart in the corners. The picked-over old clothes, already moth-eaten and not worth anybody's notice, fell into the gutters and were rolled into damp and disgusting bundles, all messed up with the fallen leaves from the camphor laurels.

What do you do with one lamp base, an arty (nouveau, I mean) mantel surround, a coil of wire, and a rather damaged print of 'The Stag at Bay'?

Easy. You put them out on the next pick-up. Let somebody else pick them over.

The Joys of Holidays

Well, that was ever so nice. My holiday, I mean. But the most interesting thing about this holiday, anticipated, I must say, with a sort of childish gleefulness ('School's out! School's out!'), was that eventually I didn't go anywhere and I didn't do anything that was at all unusual.

Excepting, in the beginning, a few things I've been wanting to do for ages, like cleaning out my clothes closet and going in to town for a day's shopping and meeting friends for luncheon and asking friends for dinner and doing the marketing in a leisurely, choosy sort of way, and indulging in hours of conversation with people I like and arranging flowers and new curtains and pages of manuscript and notebooks and wallowing in reading. There is nothing more self-indulgent than reading a novel in the morning, particularly in your own familiar surroundings where you are normally 'getting on' with things.

I suppose a holiday is really a state of mind relieved of pressure. Most of us live under pressures of one kind or another, clocks and appointments and dates and times and contracts and obligations and the necessity to 'keep up', or 'get on', and of course we become so accustomed to our pressures that we go a little peculiar and light-headed when they are removed.

Anyway, I had chosen for my holiday reading the novels of Joyce Cary. (I like to do this—that is, to take the entire corpus of work of a favourite writer and begin at the beginning and read through chronologically to the end. It is

fascinating—at least to a writer—to see how the veriest germ
of an idea or sketch of a character in an early book is
gradually explored and developed in later ones and finally
becomes a major theme.) So, I was reading *A Prisoner of
Grace*—in the morning, too, sitting in the sun with my feet
up—and I came upon these words of Nina's:

'I felt an immense calm gaiety, as if, so to speak, I had just
inherited such an immense wealth of delights that I did not
need to be extravagant; I could afford simply to feel the
comfort of being so rich without the trouble of spending.'

And I read those words with such a stinging sense of
recognition. Because, of course, that's exactly the way I was
feeling too. It was something to do with the way the morning
light was skittering among the leaves of my young trees and
the clump of papyrus at the bottom of the yard glittering like
fresh-washed hair and the silly spoilt cats frolicking and
pretending to be jungle beasts and little Wesley next door
riding his tricycle round and round the clothes hoist (entirely
for my admiration and attention) and I needn't bother with
anything more elaborate than sandwiches for lunch and there
was a dinner party in prospect with comfortable sorts of
friends. And there were voices, comfortable sorts of voices,
too, being so familiar, and birds, and an aeroplane skywriting
on the vast expanse of tender autumn blue and I could take
the time to crane my neck and watch it like a child, guessing
what each letter was to be. Also I could hear the sound of the
vacuum cleaner inside and know that my house was being
cleaned and tidied and made seemly, and I know all these
things are trivial in themselves but they added up to 'an
immense wealth of delights' and I felt like laughing out of
sheer pleasure. I was suddenly glad that I hadn't been able to
go away for my holiday as I had planned and intended,

because the going away would have been alone and it seemed nicer not to be alone, particularly with a wedding anniversary coming up in a couple of days. More friendly and, again, comfortable.

That led me on to thinking of long-ago holidays we'd had together and the realisation that the last one was all of eighteen years ago. I suppose most married people with families find it difficult to get away together, unless there is a doting granny in the background or an obliging family friend with enough time and inclination to do stand-in duty with the children.

In England, when we took holidays, we used to board ours out at an establishment in the country designed for that very purpose, and run, interestingly enough, by the English wife of Jomo 'Burning Spear' Kenyatta, a gentle lady whose son Peter was our kids' hero, not only on account of his thrilling parentage but because he took them exploring into dangerous chalk pits and encouraged them to climb the tallest trees and pinch goodies from the pantry and generally behave like the little savages they were. England used to abound with such places—one I remember with a shudder described itself as 'The Savoy for the Under Twelves'—and I have never quite recovered from my sense of guilt at having abandoned little children to such a soulless environment for the entirely frivolous reason that I wanted to go motoring around the Bordeaux area with my husband for the purpose of sloshing claret in famous chateaux.

But after we went to Greece we never had another holiday together again. We intended to. Every year. Venice, we would say. Or Istanbul. Or the Dalmatian Coast. Or the Lebanon. But of course there were no nice (or even nasty) boarding establishments for temporarily unwanted children (I sometimes think deep freeze might be the answer), no grannies, and as for family friends ... when it came to the point of trusting them with our young it was unfortunately evident that most of them were on the irresponsible side (if not downright ratty), and were in any case so involved in complicated love affairs, quarrels, feuds, works of genius, despair, drinking bouts, or what looked like (from parents' points of view, I mean) debauchery of all kinds, that they would obviously not have had much time or patience left over to run a household that required a certain dull routine or to deal sympathetically and understandingly with three highly individual little monsters who would be bound to play up on their temporary guardians on principle. Anyway, Venice wouldn't run away, or Istanbul, or the Lebanon, or the Dalmatian Coast either. We could go next year. And in the meantime the sun was shining, and we were swimming every day again, and the white yachts were coming in loaded with interesting summer visitors, and life had moved out of doors, and we always had a few extra children to care for because their parents were running away from each other (or sometimes even with each other: it happened occasionally). So we never did go.

And I suppose not going away together becomes such a habit that even since our children have far outgrown the 'being minded' stage it has never occurred to either of us that it might be possible to arrange our affairs, stock the larder, and just pack up and go.

So that is why my anniversary present was so surprising and delightful. Because I was given just such an invitation. And that is why I spent the rest of my holiday bashing the typewriter with such urgency that the keys kept bunching and sticking and the words coming out back to front.

'But I thought you were on holiday,' said a puzzled friend, discovering me at it. 'I am,' I said. 'Then what on earth are you working for?'

'So I can have a holiday.' There must be a zany logic in it somewhere. And perhaps I might even tell. When we get back.

Royal Jelly?

In the dank early morning hours of 2 June 1953, in our flat in the Bayswater Road, London, England, we rose from our warm beds, awakened the journalists who had camped the night on sofas and floor, breakfasted hurriedly but heartily (since it was going to be a long day), dressed ourselves and the children, and went to see the young Queen Elizabeth crowned.

My husband was dressed oddly for that bleak and dismal hour, in white tie and tails that were ill-fitting to say the least, he, apparently, having been the last man into Moss Bros to hire his coronation gear and finding nothing left but oddments—trousers that had been tailored originally for a man of the corpulence of Sydney Greenstreet, a tail coat turned in by a dwarf perhaps a century before, a vest designed for a very long stick-man, and a curious shirt-front, as stiff and bulging as a medieval knight's corselet. He was not consoled by his children's admiration, they likening him in his splendour to a gollywog, than which nothing could have been a greater compliment under the circumstances. The circumstances being that even after a frantic ransacking of every drawer in every room we could not find a pair of braces to hold up the voluminous laps and folds of his pants (the children having used said braces to hang a couple of rebel dolls by their necks out of the back nursery window, but not, of course, telling in that sizzling hour of the most terrifying profanity: they weren't silly).

After all, he had a row of chinking decorations on his breast, and he could hold up his pants with one hand. It was enough. And the only alternative to his festal costume, as I reminded him, would have been court dress, as laid down in the detailed order of dress for the day, and he might have felt even sillier in knee breeches and silk stockings and buckled shoon. He would have to make do as best he could. In any case it was not a question of whether he wanted to sit in Westminster Abbey for nine hours or so. He had been *ordered* to sit in Westminster Abbey, and the Lord knows what regal retribution might not fall upon his rebellious colonial head if he failed his loyal duty. What he said about his loyal duty was pointed and pungent, but not, I think, printable, even in the pages of this enlightened magazine.

How long ago and far away it seems now. That drive through the damp and soggy London early morning, dismal beyond telling, the colour of gruel, the texture of gruel, and the damp soggy banners hanging among the damp decorations, and the damp soggy gruel-coloured people who had camped all night on the gruel pavements beginning to bestir themselves and stretch and fold up their blankets and open packets of sandwiches, Scotch eggs, toad-in-the-hole, jellied eels and other national delicacies to fortify them for the long hours of waiting still ahead. In spite of the banners the streets did not have the appearance of a Triumphal Way. Coriolanus would not have thought it up to the mark. Still, the newspaper billboards on the pavements blazoned the tidings that Hillary and Tenzing had conquered Everest—'done the old bitch'—and a young queen would indubitably be crowned this very day. There might be something in it, after all. Something auspicious, I half felt, something of a high singing noble order that would lift the hearts and spirits of these poor tired depressed and apathetic Englanders, defeated in victory, austerity-weary, but surely this day, for a few hours anyway, hopeful?

For us in the covered stand outside the Abbey it was a long and weary wait, but there was pomp and panoply enough, I suppose, at last, and drums and tuckets, and fleeting flashes of great brilliance, and hot tea from the thermos to keep us warm, and a clean arrangement of lavatories under the stand. (My husband's experiences, holding up his pants inside the Abbey, were of a different, more piquant—if more distressing—order, he having left my carefully arranged packet of sustenance in the way of food and drink in the car now parked in the Foreign Office, and having no nourishment whatever, while around and below him the high and mighty of the land swilled and guzzled with every appearance of enjoyment. Besides, in the Abbey the loyal subjects were summoned to the lavatories in rows, at the command of a Black Rod, or Gold Rod, or somebody equally splendid, and my husband's timing was out that day. Then again, he was seated next to Rebecca West, with whom he had quarrelled. In print too. If he had been an anti-monarchist before the coronation, that ancient ceremony passionately confirmed him in his republican tendencies.)

Outside, I do remember thinking at one time—slapping the bored and fretful children and discovering that my bottom was quite numb—that I might have done better to accept the invitation from my charlady to watch the ceremony on her telly. 'Lord love you, madam,' she had said, 'I wouldn't cross the street to see that lot.' Which was rather a curious statement from a very conservative woman of the old school, who had been in service from the age of twelve and had the highest reverence for the aristocracy.

Long ago, as I said, and far away. If there had been, that day, a hope for a renaissance of the spirit through the person of the young queen it was obviously not fulfilled, worthy of high office as she undoubtedly is, and conscientiously diligent at her tedious duties. Somehow, in spite of all the splendour of the trappings, charisma is lacking.

The House of Windsor has not been notable for charisma. Respectable family people, mostly, with respectable tastes, average tastes, middle-of-the-road tastes. Nothing wild or scaring or original in the way of imagination. Really, under mantle and crown, just like Mr and Mrs Everybody. Only with a sterner sense of duty and propriety drilled into them and not so many opportunities to put their feet up.

Victoria, at least in retrospect, seems to have had some little additive in the way of mystique. Possibly India and the title of Empress. Even such a dowdy prudish small frump would have to take on a certain incandescence in the circumstances. And then, of course, she had the Empire, which was a reality then, a source of unquestioning pride and unquestioning belief to every stout-hearted Englishman, not to mention a limitless field of opportunity for younger sons in need of jobs and generals in need of glory. Besides, Victoria, the Symbol of Empire, lasted so very long, and a certain amount of charisma is bound to accrue just with the passage of all those years.

Edward her son did not inherit the charisma, but a certain glamour attached to him. His style was rakish and sporty. Even, perhaps, a little caddish. But definitely style. He lived largely if loosely, and set a high reckless tone, which was probably exciting. I think people like a bit of excitement to generate from their monarchs. After all, what is the point in being royal if you have to obey the ordinary dull conventions? Royalty should manage to be above and beyond convention if it's to maintain interest.

There hasn't been much to interest, really, since that jolly expansive king. I mean, apart from the brief and somehow terrible sad revolt of his grandson and namesake, Edward VIII who, one feels, didn't want to be a king anyway. Because if he had wanted to be a king how differently he might have managed the business. In another age there would have been plot and counterplot, not to mention an armed uprising of loyalists gathering to the royal standard. The Archbishop of Canterbury would have been seized, Stanley Baldwin held under duress (if not poisoned), the little princesses locked up in the Tower as hostages, the lovely Lady Wallis protected night and day by the king's own guard, while the Duke of Gloucester (or Kent, or York) marched down from Scotland at the head of a rebel army to seize the throne by force. Or some such. Glory be! Endless speculation is possible.

But of course nothing bold or breathtaking happened at all, and nothing bold or breathtaking has happened since. The House of Windsor, shaken perhaps by such untoward events, closed ranks and settled firmly into the unimpeachable pattern of respectability it has maintained to this day. The late Queen Mary had indeed a queenly air, and some eccentricities of dress and manner that set her apart from the others. But then she was a foreigner anyway. When I was first in England there were some stories, apocryphal perhaps, but in popular currency, that endeared her to me, although probably not to the noble families she was in the habit of visiting occasionally, since it was said that she admired their finest pieces of furniture and china and silver and tapestry so pointedly and with such intent that there was no loyal and honourable course for them to follow but to make their royal guest a gift of the treasure she had so particularly admired. Or hide away all the best bits before she arrived. Well, if a queen can't do that, who can?

Has the monarchy run its appointed course? What purpose does it serve any longer? There is no Empire left to speak of to make a plinth imposing enough to support this glittering symbol of majesty, and it is an extremely expensive institution to maintain in a country positively floundering in economic swamps and quagmires and shrunk to mini-size in importance and influence. What point is there in creating another Prince of Wales? There are no Welsh Marches any more, no rallying point, nothing to be gained. There is, in fact, much disaffection, and I can't see that an investiture can do anything but stir it up a bit more, although Charles seems a likely lad enough and at least has the inestimable virtue—or appears to have—of displaying an interest in cultural matters of a more complex nature than *The Sound of Music*. Of course, speaking of that, the royal family are useful for film stars to meet at command performances. The film stars, wealthy as they are, might even club in to keep the grand occasions going.

Also, royalty might be worth the expense of keeping them on and keeping them up, as it were, for the sake of tourist revenue, which Britain needs and which the royal family and the royal paraphernalia do much to attract. There are still thousands of Christopher Robins in the world, adult Christopher Robins and mostly American, for whom England would scarcely be worth visiting without the Changing of the Guard and the Horse Guards and the pageantry of Trooping the Colour. All that scarlet and jingle and jangle is very impressive as a spectacle. Or quaint. However you like to look at it. Interesting anyway. Picturesque. And well worth the trouble of coming over for the colour film to show back home. 'Did you know that if they faint they're court-martialled?' 'Not if they can prove they ate their proper breakfast. Cereal and all.' 'That's why they have bags of dry ice in their busbies.' 'They're not called busbies. Bearskins, man, bearskins. And they don't have dry ice in them, they have bowler hats.'

(My husband has just interrupted bitterly to say that he knows what peers have in their coronets. Chicken wings, he says, and breasts of grouse. And flasks of the best hooch. Funny how the memory of the coronation still rankles.)

Anyway, without a royal family all that pageantry would cease, and probably the tourist trade would drop off, which would be embarrassing just now.

Of course we in Australia accrue no advantages from any of that pomp and ritual. In fact some of us fail to see what advantage lies in having a monarch at all. We were never part of the Empire in the flag-planting sense, since the only purpose of our annexation was to provide a convenient dumping ground for undesirables. There are still the Birthday Honours and the New Year Honours, which may have some mystical significance for the businessmen, charity workers, and real estate agents who are preponderantly the recipients of such titles and decorations, but scarcely to anybody else. Court presentations are no longer the thing, so we do not even need a monarchy for the sake of the social advancement of our daughters. The fact of a monarchy gives us seven governors and a governor-general, thus, I suppose, providing jobs for persons too eminent or too fastidious to employ themselves further in the fields of commerce or politics, but hardly impinging on the lives of ordinary Australians in any way at all or imparting to them a proper sense of richness and tradition and heritage. We are honoured, every now and again, by a visit from the Queen of Australia, her husband, or a member of her family, when we may gawp if we choose or can wave a flag, or—if we are on an approved and vetted list—touch a royal hand.

Does it matter? Interest, predictably, has waned in such visits. It is not that we are rebellious or insurgent. Only disinterested and bored. There is not only no charisma. There doesn't seem to be any real meaning. Like my London charlady of long ago, most of us wouldn't be bothered to cross the street to see that lot. They might be very nice and worthy people, but what on earth have they got to do with us?

I wonder, at this time of Prince Charles's investiture, whether there will be ever again a King Charles of England. And oddly enough, even after what I've written here, I wouldn't put it past that likely lad to make it and those most peculiar English to thoroughly approve and endorse it, anachronistic as it might be.

For did not that flamboyant and discredited monarch, Farouk of Egypt, once prophesy:

'In fifty years there will be only five kings left in Europe. The King of Hearts. The King of Spades. The King of Clubs. The King of Diamonds. And the King of England.'

On *Clean Straw for Nothing*

Somebody—Frank Benier, I think it was—once called him 'a benevolent steamroller'.

The writer George Johnston, that is, with whom I have lived now for something more than twenty-three years. No woman lives with a man for that long out of sheer masochism, so there is obviously a great deal to him apart from the steamroller, or flattening out bit, although I do believe that to be a true observation. Or true in so far as he is inclined to be a conversational bully—being better informed about more things than most, liking to dominate, and having a most devastating turn of wit (it occurs to me that he is the only person I know who can make a compliment into an accusation). He is also a steamroller in his purposes.

His purposes are, of course, various. But one of them is to write novels. To say what he knows. What he knows uniquely, because everybody's experience is made up of unique particulars, and nobody can say for anybody else. I know this to be so because I have shared a great deal of his experience, and I know too that we both remember the experience quite differently. It affected us quite differently. We write about it quite differently. I suspect it is the difference between optimism and pessimism, but I am not entirely sure. All people have both in varying mixtures. Nobody is absolutely a Yea Sayer and nobody is absolutely a Nay Sayer. I tend to Yea and George Johnston tends to Nay, but then I am a good deal younger than he is, had a much happier beginning and launching into life, and haven't been so sick for so many years.

His purpose was not always to say what he knows. In his leaping time—trench coat, beret, dressing-gown from de Pinna, pigskin luggage, passport fabulously stamped with nearly every country in the world—he was inclined to hide what he knew, suspected, was troubled by, behind a glitteringly competent dazzle of professional observation. He could give you, in words, the look and the smell and the taste and the sound of an experience (usually an exotic experience, because he collected exotic experiences the way some people collect luggage labels: like travelling in Tibet and living with the Chinese communists and visiting the last of the great ivory-painters in Isphahan), but he couldn't or wouldn't tell you how it felt.

Perhaps he was afraid of how things felt. Certainly he shied away from any written expression of his own emotional reactions to things and settled instead for what he thought his reactions should have been if he had been in the skin of an elderly professor of archaeology or however he was disguising himself for that particular novel (it was most often elderly and tremendously erudite, but sometimes also heroic-male-writ-large—which I suppose was understandable enough coming from a very sensitive un-physical sort of man who had never had any education excepting for what he had scratched and scrabbled for himself, rather marvellously too: the range of his knowledge still staggers me).

Some words of Gerard Manley Hopkins come to me here. 'Sickness broke him.' But I'm not sure whether sickness broke him, or, in a cruel sort of way, made him. He raged against it for years, despaired, became bitter and hating and not easy to live with. He was, of course, affronted and outraged by the corruption working in his lungs. And there were times when he was affronted and outraged by anybody who didn't have corruption working in his lungs. (Or so it seemed then: it was the impression he gave.) Why did it have to pick on him? Him of all people who had never been sick in his life. I do not like to think much on those years because we almost foundered, but I do like to think on those years because in those years he began to write in a different way. To me, a truer way. Perhaps he thought he had nothing to lose any more. Perhaps he thought if people didn't like what he was and what he thought and what he felt they could bloody well lump him. The necessity to charm, to please, to entertain, to be approved (Golden Boy, they used to call him) dropped out of his make-up like so much unwanted baggage, and as he fined down alarmingly in weight (for a man six feet tall a weight of seven stone is alarming) he also fined down in character, persona, or whatever you call it. And of course this, in a way, was alarming too—for a wife, that is, who found she was married to somebody else entirely.

Closer to the Sun was the first novel he wrote in that time, apart from the Professor Challis series of thrillers written under the pseudonym Shane Martin (the names of our daughter and elder son) which were bread and butter and which he wrote at white-heat at the rate of a couple of months for each one as insurance policies for me and the kids.

Closer to the Sun was different. I don't think it was a good novel, but it was a very important one to me because it was halfway honest—that is, honest for half its length, when obviously uncertainty engulfed him and he retreated into storyline and the old trick of dazzling observation. And it was an important novel because it was an exploratory sort of one, feeling out the ground for the one that was to come so many years later—like now, or actually next month when Collins publish it—called *Clean Straw for Nothing*.

I've been living with *Clean Straw for Nothing* for all those years since *Closer to the Sun*. There have been novels in between, of course, because that's the man's business. After *Closer to the Sun* there was *The Far Road*, which I still think is one of the best things he's ever written and in which I have a personal pride because I nagged him into writing a novel about two men, a jeep, and 100 000 corpses. I believe it sold all of eighty-two copies in Australia, but that doesn't really matter now (although it did at the time, naturally). What matters is that he set down, as truly as he could, an experience that had shattered him. Fictionalised, but not the less true for that. Maybe even more true for that. Distilled. The very essence of the thing in all its dreadfulness. I loved that novel. I stood up and cheered for it. Perhaps my cheering mozzed it, because it was a complete failure commercially, and because the poor man had all of us lot dependent upon him he went back to what I call 'faction-fiction' and wrote a novel—quite a good novel, in fact—called *The Far Face of the Moon*. Very exotic again, set in Burma in the time of the last war and all about pilots flying the Hump and its heroine was a nymphomaniac and its hero was impotent and where he dredged that lot up God alone knows (since he has no truck with psychiatrists, mistrusting that profession profoundly).

And his publishers didn't like that novel a scrap. In fact, he was told in so many words that as a writer he couldn't afford even one more near-miss. That's an awful thing to be told when you're fifty and sick almost to death and you have all this wretched family whose very breaths depend upon your breath and you can't breathe much anyway.

But what he did, instead of tearing up the manuscript or tearing his hair or slashing his wrists or shooting his publishers or indulging in any similar despairing dramatic action (and I cannot say how I admire him for this), was to withdraw *The Far Face of the Moon*, quite quietly and reasonably, and write *My Brother Jack* instead. Which proved to be wise, not only because it has been what they call 'successful' in the trade and was the lever which moved us all back to Australia and him into the proper medical care which has undoubtedly lengthened his life by some years, but also because *My Brother Jack* committed him totally to exploring his own experiences. There would be no more aged professors of archaeology or bitter exiled Englishmen of vast erudition or rambunctious sponge-divers. There would be George Johnston being, quite unapologetically, George Johnston.

This pleased me because—even when I was hating him, and I was hating him quite frequently for a period—I always did believe George Johnston to be more interesting than the characters he made up. I know that everybody, particularly every creative body, makes himself up to a certain extent, and to that degree the narrator of *My Brother Jack*—that David Meredith who begins tentatively in *Closer to the Sun* and is expanded and developed and really begins to sing in *The Far Road*—is a fictional person. But it was obvious in the very writing of *My Brother Jack* that this person David Meredith wasn't going to be dismissed with the last page and the words 'The End'. He had a great deal more to say and to do and to suffer and to witness and to record, so in a mad way (or a writer's way, which is mad anyhow) all the time *My Brother Jack* was being written *Clean Straw for Nothing* was just as certainly evolving, although it would be five years and more before it was formed and finished, and six years and more before publication.

That is a long time between books for such a prolific and (formerly) facile writer. Of course *The Australians* came in between, and some film scripts, and a couple of longish hospital bouts, and a bit of savage surgery, but I suspect that the real difficulty about writing *Clean Straw for Nothing* was (a) finding a form sufficiently tight and still sufficiently flexible to compress such an enormous mass of material—twenty-five years of growing and suffering and learning and changing—I mean, if you're raging to say your say before it's too late you still have to find how to say it within a compass that is acceptable ('Don't do it in the street and frighten the horses'), and (b) the unfortunate fact that for the first time in all our years together I was totally incapable of giving him the sort of help he needs with work in progress. He needs a constant presence, an ear, a sounding board, an audience. Some writers are like that and it has been my peculiar pleasure to perform this function for him. In fact, while *My Brother Jack* was being written I sat on the step by his desk every day for seven months so that I would be there when I was wanted for discussion or suggestion or maybe only to listen.

But with *Clean Straw* I've had a complete emotional block, and not all my deep and genuine sympathy at the sight of him struggling and fighting with what was obviously proving to be recalcitrant (sometimes I thought intractable) could force me into the old familiar step-sitting role. Nor all my professionalism could lure me into listening dispassionately. I do believe that novelists must be free to write what they like, in any way they like to write it (and after all, who but myself had urged and nagged him into it?), but the stuff of which *Clean Straw for Nothing* is made is largely experience in which I, too, have shared and—as I said earlier—have felt differently because I am a different person.

I was concerned that it was so hard for him, and grieved that I could not help. He had dreadful fits of depression and days of such incapacity that even half a page seemed an effort that drained him. And this from a man who could, once, churn out 5000 words a day without turning a hair and 'never blot a line of it'. Of course most of the novel—as with the text of *The Australians*—was written in hospital and he was pretty heavily drugged all the time, so in a way it seems miraculous that he finished it at all. I suppose it's that inexorable steamroller quality he has. And the fact that he'd been given a Commonwealth Literary Fellowship and felt morally obliged to produce the goods.

But what was troubling too was that when the novel was finished at last he wouldn't—or couldn't—give it up. For weeks he tinkered and polished and fiddled and rewrote until, watching him, I felt that the wisest thing to do was to ring his publisher and get rid of the damn thing. For better or worse. Which I did. I think he was relieved by this action, but nervous too, more nervous than I have ever seen him. That waiting time is always jittery for a writer, but usually you have some idea of what sort of a job you've done, and this time he evidently had none at all. He only knew that he had committed himself absolutely, as a professional and as a person too, and it had been the hardest piece of writing he'd ever done in a long writing life.

Fortunately he didn't have to wait all that long. He heard from London in ten days and they liked it. There have been a lot of readings since, and all favourable. That helps. But the waiting goes on. Because now there will be the critics, and throwing your guts to the critics is, I suppose, just asking them to treat your guts like so much offal.

Most people ask what the title *Clean Straw for Nothing* means.

It comes from a sign in Gin Lane in the time of Hogarth, and the sign says: 'Drunk for a Penny, Dead Drunk for Tuppence, Clean Straw for Nothing.'

Clean straw for nothing? Whatever anybody says, I will read that book myself one day. When I'm brave enough. Or when I feel I've really earned my own small bundle of clean straw.

Anyone for Fish and Chips?

In the Sydney harbour suburb where I live there has been some controversy lately about an application for a liquor licence from a beach restaurant which intends to specialise in seafood.

The comments of residents living within a quarter-mile radius of the proposed restaurant, as reported in our local newspaper, are interesting. Of course one can't be sure that it is a completely unbiased report, or a really representative cross-section of the community, but just taking it as it reads you begin to realise why our foreshores (and this goes for Melbourne too) are for the most part innocent of any place to eat and drink more civilised than plastic-lined milk bars and pie shops.

The residents in opposition (and one, of course, is the mother of teenage daughters) are 'apprehensive' that the granting of a liquor licence to a beach restaurant would attract 'rowdy elements', 'rough elements', 'drunken louts', 'hooligan types', who are, they admit, 'with us always' and 'get drunk and cause a nuisance by throwing sand, pushing and shoving, fighting and using indecent language'.

Now it is a very curious thing that in four or five years of occasional lunching and dining out in restaurants with liquor licences, both in Sydney and Melbourne, I have never once noticed that such restaurants attract 'hooligan types' or 'drunken louts'. The restaurants I've been in have been rather quiet, discreet places, catering—or at least appearing to cater—for rather quiet, discreet people who seemed to know what knife and fork to use and the purpose of a table napkin and didn't look at all likely to push or shove or fight or use indecent language (unless they were doing so in discreet whispers, which would be their business and not mine).

On the other hand I've seen rare young specimens propping themselves up around milk bars and pie stalls and looking willing for any sort of caper. Looking bored, actually—poor sad little sillies—and I suspect that boredom might be the real cause of most of the capering. But it never would have occurred to me that these aimless packs of hair-and-Levis might be potential customers at a lunching-and-dining-and-wining seafood restaurant.

Seafood is scarcely cheap, not if it is served elegantly, I mean, with all the razzamatazz of appropriate sauces and napery and cunning lighting and deft waiters and long, comprehensive wine lists. The likely lads in the disposal store gear will probably get their seafood from the nearest fish and chip shop, just as they've always done, and their liquor in cans from the nearest pub. And go on throwing sand and pushing and shoving and fighting and using indecent language and chucking their empties over residents' front fences after they've had their fun. But it won't be anything to do with a nice civilised restaurant, because in nice civilised restaurants people, on the whole, behave themselves.

And wouldn't you say that we desperately need some nice civilised restaurants around our foreshores? With all those stupendous seascapes to look at, and the water traffic bustling or idling, and the lovely briny smell of it all, and the sweet crumpling swoosh of waves on sand, and the dance and dapple by day and the jewellery of lights by night—with all that, it seems a deprivation that when we lunch or dine out we are forced to do so in dark cellars, like furtive conspirators, peering across the candles and fumbling for our specs to even hazard a guess at the menu.

It's not that I'm against cellars, having had much pleasure in many, but I'm dead against the cellar complex which pertains here and decrees that eating and drinking, although necessary and even permissible, is tantamount to indecent exposure if you do it in full view of the world.

I think that eating by the water (all right, and drinking by the water, too) is a pleasure of a high and particular order. Of course, there are some lucky people who have their own beach views or water views, but most of us don't, even though most of us feel that all that water is actually communal property, and we ought properly to be able to live on it and around it and by it in as familiar a way as if it was our own back yard.

So all this fuss about one restaurant has saddened me rather. Because it isn't one restaurant we need, but many. With licences and without, and of all sorts of price ranges. And coffee courtyards and beer gardens and informal places as well as special-event places.

Any other country in the world with a stretch of water, even if it is only a pretty turgid-looking river, utilises it for public enjoyment. And eating and drinking are really rather enjoyable. I suspect, too, that the more agreeable and civilised you make the atmosphere for eating and drinking, the more agreeable and civilised will be the clientele.

Some of my pleasantest memories of meals are meals by the water. Lunching at Bray in the summer with the punts sliding by on the Thames and spilling over with pretty girls and tasselled cushions and picnic hampers, and the bad-tempered swans waddling up the lawn to the luncheon table to demand pickings. And a Marseilles waterfront like a stage set, peopled by costumed bit players obviously acting their heads off, and smelling of acrid French cigarettes and hot bread and the delicious dinner being prepared for us.

Oh, and all the meals, breakfasts and luncheons and dinners, along the coasts of France and Italy, and by the rivers of Europe, the Rhine and the Rhone and the Loire and the Gironde and the Mosel, and some of these meals were of the bread-and-cheese sort and some were extravagant with truffles and cream and bottles of famous vintage, but they are memorable not so much for the food one ate and the drink one drank as for the sense of ease and contentment one always has by the water. A sort of large brimming peacefulness, which I am certain must be good for the digestion, not to mention one's attitude towards one's fellow men.

I suppose I've been spoiled by living in the Mediterranean for too long, where you take your meals by the water as a matter of course and in the most public fashion, and order wine with your food with never a guilty thought that you might be helping to attract 'rowdy elements' or 'hooligan types' or contributing towards a deterioration of the language into indecency.

I must say I miss all that very much, in spite of the many excellent cellars there are around these days and the excellent food and wine that are served in them. Oh well, next time I'm asked out to a meal in the way of business or pleasure, I suppose I could suggest we have a picnic on the foreshores instead. Or would that outrage propriety? If I made it a meat pie and a milkshake I might just get away with it.

Winter Solstice

Sometimes when we were young it was winter. Not very often, because when you're young it's mostly summer. Endless. Golden. Not the 'unimaginable zero summer' you dream about now, but the real thing.

But, yes, there were a few winters too. Dramatic winters, with great turbulent aubergine skies rolling and crashing about, and moments of prescience so still you reeled in the darkening silence and held your breath and waited for signs and wonders and portents. Lightning, maybe, stabbing and forking and ripping that purple arras, or pall, that so ceremoniously looped itself over our winter world. Thunder, peremptory, barking some challenge to us. To us? God to god, more likely—in immortal combat. We believed in gods then. That much was easy.

And then the rain. Sheets and gallons and oceans of it scratching the world over with a million diagonals, or sometimes verticals, sogging up the tussocked paddocks, gurgling down the gutters, springing freshets where the cannas grew by the creek, sounding a din on the tin roof like all the kettle-drums that ever summoned Marlborough, and drawing up and out of the earth such a smell as I have never smelled since—not through all my winters—of the pungency of life. Soil, growing things, paspalum grass, seaweed, creek mud, cow dung, and bruised white flowers.

When it rained like that we didn't go to school because school was a mile away over the hills and we'd only get soaked and be sent home anyway. What we did was to kneel in a row on the cracked brown leather couch under the weeping window—long-haired Margaret, skinny Barré, and I, Charmian, the youngest—rubbing it clear, or writing our names on it, or drawing mandalas. We didn't know we were drawing mandalas then, of course, excepting in so far as children know some things instinctively, and do some things instinctively.

The window faced the creek and, in the rain, chewing on some sticky mess of confection we had just made on the kitchen range—toffee, maybe, or coconut ice—we waited and watched for its rising. Never-failing drama as the water crept up the furred rushes wading now plume-deep in the boiling brown and began to seep over the mud-flats, carrying on its errant surface bits of swirling driftwood and bobbing pumpkins washed down from the high farms.

And then: 'She's out!' we would shriek, watching the bits of flotsam twirl tentatively and begin to rush towards the beach, gathering speed as the momentum of the current caught them and flung them from side to side in the wild desperation of water about to lose its identity in the sea.

Our sluggish little creek seemed a mighty river then, and the banks of sand gouged out by its impetuous dash across the beach were wet gamboge ramparts, splitting and plopping heavy slides of sand that fanned out darkly for an instant and then were lost in the churning water.

Then we ran. Bare-legged and bare-headed, hauling on slickers as we went. Down to the wild wet beach and the squeaking sand and the enormous winter sea, dark to purple almost and frilled and frothed with the coldest white, lashing and pounding at the rocks and the cliffs but pulled back and out at the creek's mouth, and stained with the reception of that muddy flood-tide. Rippling now at the beach's edge, fast and shallow. To be waded in until the ripples rushed up your legs and made fountainy high-boots. And the wet gulls belching up like a cloud of scummy steam and hanging there, beating, with their red legs stiff and talons spread, wanting the pumpkins.

And sometimes there was hail. The sky was black-green then, a marvellous colour like the beginning and end of things, or what children might imagine the beginning and end of things to be. The sea, black-green too, exploding into millions of little jumping gushers. Silver cake-lozenges bouncing and scattering and rolling. Piles of them. Cars stopped on the roads. And the noise on the roofs to wake the dead. Ice pebbles leapt and bounded like golf balls. You rushed out and grabbed hands full and crammed them into your mouth, scrunching and scrunching. And the black world roared and your hair was hung with diamonds.

Afterwards there was always a rainbow hanging gauzy in a sky the colour of an old green bottle, blown unevenly, with flaws and whorls of thickness and darkness and one crackled patch where the sun was breaking through. Our winter world lay in a marvellous silence then. Only the brilliance of the paddocks singing, and the raw sienna sand, and every house and every wall frosted—piles of ice pebbles banked up, blue-white, green-white, polished and glittering like crystal beads.

In the winter our mother made fires. Out of wet billets of box and scoops of coal. She had a way of coaxing fires. And at night we three would sit around the dining table, covered decently with brown bobble-fringed cloth, colouring in the Virgil drawings in *Smith's Weekly*, sticking shells onto cigar boxes for birthday or Christmas presents, cutting out things, pasting things, while our mother, curled up on a cushion by the scaly grey and leaping blue-and-orange of the fire—and prodding it into a frenzy—read to us.

Blow, winds, and crack your cheeks! rage! blow! ...
I tax not you, you elements, with unkindness ...
You owe me no subscription: then, let fall
Your horrible pleasure ...

We shuddered with delicious terror at such wonderful
words and pleasure in our warm young selves, safe and
protected from the elements' horrible pleasure. We wondered
if there would be a shipwreck, and hoped there might.
Sometimes there was seaweed draped and rotting on the
picket fence in the mornings: that's how close the sea was.
Our father had been shipwrecked once, and had had to swim
five miles to shore. We thought we might quite like to be
shipwrecked ourselves. Under certain circumstances, and with
an audience. We would save somebody.

Winter tasted of hot soup and toffee and cocoa, smelled of
wet earth and burning box billets, sounded of the elements'
horrible pleasure shrieking and whining and howling and
drumming, and felt of comfort. We dressed up sometimes and
played at kings and queens: the Shakespearean influence was
strong in our house.

There have been winter solstices since. Many and many of
them. Too many perhaps. I saw snow for the first time.
London fog. Blizzard. Picked mistletoe from a Druid's oak
tree. Walked Cornish moors in the mist and watched a ship
pounded to death beneath a lighthouse. I huddled in the
Black Forest once, in dark and primitive terror. And once I
shouted in to the rumbled guts of the worst storm I have ever
known. A yellow storm. Yellow's always the worst. It's more
angry somehow. I've always shouted into yellow storms,
being defiant by nature, I suppose. And once in a yellow
storm there was a yellow balloon too, skittering madly over

the yellow sea, and a cheque in the mail that day, signifying something. The gods' favour, I thought then, being a bit exalted with the weather.

Isn't it strange how your childhood dogs you and tracks you and will not let you be?

Because of mine I have always loved weather. All sorts of weather. In a way, the worse the better. I vibrate in a storm like a tuning fork, and long for beaches, long, wave-lashed beaches, gulls, splinters, spars, dripping weed, squeaking sand, the fury of the sea roaring up the cliffs and sobbing down in impotence, and a creek breaking its banks to make a playground for wild wet children.

Eliot says: 'There are other places/ Which also are the world's end, some at the sea jaws .../ Where is the summer', Eliot asks, 'the unimaginable Zero summer?'

But I ask where is the unimaginable winter? Sometimes when we were young it was winter. But not very often, of course. Perhaps children aren't allowed too much of a good thing. They might become addicted to the elements, believe in the old gods, turn hieratic and identify themselves with old cults, old sacrifices, and neglect their civilised destinies in the most patriotic Australian wool, turning on the central heating and drying out their smart umbrellas. Wool's in this season. Lovely colours, too. Toffee and caramel and raw sienna and kelp green.

It's a long way back to the sea's jaws. The world's end.

Notes

Coming Home: This was the first of Charmian's Clift's 'pieces' to be published. It appeared in the Melbourne *Herald* on 6 November 1964 and in the Women's Section of the *Sydney Morning Herald* on 19 November.

On Debits and Credits: EOKA was the National Organisation of Cypriot Fighters, which revolted against the British colonial rule of Cyprus in 1955. When negotiations between the British governor and the Greek leader, Archbishop Makarios, broke down in early 1956, the British deported the much-loved patriarch to the Seychelles. This trouble erupted just after the Johnstons bought their Hydra house—and while they awaited the birth of their second son, Jason.

On Painting Bricks White: Robin Boyd's *The Great Australian Ugliness* (1960) was an unexpected bestseller. Donald Horne (in *A Time of Hope*) describes Boyd's book as 'an assault on Australian suburbia that, with meticulous pitilessness, lampooned Australian traditions of design, then went on to mock the tastelessness of both the Australian elites and the Australian masses'.

On Lucky Dips: On 10 November 1964 the Menzies government introduced conscription for twenty year old males. Under a bizarre intake system, birth dates were placed in a lottery barrel and the army only took those youths whose date was drawn. The Johnston's elder son, Martin, turned seventeen on 12 November 1964, so this piece was clearly written just after the draft was announced. I have been unable to find this essay in published form.

The Rare Art of Inspiring Others: The artist described in this piece is Sidney Nolan.

On Letting Asia In: This essay was published in August 1965. Australia at that time still followed the White Australia Policy.

A Birthday in the Kelly Country: In July 1965 George Johnston went into hospital to be treated for his tuberculosis. Charmian took their youngest child, Jason, to stay with relatives in Victoria, so that he would be out of the infection zone.

Getting with the Forward-Lookers: In September 1965 Charmian and the two older children moved into a three bedroom rented home unit in Neutral Bay.

The Right of Dissent: In October 1966 the American President, Lyndon Baines Johnson, visited Australia as a reward for the loyalty of Australian prime minister Harold Holt, who had declared that we would go 'all the way with LBJ'. The official program of triumphal motorcades was frequently disrupted by demonstrators. In Sydney, the President's visit to the Art Gallery was a particular focus for protest.

Where My Caravan Has Rested: At the end of 1966, Charmian and George bought a two-storey house in Raglan Street, Mosman. This was the family home for the next four years.

Report from a Migrant, Three Years After: At this time the ABC was under the department of the postmaster general, and received very little funding for the production of local television drama. The 'tragedy' of the Sydney Opera House refers to the fact that the architect, Joern Utzon, had resigned from the project in February 1966, after state government interference with his design. *Till Death Us Do Part* was a British satirical sitcom, featuring a working class Tory bigot named Alf Garnett.

On Trouble in Lotus Land: In regard to 'Bolte and Holtie'—Holt was, of course, the prime minister, and Bolte was the extreme right wing premier of Victoria. In contrast, the 'swinging Mr Dunston' was the Labor premier of South Australia.

The Centre, The Rock, The Olgas: In September 1967 Charmian Clift accompanied Sidney Nolan and an ABC television crew to the centre of Australia, for a documentary that was being made about Nolan. It was Clift's job to interview the painter. After this, the author flew to Cairns, then visited Karumba and Thursday Island.

The Voices of Greece: On 21 April 1967, while the Greek parliament was in recess pending elections, a military coup transferred power to a group of army officers. This military Junta established strict censorship and began arresting large numbers of politicians, academics, civil servants and outspoken citizens. In December trial by jury was abolished, and Colonel Papadopoulos and Brigadier Patakos took over as prime minister and deputy prime minister.

In Australia, protest meetings were organised by the Committee for the Restoration of Democracy in Greece, of which Charmian Clift and George Johnston were honorary vice-presidents. Their daughter, Shane, worked at Sydney's *Hellenic Herald* newspaper, which was one of the voices of opposition to the Junta in this country.

A Matter of Conscience: In May 1968 Private Simon Townsend, a registered conscientious objector who had been conscripted into the army, was sentenced by court martial to twenty-eight days detention at Ingleburn military camp for disobeying an order. This received wide media coverage, at the time when the anti-Vietnam and anti-conscription movements were starting to swell.

This same month, the federal government introduced a bill which obliged employers, teachers, church leaders and other citizens to report any young man whom they suspected of not registering. A *Sydney Morning Herald* editorial attacked this 'obligation of pimping'.

The Habitual Way: In May 1968 George Johnston went back to hospital for further treatment of his tuberculosis.

A New Generation of Protestants: 'Mr Askin's little blunder' refers to the famous order given by the premier of New South Wales to 'Run over the bastards'—the bastards in question being anti-Vietnam demonstrators having a peaceful sit-in on the street.

In July 1968 Eric Willis, the New South Wales chief secretary, banned the last short play in *America Hurrah* because four-letter words were spray-canned onto a wall. When announcing this act of censorship, Willis declared that 'only hippies and the lunatic fringe would object'.

Last of the Old: 'It is seventeen years ago today ...' Clift meant from the day of publication—6 February 1969. However, the author was muddling the date of George VI's death and Elizabeth's accession (6 February 1952) with the date of the Coronation (2 June 1953).

Royal Jelly: Clift again gave the date of the Coronation as 6 February 1952. It has been corrected in the text.

On *Clean Straw for Nothing*: This essay, which was one of ten long pieces produced for *Pol* magazine, was probably written during the author's 'holiday' from her column in May 1969. The second novel of George Johnston's autobiographical trilogy, *Clean Straw for Nothing*, was due to be released in August; Clift filed this piece so that it would come out in the same month. She died before publication either of the novel or of this essay.

Anyone for Fish and Chips?: The author filed this piece four days bef her death in July 1969. In the second column piece she publishe 'Social Drinking'—she had made a similar plea for more outdoor e and drinking places.